THE NEGLECTED
VOTER

THE NEGLECTED VOTER

WHITE MEN AND
THE DEMOCRATIC DILEMMA

DAVID PAUL KUHN

First published in 2007 by
PALGRAVE MACMILLAN™
175 Fifth Avenue, New York, N.Y. 10010 and
Houndmills, Basingstoke, Hampshire, England RG21 6XS.
Companies and representatives throughout the world.

PALGRAVE MACMILLAN is the global academic imprint of the
Palgrave Macmillan division of St. Martin's Press, LLC and of Palgrave
Macmillan Ltd. Macmillan® is a registered trademark in the United
States, United Kingdom and other countries. Palgrave is a registered
trademark in the European Union and other countries.

ISBN-13: 978–1–4039–8274–2
ISBN-10: 1–4039–8274–0

Library of Congress Cataloging-in-Publication Data

Kuhn, David Paul.
  The neglected voter : white men and the Democratic dilemma / by
David Paul Kuhn.
    p.   cm.
  Includes bibliographical references and index.
  ISBN 1–4039–8274–0
    1. Elections—United States.   2. Voting—United States.
3. Political participation—United States.   4. Men, White—United
States—Attitudes.   5. Sex role—Political aspects—United States.
I. Title.
JK1965.K84   2007
324.973'092—dc22

                                                          2007010326

A catalogue record of the book is available from the British Library.

Design by Letra Libre, Inc.

First edition: October 2007

10 9 8 7 6 5 4 3 2 1

Printed in the United States of America.

To my father, Robert M. Kuhn

CONTENTS

White Male and Female Presidential Voting 1948-2004*—*grey column represents the White Male Gap.*

Year	Gender	Republican Advantage	Dem % of Vote	GOP % of Vote	Indep % of Vote
1948	Male	1.1	47.4	48.5	4.1
	Female	5.4	43.4	48.8	7.8
1952	Male	15.2	41.9	57.1	1.0
	Female	19.4	40.3	59.7	0.0
1956	Male	13.7	42.8	56.5	0.7
	Female	29.6	35.2	64.8	0.0
1960	Male	−0.2	49.9	49.7	0.4
	Female	11.3	44.2	55.5	0.3
1964	Male	−11.8	55.8	44.0	0.2
	Female	−16.0	57.9	41.9	0.2
1968	Male	14.1	33.0	47.1	19.9
	Female	13	37.7	50.7	11.7
1972	Male	35.7	31.2	66.9	1.9
	Female	37.3	30.8	68.1	1.2
1976	Male	5.0	47.0	52.0	1.0
	Female	7.3	46.1	53.4	0.6
1980	Male	29.0	32.2	61.2	6.5
	Female	14.2	39.2	53.4	7.3
1984	Male	37.3	30.9	68.2	0.8
	Female	26.7	36.4	63.1	0.5
1988	Male	29.0	34.9	63.9	1.3
	Female	14.8	42.2	57.0	0.7
1992	Male	4.6	36.3	40.9	22.8
	Female	1.9	39.6	41.5	18.9
1996	Male	12.2	38.3	50.5	11.2
	Female	−4.5	48.3	43.8	7.9
2000	Male	26.5	35.2	61.7	3.1
	Female	3.4	47.1	50.5	2.4
2004	Male	26.1	36.8	62.9	0.3
	Female	12.7	43.5	56.2	0.3

* 1948–1968 source: American National Election Studies
* 1972–2004 source: CBS News and combined media exit polling
* Whites include self-described Caucasians, who are not Jewish or Hispanic.
* See Appendix for methodology of the White Male Gap (W.M.G.) study

THE WHITE MALE GAP

Ronald Reagan was once a Democrat, like the white men who followed him to the Republican Party. As Franklin Delano Roosevelt ran for the presidency, Reagan returned home to Dixon, Illinois, a 21-year-old college graduate. It was 1932 and twelve million Americans were jobless. "A job, any job, seemed like the ultimate success," Reagan recalled.[1] He found one, voted four times for Roosevelt through 1944, and joined America's workingmen in constructing the Democratic era.[2]

Six presidents later, with the United States suffering another economic downturn, Reagan won the White House by sundering the very coalition Roosevelt had built. His election marked the arrival of the modern Republican majority, a majority built on the ballots of white men who still called themselves Democrats but no longer saw their future in liberalism. At the very time Democrats were reaching out to all others, white men found in Reagan a future that could be theirs. Reagan won 61 percent of white male voters in 1980, and with them, he won the Republican Party's future. Four years later, he garnered 68 percent of the white male vote. The Democrats won only 32 and 31 percent of white men in 1980 and 1984 respectively. In every presidential election thereafter, Democrats never won more than 38 of every 100 white men who voted. No factor has been more instrumental in causing the Democratic decline in presidential politics than the loss of white men.[3] Never again did Democrats win the male vote overall. Soon, Republicans seemed to own masculinity itself. The White Male Gap had arrived.

The United States remains the only nation in the western world where the conservative party consistently wins the vote of the workingman, poor and middle class alike. Imagine Britain's Labour Party, over a period of decades, losing the majority of men in the working-class neighborhoods of Manchester or Birmingham. Imagine it as a trend reaching back to Winston Churchill, emerging with the rise of Margaret Thatcher, and continuing unimpeded beyond the government of Tony Blair. The idea is absurd. Yet exactly that has occurred in the United States.

Between Harry Truman's narrow victory in 1948 and George W. Bush's victory in 2004, every strata of the white male vote shifted in the Republicans' favor. For the poorest third of Americans, white women's support for Democratic presidential candidates went *up* 3 percent. For white men in the same income bracket, there was a 25 percent decline! The much-discussed success of the GOP in reaching poor whites over the past half century is a story of men. Within the middle third of white Americans, the Democratic Party saw a decline of 15 percent among white females. But white men left Democrats at twice that rate. Their support for Democratic presidential candidates declined 29 percent between 1948 and 2004. A third of white middle-class men left the Roosevelt coalition in the past six decades. Even within the wealthiest third of whites, a group that is traditionally Republican, Democrats lost 6 percent of white men since 1948, while they earned the support of 3 percent more women.[4]

However the polling is deciphered, the white male migration from liberal to conservative politics is the fundamental reason Republicans have won five of the last seven presidential elections.

After the 2004 election, Bruce Reed, president of the Democratic Leadership Council (DLC), was bothered by one fundamental fact: Despite a Republican tax policy that favored the wealthy, widening income gaps between the ultrarich and everyone else, corporate impropriety topping the news, and millions of job losses, Democrats lost 26 of the 28 states with the lowest per capita income. The Republican candidate won nineteen of the twenty states with the lowest median income.[5] And President Bush won *every* economic class of white men, like so many Republicans before him.[6]

The irony is palpable. Liberals believe they are standing up for the working-man, while the white workingman believes the culture of liberalism stands against him. Years after the DLC raised the first alarm in 2001 about the "white male problem," Reed is frustrated, if only because it took two decades to be noticed, and as the 2008 election nears, the loss of white men remains substantively ignored.

"Look," he tells me, "if we are losing the second largest demographic group in America by nearly two to one, we don't deserve to be a majority party! And we don't have to do that. You know, men are from Mars and women are from Venus, but a lot of them are married and live together in households with the same general interests and, as Clinton would say, part of it is just showing up."

There are second acts in American politics. The Democrats' revival depends on reconnecting with the voter they left behind. At midcentury, white men were the most loyal Democratic constituency. But as the party of Harry Truman and John F. Kennedy became the party of George McGovern—as the counterculture rose—many white men felt they were now the liberal antagonists. As they left, so did the Democrats' presidential viability. By 1980, the GOP won the barbers, the lawyers, and the policemen. The Republican presidential era was born and Democrats kept pushing on, a new liberalism without the people to win back a majority.

Bob Dylan once commented, "You can't be wise and in love at the same time." Democrats fell in love with the cause. They soon lost themselves in the fight, and the greater good went down with them. To be on the right side of history can be a curse, indeed. The party of plutocrats became the party of the people by redefining populism in terms of culture instead of class, deftly turning the word "liberal" into a pejorative antagonistic to the American ethos. In doing so, Republicans fractured the FDR coalition that had defined the Democratic Party. In fighting the good fight, liberals believed, Democrats lost their majority.

It did not have to be that way. As the fight for civil rights advocated "forced busing"; as equal opportunity became equal outcome through quotas; as affirmative action placed the condition of a rich white woman above that of a poor white man; as feminism concluded that the fight for women's rights meant classic notions of manhood were wrong; as Lyndon B. Johnsons's failure in Vietnam branded John F. Kennedy's "peace through strength" a failed policy; as tolerance and multiculturalism became intolerance of the majority's culture (an issue at the heart of the debate over religion in the public sphere)—white men began to reconsider their partisan vows. Although some on the political left denied that the paradigm shifted over the years between Henry Wallace and George McGovern, white men believed that it had. Like the rejected husband, they walked out on liberalism for good.

The slam of the door on the way out was the White Male Gap: the margin between the strong majority of white men who support Republicans in presidential elections, in comparison to the minority who vote Democratic. Without a major third party candidate, between 26 and 37 percent more white men have supported the Republican candidate in each contest since Reagan's 1980 election.[7] Meanwhile, the last seven presidential elections were won with an average popular vote only slightly greater than 50 percent.[8]

In a nation where slim margins make presidents, the White Male Gap should have raised alarms in 1980. It did not. Leading modern liberals believed that to champion equality they were compelled to challenge white men. This was an unnecessary choice. The majority of white men *and* women were slow to support civil rights. Many men, both white *and* black, were slow to accept women's equality as well. But in years that turned to decades, white men came to believe that this new form of liberalism branded the ills of the American nation as solely theirs, while their contributions were forgotten. They were a race and gender blamed for the worst actions of their fellow Americans. So they left the Democratic Party.

Liberals watched white men walk out and never considered sharing the blame. From George McGovern to John Kerry, the Democratic apparatus became progressively disconnected from the very working and middle-class voter who once defined it. But, contrary to conventional wisdom, the voters who left and did not return were not merely white; they were also overwhelmingly men. That's the part journalists and academics got so remarkably wrong, particularly following Reagan's ascension in 1980. The white flight from the Democratic Party was, above all, a movement of men.

Jimmy Carter never saw it coming. The patriarch of today's Democratic Party, once the "new man" of the new South, is seated beneath a photograph of a lake beside a snow-covered mountain, a gift from Ansel Adams. His blue veins push against his pale skin. There are pictures of his wife and daughter and the Jimmy Carter of the 1970s. The nuclear engineer, the man who left his naval career to save the family farm, the last rural American to win the White House—every chapter of his life is present in Carter's long blue stare.

"You are the last Democrat to nearly split the white male vote," I tell him.

"Oh really," Carter replies, pausing, and tilting his chin upward.

"When Ronald Reagan won the presidency, he won a slim majority of white women. But he dominated white men. Mr. President, you went from 47 percent of the white male vote in 1976 to *only* 32 percent in 1980. White women returned to Democrats. White men never did."

"Oh really," Carter repeats, "that's surprising." He turns away, looking toward the 1970s portrait of himself. "Women are more inclined toward peace and social issues—education, health care, the avoidance of war," he says, returning to the female vote.

Carter lives today in the same town where he was born. His red brick ranch house is "just two football fields" from the center of Plains, a small town in the Deep South of Georgia. "I think," he replies, "that a lot of those middle-class men are beginning to ascertain that this Republican administration has been both wasteful, has put an extraordinary and unprecedented burden on our children and grandchildren for debt, and has subverted any possibility in the future for escalated improvements in education or health and has grossly favored extremely rich people."

Carter references the widening wage gap between executives and workers. In 1980 the CEO-to-worker ratio in annual earnings was 42 to 1. By 2005, it was 411 to 1.[9]

"Those kinds of trends are sometimes esoteric but sometimes they become absurd," Carter adds, "just a general feeling that I'm getting screwed, my bosses are getting rich and I'm not getting any better. So I think the omens, for even white men, for the Democratic Party might be encouraging."

It will take more than omens. For a quarter century white men have been estranged from the Democratic Party, though the marriage was on the rocks far earlier. By the late 1960s white men were already deemed racist and sexist, and that sufficed for explaining the collapse of the Democratic presidential majority. Historian H. W. Brands once observed, "The purpose of history is not to make people happy, it is to make them wiser."[10] This is the tale of how white men saw the world erupt all around them. It's their story—how those fighting the good fight mistakenly chose the workingman as their adversary, and how liberals misjudged tens of millions of men.

By the time George W. Bush accomplished what his father could not do—that is, win a second term—only about a quarter of white male voters identified as Democrats, while nearly half identified as Republicans.[11] In comparison, when Bush and Bill Clinton were children in 1952, about 47 percent of white men said they were Democrats and about 26 percent said they were Republicans.[12]

Highly represented in rural states, the 97 million white men of America are even more influential than their portion of the electorate.[13] They make up between 36 and 39 percent of voters, roughly five times more than Hispanic male and female voters combined. White women are about a 5 percent larger voting bloc than white men, but they have largely returned to the Democrats. White men have not.

Had John Kerry narrowed the White Male Gap from 26 to 21 percent he would have gained more than 2 million votes, and almost assuredly won the presidency. The same gain among all minority men would have won Kerry less than a third of that total.[14] But like every Democrat since Carter, Kerry did not substantially seek the white male vote, and therefore one more presidential election passed with new Democratic hopes but the same mold of candidate, the same platform, and the same inability to win a majority of Americans.

"Gore got 90 percent of the black vote; you are not going to do better than that," the Democrats' leading demographer, Mark Gersh says, adding that Kerry earned 88 percent as well. "So how are you going to win? I have this theory that the *only* way he could win the state was by really jumping the numbers up in Democratic performance in blue-collar Northeastern Ohio." This means winning white men.

In the last three decades, hundreds of books were published discussing the Democratic decline. But none got to the pith of the problem. From the defeat of Hubert Humphrey to the failed bid of John Kerry, the very voter who built the edifice of Republican presidencies remained substantially ignored by liberalism, the media, and the academy. The gender gap was seen through one gender's eyes—and they were not male.

"Women Shifting Sharply Away from Reagan, Republican Party," the *Washington Post* headlined in May 1982, looking toward the midterm elections. The political director of the Democratic National Committee, Ann F. Lewis, told the *Post*, "'The right-wing takeover of the Republican Party' has driven moderate women from the party."[15] But the facts demonstrated otherwise. The left wing was driving far more men from Democrats. Lewis was wrong about women as well. Reagan won the votes of *more* women than Carter with a slim majority of white women.

By September of 1983, *Newsweek*'s coverage typified the mainstream media. Its headline asked, "What Do Women Want?" The gender gap, it told us, was "shorthand for the president's persistently lagging support among women."[16] A decade later *Business Week* asked in a headline, "Can the GOP Bridge the Gender Gap?" explaining, "The party tries broadening a base beyond angry white men."[17] But it was the Democrats whose base was thinning. Two decades of wrongheaded reporting and political science research about one of the most fundamental issues in modern presidential politics persisted. It was not simply a question of considering the male side of the issue. The media and political analysts ignored the fact that the gender gap was fundamentally a male issue! They were intellectually negligent in failing to consider that civil rights, the culture wars, and the shifting perceptions of gender, war, urban upheaval, the economy, and the welfare state were drastically changing how white men voted. And the reasons were far more substantial than backlash.

Reagan's chief strategist Richard Wirthlin first coined the term "gender gap." "The context of the gender gap—once it was identified and the press ran with the idea—the question they always asked was, Why is Reagan doing so poorly among women? But that's only one blade of the scissors. The question I was always interested in was, Why was Reagan doing so well among men?" Wirthlin tells me over breakfast. "It's been a mystery to me for 25 years why that wasn't recognized. When the question is refocused on the issue of our strength, then it provides a very different point of view. Mainly, why spend tremendous campaign resources in trying to soften the harsher, negative image of women and rather reinforce the strength among men?" He adds, "One of the political axioms, I have always felt, was you concentrate on your strength."

Democrats believed that's what they were doing. By 1984, the Democratic platform spoke of the "feminization of poverty," emphasizing the crisis of single mothers. It ignored that more than eight out of ten homeless people were men.[18] The platform cited the "millions left behind" while focusing on subgroups of women and minorities, with abstract mentions of working men and women. But white men had specific problems as well. Between 1979 and 1983 alone, more than 9 million Americans were added to the poverty rolls and more than half were from white, male-headed families.[19]

"There was a morphing of the Democratic Party from a sense of a common good or a common commitment to each other as fellow citizens to being an advocate for groups," Mark Warner says. Warner was the Democratic governor of conservative Virginia, and he won his election by outflanking Republicans on traditionally male issues such as gun rights. "And I think," Warner adds, "that Democrats were advocates for every other group except for white males."

In time I came to see that one core fact can explain the forty-year decline of the American political left in presidential politics. And that fact was the White Male Gap. Yet it concerns a "problem with no name." Betty Friedan used these words in the first chapter of her landmark 1963 book, *The Feminine Mystique*. She told us of a muzzled existential angst, a "desperation," among American 1950s housewives.[20] By the turn of the century, there was also a white male problem with no name, and the silence Friedan wrote of is progressively a masculine murmur—one hardly understood and one continually demeaned as "exaggerated" and "angry." But this problem of the rejected man is as real as the presidents it made.

After Bill Clinton won the presidency in 1992, columnist Donna Britt received letters from men disgusted with her comment that the nation should begin electing presidents who are not white males. Colleagues advised her to disregard the angry letters. But instead, Britt listened. She wrote that some white men, "are weary of being the ultimate lightning rod for grievances; responsible for every problem facing American minorities, white women, Mother Earth." She added that "'white man' is so loaded now, it's almost an epithet," and though it may be the price of power, "many white guys just don't feel that powerful." She added that they "don't relate to being blamed any more than do black folks who are sick of being seen as the group responsible for what's wrong with inner cities."[21] It was a significant insight, if only because it was so rarely made in post–counter culture America. That it came from a black woman made it all the more poignant.

The following year *Newsweek* explained why white men did not support Bill Clinton: "partly out of fear that his multicultural ecofeminist storm troopers would take away their guns, steaks, cigarettes, V–8 engines—and jobs."[22] No other explanation was given. It was indicative of the mainstream. All white men who were not voting Democratic were branded as "male chauvinist pigs," bigots, or merely greedy.

By 1994, four decades of Democratic control of Congress had ended. The loss was blamed on "the angry white male." White men's political beliefs were reduced to spiteful blowback. Between 1980 and November 1994, "angry white male" was used 12 times in newsprint and broadcast transcripts according to a LexisNexis search. In the year following the 1994 November election, the term was used in 1,574 news reports. But the substantial reasons these men left the Democratic Party were hardly considered.

Television commentator Chris Matthews popularized the concept that Democrats are the "mommy party" and Republicans are the "daddy party."[23] In this frame of thought, Daddy was concerned with protecting and Mommy was concerned with nurturing. While Democrats, by 1984, made explicit overtures to women, what received less notice were the Republican overtures to men. The result was an electoral imbalance. Republicans were winning more white men than they were losing women. It turned out many white women were also attracted to, or comfortable with, the traditional masculine appeal.

Republican's "proactive attempt" to reach white men, says Harvard University social psychologist William Pollack, was "a programmed message to say what was heroism, what was true masculinity, what was being a man—which is standing up for yourself, being the man of the household, which is being the breadwinner—has been stolen from you and we are the party that is going to give it back." Pollack believes Republicans affirmed the destabilized footing beneath the average white man. The GOP "recognized the pain and offered sort of a solution, which is to say, you are worthwhile in this way and it's not fair for you to be mistreated," adds Pollack, a leader in the humble field of men's studies and director of the Center for Men and Young Men at Boston's McLean Hospital. "From the other direction, when you think about Democrats," they were, "to some extent pooh-poohing it, or saying things that might be negative and uncaring."

Democrats came to be seen as not only the advocate for all others, but also as *against* white men. An entire generation of white men was raised in a system in which *they felt* disadvantaged. It did not matter if the perception was true; the perception itself had political consequences.

By 1999, Susan Faludi charted the "male crisis in America" in *Stiffed, the Betrayal of the American Man.* "I was operating under the assumption," Faludi wrote, "that the male crisis in America was caused by something men were *doing* unrelated to something being done to them." And Faludi found, "If men are the masters of their fate, what do they do about the unspoken sense that they are being mastered. . . . Women were able to take action, paradoxically, by understanding how they were acted upon."[24]

Although women came to see "how they were acted upon," white men have not. Their manhood is dependent on the perception that they shape their own lives. Minority men rightly understand that forces act upon them and society recognizes their plight. It is principally the American white man who is told to "be a man and take it." If white men were confined to a cultural cell at the dawn of the twenty-first century, it was seen as a cell of their own design.

By the 1970s, when white men were being caricatured as the bigoted Archie Bunker from *All in the Family*, the rejected man looked elsewhere. In the years between the presidencies of John F. Kennedy and Bill Clinton, there was a 14 percent decline in Democratic support among whites without a four-year college degree. When this working-class white population is looked at by gender, the White Male Gap presents itself. Working-class female support fell 9 percentage points over this period while support for Democrats by white male voters without a bachelor's degree declined an astonishing 21 points.[25]

"Not only are women starting to outpace men in going to college but we are starting to see that even in law school, medical school, and not so much in business school," Democratic analyst Anna Greenberg says, who was one of the first to study the white male political migration in depth. "Look, the people that are screwed the most are men without a college education," she says.

"If you look at government and who government helps, it's not white men, especially if they are younger," Greenberg adds. "Your role being the breadwinner, the person responsible for your family, became undermined by policy changes," she continues. "And there's a way in which this white male anger is legitimate and I know that's something that liberals don't say," Greenberg laughs, clears her throat, and adds, "I do think the Democratic Party has forgotten about the white working class."

Altruism is rarely the source of a presidential vote. From the mid-1960s onward, white men said no to a government that served them least, while other groups said yes to a liberalism that acted on their behalf.

"Liberals didn't realize they had a whole constituency of disenfranchised people without rights who were called standard masculine men," Pollack explains. "I'm not saying that all liberal Democrats saw these men as the enemy, but they didn't see them as the victim—but these men felt more and more victimized."

At times, though, the dogmatic liberalism that arose in 1968 and won the party in 1972 viewed white men as the enemy. Liberals seemed incapable of arguing for the rights of the oppressed without pinning white men as the scapegoat—as if white racism was exclusively the vice of men, as if sexism was exclusively the vice of whites.

So white men became "the man." He held all the cards, and everyone else's bad deal was *his* fault. But the bulk of white men did not feel like dealers or players. They felt like pieces on someone else's table, and their livelihood, their family's very stability, was in richer men's hands as well. The harsh fact of American male modernity was his too. The pressure on him persisted as the potential for success lessened. Despite hard times, white men particularly believed that hard work earns a good life. But increasingly, white men found a world of instability on the other end of American manhood.

Among voters in 2004, only 3.7 percent of white males' household incomes exceeded $200,000 annually, while 3.5 percent of white females were in the same income bracket (for singles: it was 2.9 percent of men and 1.8 percent of women). Among the middle class, there is only a slight difference in earnings of white men and white women voters, single or married.[26]

White men constitute the vast majority of leading CEOs, but that small fraction of white male success falsely represents a group that remains intimate with failure. White men still live the hardscrabble life. About 21 percent of white men and 22 percent of white women make $30,000 to $45,000 in household income.[27] In the end, do these meager margins correlate with the perception of white male dominance?

Today, there are two exceptions to the White Male Gap. White Jews, men and women, remain the only upper-class sociological group to continue to vote Democratic, often due to religious and cultural values. More than three out of four Jews supported Kerry in 2004.[28] White gay voters believe it is Democrats who champion their cause for equal protection under the law, so the majority of gay men support Democrats. In every other sociological, religious, and economic category, white men are likely voting Republican in presidential elections, and the reason is rooted in their worldviews as well as in specific issues.

White men continue to feel disempowered, distant from liberal mores, and unmoored from the stability that their fathers and grandfathers enjoyed. The expectation persists that they can not only make a living for themselves, but also support a family. Seven out of ten men remain the lead wage earner, while a higher percent of men, three out of four, say it is family that gives them a "real sense of belonging."[29] Like others, white men feel controlled by bosses and compelled by fiscal responsibly. They take on thankless work to meet their obligations, and it often creates a sense of compromised manhood. If a white male's salary places him in the upper class, his self-worth is often tied to that wage. For many, the definition of being a man has meant surrendering what one wants to do for what one must do. This has long been true. But modern liberalism no longer saw it that way. The hard life was said to be the easy life if one was born white and male.

It is not only the perceptions of white men that are often misunderstood, but also the gender politics surrounding them. Today, white men hold similar opinions to white women on whether government should take care of people who cannot take care of themselves, as well as on whether we have gone "too far pushing for equal rights." The same numbers of white men and women agree and disagree that blacks get "preferential treatment," that the poor are "too dependent on government assistance," and that men and women are "better at different things in the workplace."

But among whites, significantly more women believe that "leaders should make compromises." More men "completely agree" that we should "ensure peace through military strength," and those that completely agree are twice as likely to call themselves Republican. More men "completely agree" that the tax system is "unfair to people like me," while more women "completely disagree."[30] Significantly more men wanted Bush's tax cuts to be made permanent. And hinting at the belief in realizing one's economic aspirations, detailed later in this book, more men "strongly" believe that hard workers get ahead, while more women "strongly" believe that hard work does not guarantee success.[31] These gender differences run even deeper in presidential politics. Until 1999 those differences, when applied to men, remained largely ignored. Ideology seemingly blinded logic for the party of intellectuals.

MISUNDERSTANDING THE GENDER GAP
AND THE DEMOCRATIC DECLINE

"All during the '80s, the major media constantly wrote about the gender gap, but it was all about Republicans problems with women," Gary Bauer says from his office just outside Washington, D.C. Bauer became one of the most influential social conservatives following his service in the Reagan administration. "What some of us were very frustrated about at the time is that you really can't have a one-way gender gap. If Republicans were doing worse among women than among men, the reverse was true."

From the first days of the Reagan presidency to the last days of Clinton's, there were thousands of stories in the media and hundreds of articles in academia on the gender gap. With a handful of exceptions, the male side of the gender gap was almost entirely disregarded.

"Everything you read about the gender gap is about the Republicans not getting women," a strategist behind Newt Gingrich's Contract with America, Frank Luntz, recalls. "Do a ratio, do a study. How many times have you read articles, books, about why Democrats don't win men?"

There were few exceptions. Nineteen years after the White Male Gap first appeared, both academics and political strategists were finally reconsidering their understanding of the gender gap. "American women have been the central feature of the gender gap story for the past twenty years" but that "could not be further from the facts," wrote two political scientists in 1999.[32] A year later, two leading Democratic strategists, Stan and Anna Greenberg, authored a memorandum warning Democrats that, "No amount of targeting of women will get Democrats beyond the near parity," because "to make real gains, Democrats will have to re-open the channels of communication with white men."[33]

That year, Al Gore lost the presidential election, notorious for its narrowest of outcomes, due to the White Male Gap. White women favored George W. Bush by only 3 percent, but white men favored Bush by a whopping 27 percent![34] Democrats begrudged Ralph Nader winning tens of thousand of liberal voters in key states. But the slightest improvement with the tens of millions of white men would have made Al Gore president and commander in chief.

The conservative appeal to the white everyman was based on five consistent themes once upheld by classical American liberals.

1. Grit—an inward quality of strength of character.
2. Safety and security issues—the outward quality of strength, both domestic and international, as well patriotism, which is pride in what one defends.
3. The western man sensibility—combining rugged individualism and small government.
4. Common culture—a sense that candidates share voters' values, beliefs, and customs, which can include social issues like gun control and religion.

5. Guardian's politics—the strong father in FDR or JFK, or the matriarch
    in the tradition of Margaret Thatcher or Queen Elizabeth.

Grit affords leeway on the four other issues because it is the character of a
politician that shapes every issue.

For every 100 white men, roughly 16 identify themselves as liberal, 40 as
conservative, and 44 as moderates.[35] The White Male Gap exists because so
many of these moderates lean strongly Republican. For this reason, unlike the
successes of Reagan in 1980 and Bush in 2004, Democratic presidential elections
are won on the middle road.

Despite this fact, triangulated centrism is not the answer. Bill Clinton's candidacy, when national security was not an issue and economic insecurity was,
might never have succeeded without Ross Perot in the race. In 1992, Clinton
made only slight percentage gains with white women and men compared to
Michael Dukakis four years earlier.

Equally, the Democratic answer does not spring from the leftist base. The dogmatic liberal movement that rose with George McGovern is compelled to compromise on some issues in order to widen the coalition to a winnable majority. The
alternative to this compromise has been to lose on every issue by failing to win and
hold a Democratic White House. It is, in the end, a matter of the electoral math.

"Democratic activists fundamentally misunderstand the arithmetic of elections," DNC president Bruce Reed says. "They think the way to win is to motivate the base and make people come out of the woodwork. And our view is you
have to excite the base and find ways to persuade people who didn't vote for you
last time," adds Reed, who also served as a domestic policy advisor in the Clinton
administration. "In much of the country there's nobody hiding in the woodwork.
Both parties are doing a superb job of motivating and exciting the base and getting them to the polls."

Liberals amount to about one out of five voters. But as long as they expect
presidential candidates to adhere to their strict platform, they will estrange their
candidate from the center. Even John Kerry, the supposed compromise candidate in 2004, never would have survived the primary gauntlet if he had not been
liberal on every key social issue.

The further front-loading of the primary process also makes such compromise more difficult. Primaries veer the parties toward their flank, and indeed, the
liberal flank is farther from the American majority. In 2005, the Pew Research
Center for the People & the Press divided political persuasions into nine groups.
Liberals were found to be the least religious, to hold the strongest preference for

diplomacy over military force, and to be most supportive of gay marriage, abortion, and environmental protection. They also had the most sympathy for illegal immigrants, likely because their jobs are the least threatened since liberals are the wealthiest and best educated group. More than 80 percent are white, and among them significantly more are women. Among the three Democratic blocs, including poor and conservative Democrats, liberals are the least enthusiastic about the party, and are therefore the least likely to put the coalition before the cause.[36] This, in part, explains their unwillingness to compromise with moderates. But it is moderation on social issues that defines America.

Americans are conservative in their opposition to gay marriage and gay adoption but liberal in their support for embryonic stem cell research and granting same-sex couples the same legal rights and protections as those in traditional marriages, based upon polling. Most Americans are centrist, rather than extreme, on the abortion issue.[37] But from abortion to gay marriage, Democrats' positions have been more successfully wielded against them. The left flank of the party continues to rely on tax policy to achieve their goals rather than consider why they offend so many regular Americans.

When Thomas Frank's best-seller *What's the Matter with Kansas* hit bookshelves in 2004, it fed the dogmatic liberal desire to believe the Republican ascension was a con.

> The problem is not that Democrats are monolithically pro-choice or anti-school prayer; it's that by dropping the class language that once distinguished them sharply from Republicans, they have left themselves vulnerable to cultural wedge issues . . . whose hallucinatory appeal would ordinarily be far overshadowed by material concerns.[38]

In other words, a liberal was arguing that working-class whites should care less about the state of society and be more materialistic. To win, Frank argued, Democrats need to champion the economic populism of William Jennings Bryan and the like-minded. "One example is worth a wilderness of abstractions," Henry Steele Commager once wrote.[39] There are no examples of winning campaigns that placed economic populism at the center of a presidential race.

Not even FDR's "New Deal for the American People" was a populist movement. Hoover's undoing was a response to the Great Depression. From Andrew Jackson's "sinews of the republic," his "producers" versus the "nonproducing elite," to William Jennings Bryan's "brow of labor," to the "average man" of the American Federation of Labor's heyday in the early twentieth

century, to prohibitionist preacher Billy Sunday's "rubes" against the "dia-
mond-wearing bunch," to George Wallace's working man, to Richard Nixon's
"silent majority," to Al Gore's "people versus the powerful," to George W.
Bush's "values politics," and John Edwards's "two Americas," populism has always been woven into presidential politics. Yet, the class politics of Europe has
not won presidencies stateside. Economic populism is the chimera of American
liberalism. Thomas Frank idealizes a strategy that did not win any of William
Jennings Bryan's three bids for the presidency. Equally pertinent, Bryan's populist movement, the most successful the left has known, was never merely about
class. It was born of his Christianity and his era's drastic economic downturns. In
Kansas alone, between 1890 and 1894, 11,000 farm mortgages were foreclosed
because of the drought.[40] And like all populism, Bryan's had its dark under-
belly—instead of the racism of George Wallace, Bryan's was saturated in anti-
Semitism and nativist politics.

Despite history, many Democrats expected middle- and lower-class whites
to ignore their grievances with liberalism and vote Democratic based on tax
policy. But in a nation whose people believe they or their children can be rich
someday, cultural populism is the only populism that has proven worth its weight
in electoral votes.

While values *may* matter most, cultural issues are neither contrived nor
separate from a person's economic state. For example, financial struggles cause
divorces, divorces create instability, and instability creates the search for a moral
center.

"I don't believe the Thomas Frank argument that there has been this
sleight-of-hand and cultural values are trumping economic interests," Anna
Greenberg says. "It is completely ridiculous." But it was also exactly what activist
Democrats wanted to hear, so they bought it. After all, you can defeat propaganda with better propaganda.

By November 2003, as the presidential primaries neared, the Republican
dominance of the white male voter earned new concern among Democrats.
"NASCAR dad" referred to rural white men, "the guys with the red-and-white
'3' decals on their trucks signifying their loyalty to the late Dale Earnhardt, not
the late Jefferson Davis," as one *Boston Globe* columnist put it.[41] Akin to the
"angry white male" and "soccer mom" articles, "NASCAR dad" dealt far more in
stereotypes than in substance.

After the 2004 election, the White Male Gap was vast, and again ignored.
Forty years in the wilderness, with brief reprieves, is no way for a political party

to persist. One year later, liberal *New York Times* columnist Maureen Dowd took her provocative wit to new levels, publishing her 2005 best-seller *Are Men Necessary?* The answer was a blunt *yes*, in terms of politics, if Dowd's Democratic Party was to again have a sustainable presidential majority to win and *keep* the White House.

THE 2006 MIDTERMS AND WHITE MEN

The midterm election of 2006 was not a reclamation of liberalism. Had the Republicans not been mired in scandal, had the war in Iraq not appeared to be more like the Vietnam War by the month, Republicans might have held Congress. "There is no political boon greater than the ineptitude of one's foes," Michael Kazin wrote in *The Populist Persuasion*.[42] The Democrats' boon may turn out to be fleeting. Prior to the election, Clinton strategist James Carville called 2006 the most "favorable environment" for Democrats since Watergate.[43]

And they did win. Yet, the 2006 contest was little more than history asserting itself. In the sixth year of every two-term presidency between 1862 and 2002, the president's party has lost on average 40 representatives and about seven senators to the minority party.[44] Democrats upheld history perfectly.

However, temporary victories during scandals or economic downturns and against poor opponents cannot change long-term electoral trends. Democrats also did well in the midterms of 1998 and 1986, only for Republican presidential victories to follow.

Most telling, the three most prominent Senate seats narrowly won by Democrats in 2006, which allowed for their slim majority in the upper chamber, were not won by the Democrats of the urbane sort. They were exactly the sort that Democrats need to bridge the White Male Gap—and they did.

It took the son of Bob Casey of Pennsylvania—barred from speaking at the 1992 Democratic convention because of his antiabortion views—to unseat the social conservative Rick Santorum, the Senate's third most powerful leader. Like his father, this Casey was also pro-gun. Casey Jr. won white men by a margin of 6 percent in 2006. It marked a 15 percent improvement with white men since 2000 for Democrats, compared to a 4 percent improvement with white women over the same period.

Also a strong Second Amendment type, Montana Democratic farmer Jon Tester—a big man who farms, owns a pickup truck, sports a flattop, baggy jeans, and cowboy boots—wrested a senate seat from the incumbent Republican with conservative stances, which accounts for Tester's opposition to amnesty for illegal immigrants. While doing slightly worse among white women than the Democrat did in 2000, Tester lost among white men by *only* 4 percent. In comparison, the 2000 Montana Democratic candidate had lost white men by 21 percent—and with them, the race.

Virginia's senate race was more complicated. It took Ronald Reagan's former naval secretary, Jim Webb, to unseat George Allen, once a prominent Republican presidential prospect. Webb won about 3 percent more white men than Allen's 2000 Democratic challenger. It was a slight improvement and one Democratic presidential contenders have rarely accomplished. Webb also gained 2 percent with white women and improved 2 percent with minorities. But had Webb not made the meager improvement with white men, Republican George Allen would still be representing the Virginia Commonwealth.[45]

The day after the 2006 midterms, presidential politics was immediately the topic of the Washington chattering class. The Republican "thumping," as President Bush portrayed it, emboldened John McCain's moderate campaign, until McCain too was dragged downward by the Iraq war. The night before Bush spoke, as returns were still coming in, Fox News's Chris Wallace was interviewing McCain. Wallace asked the Arizona senator about the race of 2008. "Look," McCain said, "We've taken setbacks before. In '76, we lost just about everything, and Ronald Reagan gave us new direction, new focus." On the night of Republicans' most significant electoral defeat since 1992, McCain believed that the GOP's future would be born in the Republicans' most successful past, one created by the white men who had left the Democratic fold in the 1960s. "The story of the white male voter moving to the Republican Party is still going," presidential scholar John Fortier says. "It's such an old story that people don't think it is still happening."

Yet the future is not fated. A Democrat with the leadership of Franklin D. Roosevelt, and not merely the charisma of John F. Kennedy—but with the hero's tale behind him—can win back enough white men and thereby begin a new Democratic era. It will, though, take a political party that places the pragmatism of the moribund FDR Democratic coalition at the forefront, and in that look toward its most successful past heeds the lessons of history.

This is easier said than done. With leading news organizations once more discussing the female swing vote during the 2006 midterm elections—"mortgage mom" replaced "security mom" on the front page of the *Washington Post*—the myth of the Democrats' future resting primarily on the female vote continued.[46] The white male voter remained rejected and forgotten.

So the plot line persists. Mark Twain observed that history does not repeat itself, but it does rhyme. The same politics that made presidents in George Washington's and John F. Kennedy's day still makes them today. The technology changes but people's passions do not. And so as the 2008 election nears, Democrats are like an old record slowly being set in a jukebox. The dirge seems to be playing all over again. It sounds something like "Bye, Bye, Miss American Pie," if only because it all began back then, in the mid-century that the lyrics mourn.

UP FROM THE ASHES
The New Conservatism and the White Everyman

"I don't happen to be a rich man," Richard Nixon told America. He spoke of the "modest circumstances" of his boyhood and working at his father's store. He recalled his service in World War II. "I guess, I'm entitled to a couple of battle stars. I got a couple of letters of commendation. But I was just there when the bombs were falling." Dwight Eisenhower was the hero. Nixon was the grunt, like most of the other men of America. Three out of four infantrymen never fired their weapons during the war, but they were there when the bombs fell.[1] These were the white men Nixon sought for a new Republican majority.

Nixon spoke to the nation in 1952. It was the lowest point of his career at that point, as he defended an $18,000 secret political fund made public by press reports. Eisenhower was considering dropping Nixon from the ticket. Thomas Dewey urged Nixon to resign the vice presidential nomination. But Nixon was intent on one last effort to save it. He sat, resting his elbows on the desk, clasping his hands, his long sagging face overpowering his small shoulders, as all three television networks broadcast his speech.

Nixon said he owned a 1950 Oldsmobile, had mortgages, and owed $3,500 to his parents on which he paid interest. "Pat and I have the satisfaction that every dime that we've got is honestly ours," he said, famously adding, "I should say this, that Pat doesn't have a mink coat. But she does have a respectable Republican cloth coat, and I always tell her she'd look good in anything." Nixon added that there was one gift he did take for personal use—his dog Checkers. "The kids, like all kids, love the dog" and "we're gonna keep it." Nixon pointed out that the chairman of the Democratic National Committee said, "If a man couldn't afford to be in the United States Senate, he shouldn't run for the Senate. . . . I don't agree with [Chairman] Mitchell when he says that only a rich man should serve his government." Nixon, pushing the point, said that he was not like Democratic nominee Adlai Stevenson, "who inherited a fortune from his father."

After Nixon established his everyman bona fides, he said that the very same columnists who were criticizing him also criticized his prosecution of communist spy Alger Hiss. "But I continued to fight because I knew I was right." It was an early effort to invalidate media reports as liberally biased, to portray the Republican fight as the fight against communism, and the conservative party as the party of the common man.

Nixon concluded with a quotation from Abraham Lincoln, the first Republican president. "God must have loved the common people—he made so many of them." Finally, Nixon said that he was going to keep on fighting and so would his wife, Pat. "After all, her name was Patricia Ryan and she was born on St. Patrick's Day, and you know the Irish never quit." And neither would Nixon, like all those working-class descendants of Irish immigrants who Republicans were intent on winning.[2]

Republicans dearly desired a victory in 1952. Democrats had won five presidential elections in a row. A 1949 *Wall Street Journal* editorial described the common American perception of conservatives: "If a man is described as a 'conservative' in politics," it read, "he is likely to be suspected of wanting to cheat widows and orphans and generally to be a bad fellow."[3] Conservatives' two central ideas had become suspect. The belief in absolute laissez-faire economics ended with its failure during the Great Depression. Isolationism became untenable with America's new role following the Second World War. By the summer of 1951, a Gallup poll asked, "What does the Republican Party stand for today?" More respondents chose "for privileged few, moneyed interests, big companies" over any other options.[4]

The same year of the *Wall Street Journal* editorial, George Orwell's *Nineteen Eighty-Four* was published, contributing to the reemerging American skepticism of big government. Two years later William F. Buckley published *God and Man at Yale*, in which he castigated Yale as antagonistic to both Christianity and capitalism. And in 1953, Russell Kirk's monumental book *The Conservative Mind* became the intellectual bulwark of the right. Kirk believed that a religiously based morality was the mortar of society. True conservatism, in his view, treasured the best of traditional customs and institutions while reconciling itself with the times. The past was to inform the future; conservatism was to be the defense of the permanent things in life.

Washington was without an organized conservative movement in the early 1950s. Magazines such as the *Nation* and *New Republic* were the brain candy of the New Deal coalition. They had no equivalent conservative counterweight until the young and intellectually irrepressible Buckley came along to create the foundational publication of a new coalition. Buckley was of the manor born, and with his enunciated inflection and his father's $100,000 of seed money he founded the *National Review* in 1955.[5] In the premiere issue Buckley declared that the magazine "stands athwart history, yelling Stop, at a time when no one is inclined to do so."[6] Buckley provided the forum to fuse social conservatives, libertarians, and national security hawks.

"What's happened in the last 50 years is the intellectualization of the conservative movement," Buckley recalls in an interview. "So it no longer could be simply dismissed as an anti–labor union and a prodiscrimination movement, which essentially it was associated as up until the late '50s."

JOCK POLITICS: ANTI-INTELLECTUALISM AND THE DOUGHFACE DEMOCRAT

That Dwight Eisenhower defeated Adlai Stevenson in 1952 didn't irk Columbia University historian Richard Hofstadter. Both political parties had attempted to recruit the Allied supreme commander, as they had the century before with "Old Rough and Ready" Zachary Taylor. What stunned Hofstadter was that despite being "conventional in mind" and "relatively inarticulate," Ike won a "decisive" 55 percent of the vote by turning Stevenson's "uncommon mind" into a personal weakness. *Time* wrote that Stevenson's defeat "discloses an alarming fact long suspected: there is a wide and unhealthy gap between the American intellectuals and the people."[7]

If the rise of the Republican Party was due to its intellectualization, as Buckley contends, it was a decidedly anti-intellectual ascendancy. In this first televised campaign, Stevenson was the quick-witted and erudite Illinois governor. Eisenhower had a broad smile, a calm disposition, and was intent on appearing folksy. He hid his taste for classical music and confessed to his secretary that he was "deathly afraid of being considered highbrow."[8] Ike discreetly governed his administration. To Americans, he was the good-natured paternal general, and that's how Ike wanted it.

In comparison, Stevenson had been a civilian in World War II. After a 1952 *New York Herald Tribune* columnist branded Stevenson as the "egghead," the term stuck. Stevenson was ruthlessly attacked thereafter. This was the "thinking man's candidate," hence no man at all in many American minds.[9] Stevenson did not laugh, he "giggled."[10] The *New York Daily News* described Stevenson's "fruity" and "trilled voice." His Democratic supporters were described as "Harvard lace-cuff liberals" and "lace-panty diplomats," in contrast to Nixon's "manly explanation of his financial affairs" in his Checkers' speech.[11]

Eisenhower was the jock and Stevenson was the nerd, in pop-culture terms. And in America, the jocks were the men in charge. Only by shedding his glasses can the nerd find his inner superhero—Clark Kent becomes Superman; Peter Parker becomes Spiderman. The American man was supposed to be the strong, silent type. John Wayne in *The Quiet Man* (1952) played a self-made boxer who came from nothing, a man who said what he meant, meant what he said, and who backed up his silence with a punch.

Conservative populism appealed to the commonly held view that the intellectual was wimpy at best. But at worst, he was said to be amoral, sympathetic to the wrong, and skeptical of the good. He was weak in character and weak in body. He lived in books instead of reality. He was a thinker and not a doer. He was paralyzed by alternatives, socially awkward, and godless. Puritan Reverend John Cotton warned in 1642 that, "The more learned and witty you bee, the more fit to act for Satan you bee."[12]

In the American mind, it was not good to be dumb but it was better to be good, a theme reinforced from Mark Twain's *Huckleberry Finn* (1851) to the film *Forest Gump* (1994). When Andrew Jackson ran against the intellectual son of an intellectual president, John Quincy Adams, in 1824 and 1828, the race was described as the people's practical warrior versus the patrician thinker. Jackson's supporters declared that "natural sense" prevailed with his victory in 1828.[13] From Jackson on, "the people's candidate" was continuously portrayed as not simply having the best interests of voters in mind but being *one of the people*.

By 1901, Americans had a president who charged up San Juan Hill, would box in the White House, and later establish himself as a big game hunter. Although Theodore Roosevelt had a photographic memory and was a Phi Beta Kappa Harvard graduate, the physical was emphasized over the mental. "An educated man must not go into politics as such," Roosevelt wrote in 1894. "If an educated man is not heartily American in instinct and feeling and taste and sympathy, he will amount to nothing in our public life."[14] After Woodrow Wilson hesitated to enter the Great War, Roosevelt raged that he had "Done more to emasculate American manhood . . . than anyone."[15] To Roosevelt, Wilson's intellectualism was embodied in his aptitude for thinking and his failure to act.

"No party whose appeal was primarily intellectual could command [the American man's] support," Henry Steele Commager wrote in *The American Mind*. Democrats from Adlai Stevenson to John Kerry learned this fact the hard way. "No people was more avid of college degrees," as Commager described Americans, "yet nowhere else were intellectuals held in such contempt or relegated to so inferior a position."[16]

Even the intellectuals in the United States are critical of intellectuals. In Woody Allen's 1979 film, *Manhattan*, Allen stands in a circle at a black-tie benefit, chatting away with a group of upper-crust New Yorkers—

> *Allen:* Has anybody read that Nazis are gonna march in New Jersey? You know—We should go there, get some guys together. Get some bricks and baseball bats and explain things to 'em.
> *Man:* There was this devastating satirical piece on that in the *Times*.
> *Allen:* Well, a satirical piece in the *Times* is one thing, but bricks get right to the point.
> *Woman:* But biting satire is better than physical force.
> *Allen:* No, physical force is better with Nazis.[17]

During the 1980 presidential race, Jimmy Carter's campaign advertised that "the life of every human being on Earth can depend on the experience and judgment and vigilance of the person in the Oval Office." Carter anticipated that he could win reelection by appearing the smarter man, asserting that "The president must be able to grasp the issue."[18] But Reagan was viewed as more "heartily American" and so the Republican won.

By the turn of the century, George W. Bush touted that he did not read newspapers. Throughout the election, the Texas governor was ridiculed for his "Bushisms," a term first applied to his father's gaffes. But the younger Bush's garbled syntax ("Is our children learning," or his pledge that, if he lowers "the terriers and bariffs," the economy will grow) humanized the son of privilege.[19] Bush fumbled with his words like one of the guys. But men knew what he meant, and they trusted that he really meant it, in contrast to the professorial Al Gore. Bush's ignorance and misstatements also reeled political opponents into "miss-underestimating" him, to use Bush's wording. Many forgot that Bush scored in the top 10 percent of the country on his SATs, the same as Gore.[20]

The year Bush assumed office, he gave the commencement address at Yale, his alma mater. "To those of you who received honors, awards, and distinctions, I say, well done. And to the C students—I say, you, too, can be president of the United States," Bush joked. "I did take English here," he later said, adding, "I want to give credit where credit is due. I want the entire world to know this— everything I know about the spoken word, I learned right here at Yale."[21] Portions of the address were carried by the national news, and it was always the self-deprecating quips that made the two-minute segment.

In the presidential election of 2004, when voters were asked which attribute mattered most in deciding on their candidates, the characteristics of "strong leader" and "has clear stands on the issues" were selected at three times the rate as "intelligent." This emphasis on character was even more potent among white men.[22] As long as Democrats campaigned as the intellectual, they were practicing a losing strategy.

"There is nothing wrong with being articulate and intellectual, but I don't think tort lawyers, professors, and the superrich, or the ones who seem that way, are the ones who are going to win," says social psychologist William Pollack, who has held psychological sessions with hundreds of white men. "The Democratic Party has to find leadership from within that has strength, that has its roots in white, male, working-class experience, but cares about the rest of that Democratic tent of people of color."

At mid-twentieth century, the Northeast held the elite universities and prep schools, banking, fashion, Wall Street, and the media. The rising left's intellectualism was, if not sympathetic to socialism, unwilling to castigate communism as morally wrong. Socialist Henry Wallace's liberals were not suspicious of communism: They were suspicious of the nascent American superpower. To conservatives, it was no coincidence that Wallace won half of his 1948 support in New York. His success spawned men like Joseph McCarthy, who swooped down and sought working-class white men with his demagogic crusade against communism.

As early as 1947, leading FDR liberals pushed back. Historian Arthur Schlesinger Jr., Protestant theologian Reinhold Niebuhr, economist John Kenneth Galbraith, as well as Eleanor Roosevelt, joined a hundred others at Washington's Willard Hotel to formalize the liberal anticommunist group

Americans for Democratic Action (ADA).[23] By 1949, Schlesinger detailed in *The Vital Center* his concern that Democrats not follow the "doughface progressive" who has:

> A weakness for impotence, because progressivism believes that history will make up for human error; a weakness for rhetoric, because it believes that man can be reformed by argument; a weakness for economic fetishism, because it believes that the good in man will be liberated by a change in economic institutions; a weakness for political myth, because Doughface optimism requires somewhere an act of faith in order to survive the contradictions of history.

Later Schlesinger, directly criticizing the absolutism of leftist ideologues, wrote that the doughface's comfort in fighting the "lost cause" allows him to relegate Democrats to becoming a "permanent minority" due to their unwillingness to compromise. Politics, which requires realism to recognize what is possible, is not a means to action for the doughface, but the means to express one's "private grievances and frustrations."[24] In contrast, classical liberalism requires the engagement of an imperfect world with imperfect actions in order to reach better ends.

But by the late 1960s, the doughface liberals won. The new wave of liberals were soon to drive out the white workingman and park the Democrats in permanent minority status.

II

FROM THE APEX OF LIBERALISM TO THE DECLINE OF DEMOCRATS (1962–1968)

Eleven months after John F. Kennedy declared the nation would land a man on the moon, just as Congress was debating civil rights legislation, Martin Luther King Jr. stood in front of the Lincoln memorial and spoke before at least 250,000 Americans. It was the March on Washington, August 1963. Like the man whose memorial he stood beneath, King now too belongs to the ages. Three months later, as J. Edgar Hoover called Robert Kennedy to say the president had been shot, Vice President Lyndon Johnson, the consummate legislator, had already left the Dallas hospital. He was flown off to Washington, sworn in on the plane, and tasked with completing Kennedy's promise.

The next year, when Johnson sat down and put his name to the 1964 Civil Rights Act, he was "euphoric." But later that night, Johnson seemed "melancholy," confiding to an aide that, "I think we have just delivered the South to the Republican Party for a long time to come."[1]

Barry Goldwater hoped exactly that was true. Goldwater voted against the act, and in doing so sent word to southern whites that the Republican Party—under the political euphemism of "states rights"—would defend segregation.

"We're not going to get the Negro vote as a bloc in the 1964 and 1968," Goldwater declared in 1961, "So we ought to go hunting where the ducks are."[2]

Southern Democrat George Wallace wanted those ducks as well. He was to mark a new conservative populist era, building his candidacy as a die-hard defender of segregation. Wallace was a fighter by nature, a bantamweight who won his state's Golden Gloves title twice. He had a flat face and overbearing eyebrows that arched upward. He once told a politically allied crowd in Cincinnati, "When you and I start marching and demonstrating and carrying signs, we will close every highway in this country!" A child of the evangelical South and a country music fan, Wallace spoke against those "pseudo-intellectuals" and asked voters, "Can a former truck driver married to a dime store clerk and a son of a dirt farmer be elected President?"[3] It was an appeal that won many whites. During the Democratic primaries, Wallace won roughly a third of the vote in Wisconsin and Indiana, and more than 40 percent in Maryland, proving his popularity above the Mason-Dixon line.[4]

Meanwhile, Democrats bravely pushed the civil rights cause. Two months after Johnson signed the Civil Rights Act, Democrats agreed not to accept convention delegates from states that did not let blacks vote. The first southerner to win the Democratic nomination for president in 120 years was breaking from the segregationist history of the region.[5]

In the moderate Republican Northeast, Goldwater was increasingly criticized. The *Saturday Evening Post* editorialized, "Goldwater is a grotesque burlesque of the conservative he pretends to be. He is a wild man, a stray, an unprincipled and ruthless jujitsu artist like Joe McCarthy." Conservative forbearer Peter Viereck wrote in 1962, "American history is based on the resemblance between moderate liberalism and moderate conservatism," and there was little that was moderate about Goldwater.[6] Goldwater was once a Thunderbird-driving fighter pilot. His campaign was conservative, but he was as reckless as his background. While Johnson pledged to deescalate the war in Vietnam, Goldwater argued for the use of low-yield atomic weapons against the Vietcong and favored the use of a portable nuclear device called a Davy Crockett.

Goldwater knew he could not beat Johnson. His goal was to force moderate Rockefeller Republicans to relinquish the party. The blue bloods were to be overthrown to make room for the blue collars. Goldwater did defeat Nelson Rockefeller and then lost the general election spectacularly.

Johnson won 44 states and 61 percent of the electorate. He tied Franklin D. Roosevelt's 1936 electoral record. Democrats not only had the largest House majority since 1936, they outnumbered Republicans two-to-one in the Senate. Nationwide, Johnson won 43 million votes. Yet, for all Goldwater's poor politicking, 27 million Americans backed the conservative. Goldwater won the votes of five states in the Deep South. It was the last time a Democrat won the majority of whites.

The first hints of the emerging White Male Gap came in 1964. Since 1948, white men had voted Democratic at higher levels than white women. But in 1964 slightly more white women supported Johnson than white men.[7] The tectonic plates of politics were shifting.

"THE GREAT SOCIETY"

As a boy, Johnson had listened to William Jennings Bryan's oratory.[8] Men said they could hear Bryan speak from blocks away. When Bryan stood before the Democratic convention in 1896 and made his "Cross of Gold" speech, he declared, "You shall not press down upon the brow of labor this crown of thorns. You shall not crucify mankind upon a cross of gold." Afterward, he was carried off on delegates' shoulders.

The Nebraskan represented agrarian America in what was likely the most class-conscious election in presidential history. In the Panic of 1893, railroad companies failed and a four-year depression followed. The gold reserves rapidly decreased. The South and West suffered from poor harvests amid a five-year drought.

Business interests back East were concerned about Bryan's ascension. In New England, firms put up signs that read: "This factory will be closed on the morning after the November election if Bryan is elected," and railroads put notices in pay envelopes warning that if Bryan won, they would shut down.[9] Support for Bryan was strong in the Midwestern open ranges, where the cattle population had been destroyed in the blizzard of 1886–87, and in the South as cotton and tobacco prices precipitously declined. Wagons came back East with signs stating "in God we trusted, in Kansas we busted," but even that was not enough to win the great populist the presidency.[10] William McKinley won by a margin of 4 percent of the electorate. The class politics of Bryan failed, even amid dire economic circumstances nearly unparalleled in American history.[11]

It was Johnson who beat back the divisive cultural populists of 1964. Following the election, this man—who was famous for breaking down legislators by standing close, towering over them, his receding slick hairline reflecting the ceiling lights as he gripped their hands and their shoulders, cajoling, smiling, and insisting all at once—instituted domestic reforms that possibly exceeded even FDR's.

Johnson took his 1964 landslide as a mandate to shift the focus from civil rights to a war on poverty. FDR's administration had been the strong father: If Americans did their chores, their allowance was deserved. But in Johnson's time, liberalism began to define itself only by the allowance. Direct benefit programs replaced direct relief programs. Johnson targeted groups instead of needs. Though the two correlated, they were not one and the same. Doris Kearns Goodwin wrote in *Lyndon Johnson and The American Dream*, "Johnson seemed to regard the programs of the Great Society in the way overly fond parents look at their children."[12] Surely, if he was a more giving father than FDR, he could be greater. Johnson's "overly fond" tendencies surged government spending. From 1965 to 1969 federal outlays for health programs alone increased sevenfold. Johnson's Voting Rights Act, his Social Security Act, his food stamps that fed millions of Americans, and the National Endowment for the Arts were the crowning achievements of twentieth-century liberalism. But as presidential historian Allan J. Lichtman put it, capturing the conservative grievance, the federal government increasingly became a "check writing entity."[13] And in that capacity, the Great Society's failures were emphasized far more than the larger successes.

Initially, many white Americans supported some programs—the early broad racial coverage of the assistance was vital to this approval. As Cornel West wrote in *Democracy Matters*, "the uniqueness of Lyndon Johnson was that he recognized that the interests of poor whites were the same as those of the vast majority of black people in America."[14] Between 1966 and 1969, the black poverty rate sunk from 42 percent to 32 percent, while the white poverty rate over the same period fell from 15 percent to 10 percent.[15] But, just as quickly, many white men were left out of public assistance, unlike during the New Deal. Programs focused on the ultrapoor, often those with dependents. As many working-class whites struggled to maintain a basic quality of life, they saw others gaining equivalent stability through welfare.

Not only did the new liberals following the Great Society ask white men to be altruistic, but some of the government services seemed not to be correcting the troubles of the time. Whites noticed that public housing projects became hives of crime. When white men saw this new breed of liberal championing failed programs, not merely the successes, they lost trust in Democrats' "natural sense." At the same time, the remarkable achievements of programs like Head

Start were lost on many whites, often because as recently as 2003 more than seven out of ten recipients were minorities.[16] The great failure of the Great Society was that programs did not target the poor and the working poor and lower-middle classes equally. In time, the mandate of liberalism narrowed as liberals narrowed the beneficiaries of their mandate.

The legacy of FDR's liberalism was that "government didn't simply prevent evil but actively promoted good," as H. W. Brands put it in his book *The Strange Death of American Liberalism*.[17] Under Johnson, the good from government began shifting. FDR's paternal expectation that citizens must work to earn the government's assistance became LBJ's expectation that the government's assistance could be had without work. Active state liberalism gradually acted for everyone except white men. Meanwhile, many liberals began pushing equal outcomes instead of equal opportunity, creating quotas that often left out only white males. The pace of the liberal push to correct for systemic injustices against blacks also ran against white opinion. A Gallup poll in 1966 found that 52 percent of nonsouthern whites believed Lyndon Johnson was "pushing integration too fast" and only 8 percent said it was not fast enough. The push was true to Democratic credo. However, most whites did not feel included in the government's fight. The legacy of liberal politics was soon reduced, in the eyes of many whites, to the politics of entitlements. In 1966, Gallup found that less than half of Americans supported Johnson's antipoverty programs, while three out of four opposed an income tax increase even to reduce inflation or lessen the deficit.[18]

LBJ had no great majority backing his Great Society. To the white men whose tax dollars supported a large portion of this assistance and who came to question its judiciousness—as well as its effectiveness in some cases—Republicans soon represented far more than a return to order. The GOP symbolized the traditional notion of what it was to make it as a man. Rugged individualism was becoming a right-leaning political notion.

After the Democratic congressional losses of 1966—the year *Time* selected the 25-and-under generation as Man of the Year—the Democratic allies in the labor movement produced a report that found "the repudiation of the Democratic Party reaches deeply into the political structure." The vote against Democrats, the report said, was a statement of "white backlash" not only in the South but also in white blue-collar and middle-income areas of the North.[19] That same year, Ronald Reagan won the governorship of California and pledged to "clean up the mess in Berkeley."[20] Two years earlier, the Berkeley

Free Speech Movement stimulated an emergent culture of student activism. Bob Dylan sang "The Times They Are A-Changin'," and from 1964 to 1972, few could have predicted how much.

THE TIDAL SHIFT OF 1968

As the Great Society focused on ending poverty and black inequality, whites became increasingly concerned with the rising wave of urban upheaval. By 1965, the same year the Voting Rights Act passed, the Los Angeles neighborhood of Watts was ablaze with rioting, causing more than 30 deaths and tens of millions of dollars in damage. Two years later, there were 164 riots, several lasting days and only put down by the National Guard. Overall, between 1964 and 1968, 257 cities experienced 329 violent upheavals.[21] Nationally, between 1960 and 1972, the violent crime and robbery rate tripled. The aggravated assault, rape, and murder rates all doubled.[22]

As Gary Gerstle points out in *American Crucible: Race and Nation in the Twentieth Century*, working- and middle-class white neighborhoods abutted black neighborhoods in which nearly half of young blacks were unemployed.[23] As the unrest rubbed against white neighborhoods, the men who were working to leave the cities, who were charged with the security of their households, felt that criminals were being coddled. They became increasingly open to Republicans' law-and-order rhetoric and stricter policies. Democrats seemed either not to care or were deaf to the growing discontent among whites.

"Civil rights was the issue of the century," says former Massachusetts Governor Mike Dukakis, who was the Democratic presidential nominee in 1988. But, "we kind of forgot about some other issues like decent jobs, and safe neighborhoods, and good schools" and "we began taking this traditional constituency for granted."

In John Updike's *Rabbit Redux*, second in the four-part series, the white workingman Harry "Rabbit" Angstrom is talking to a black power activist and Vietnam Veteran named Skeeter. The two enter into a debate over race relations, rioting, the chaos of the day.

> "Trouble with your line," Harry tells him. "It's purely self-pity. The real question is, where do you go from here? We all got here on a bad boat. You talk as if the whole purpose of this country since the start has been to frustrate Negroes. Hell, you're just ten per cent. The fact is most people don't give a damn what

you do. This is the freest country around, make it if you can, if you can't, die gracefully. But Jesus, stopping begging for a free ride."

"Friend, you are wrong. You are white but wrong," Skeeter replies, later adding, "We are what has been left out of the industrial revolution, so we are the next revolution."[24]

America grows younger as the character of Harry ages. Harry watches the revolution pass by his streets. Sometimes he feels hated for being a white man, sometimes he exhibits white ignorance, sometimes he feels like a wrench too rusty to work. Harry is perpetually left behind when the times quicken, until he is too far from the American dream to claim it, and is simply trying to stay one step ahead of survival. He later gets a stable job, setting linotype, but he gets the pink slip. There is no need for linotype anymore. There is no need for regular white men like Harry either. He feels as outmoded as his now useless trade. But like so many workingmen, he continues to grasp at hope, until middle age hits hard and eventually he must let go, unfulfilled and struggling for a cause to justify his life.

Harry is indicative of the same white men whose sons were *not* getting college deferments to escape the war in Vietnam. Working-class whites were less upset that their sons had to go to war than that some sons did not go. "The rich kids in college could opt out of the war and that does start to create some real class friction there," recalls presidential historian Stephen Hess. Divisions over the Vietnam War turned vitriolic as some of those men who avoided the draft began to protest against the war and those that fought it. To those who went to war, it was often a matter of manhood and their patriotic obligations.

During World War II, nearly all healthy men, about 12 million, entered the armed forces. Through the Korean War, about 70 percent of those who could serve, did serve.[25] By the Vietnam era, of the 27 million men who came of draft age from 1964 to 1973, less than 10 percent, about 2.5 million, served.

To the white men whose consciences wrestled with the Vietnam War, an entire generation was split over whether they went or stayed home, whether they did their patriotic duty or stood against that duty. In the conception of the time, a man's masculinity rested on his decision for the rest of his life. It haunted nearly every presidential election through 2008. Liberal upper-class whites were now at odds with FDR Democratic whites. It was an existential split. Manhood is self-worth. To so many men of the day, Vietnam became a test of that worth, particularly among working- and middle-class white men. While most minorities did not have the means to avoid the draft, some white men did. Therefore, military service became a checklist of bravado within white America. In the common workingman's mindset, those who volunteered were brave, those who answered the call to duty were honorable, and those who avoided the war were considered to be dishonorable, cowardly, not truly men. As American troop levels topped 200,000 in 1967, the boys of the white working- and middle-class disproportionately risked death overseas, while most boys of the white upper class went to college and were assured adulthood.

From 1962 to 1972, Harvard and M.I.T. graduated 21,593 students of whom 14 died in Vietnam. Over the same period, in nearby working-class South Boston, of the 2,000 men who came of draft age, 25 died in Vietnam. A study of the male population in Chicago found that men from poor neighborhoods were three times more likely to die in Vietnam than those from rich neighborhoods. Studies from Utah to Wisconsin echoed the findings.[26] And though the passionate antiwar protests occurred only on a small minority of college campuses, the activism topped newspapers and television news and therefore consumed the American consciousness.

"It flows from a feeling that the college campuses, the intellectuals, the cultural elites were all against the war and they were for common criminals, and were for bringing about a culture of welfare and race relations," political analyst Charlie Cook says, as we sit in his office in the Watergate complex in Washington. "These themes just really didn't exist or were perceptible back in the Eisenhower days."

In late February of 1968, CBS anchor Walter Cronkite returned from Vietnam and told viewers, "It is increasingly clear to this reporter that the only rational way out then will be to negotiate, not as victors, but as an honorable people who lived up to their pledge to defend democracy, and did the best they could." Afterward, Johnson told an aide, "If I've lost Cronkite, I've lost Middle America."[27]

Johnson had. By March, soon after liberal Eugene McCarthy came within a few hundred votes of beating LBJ in the New Hampshire primary, Robert Kennedy announced his intention to run for president. Before the month closed, with about a half million U.S. troops in Vietnam, Johnson went on national television, pledged to deescalate the war, and unexpectedly announced "I shall not seek, and I will not accept the nomination of my party for another term as your president." "Lyndon Johnson," Patrick Moynihan later said, was "toppled by a mob of . . . flower children and Radcliffe girls." And as Theodore White wrote about the very same activists, they "would, in due course, during the fall season, undermine and destroy the candidacy of Hubert Humphrey, the most committed liberal of the twentieth century."[28] Indeed, they soon did.

This was a different country than when Johnson, as a boy, had listened to Bryan. In 1968, college students outnumbered farmers by three to one, railway workers nine to one, coal miners fifty to one.[29] At the end of March, the culture of these students hit Broadway with the debut of *Hair*. If the simplicity of that musical about hippie idealism captivated liberal society, the idealism was soon shot once more with the assassination of Martin Luther King Jr. on April 4 in Memphis. Riots overran more than 100 cities that night, leading to about 24,000 arrests and $40 million in property damage. Nationally, 72,800 Army and National Guard troops were called to duty in the largest civil deployment in U.S. history.[30] But once the storm calmed, the movement had to go on. "Gibraltar may be strong," Ralph Waldo Emerson wrote, "but ideas are impregnable, and bestow on the hero their invincibility."[31] King was the Gibraltar of the greatest social movement in American history. Yet the idea was larger than even him, and so the potential of the times passed to another, soon resting solely on Robert Kennedy's shoulders.

"There was a frenzy in that environment, when he was out there, and that seemed to symbolize to a lot of Americans, I think, the fear that America itself was out of control, that we really didn't have a lid anymore on our social problems and that revolution was really around the corner," historian Doris Kearns Goodwin recalled. "On the other hand, there was a group of Americans who felt that only Bobby could heal the divisions, that because he was tough and because he was straightforward and because he was passionate, he could bring the blue collar workers and the blacks together."[32]

In mid-May, Nixon took to the radio to advocate "a new alignment for American unity."[33] Robert Kennedy looked increasingly likely to be Nixon's opponent. Kennedy won the Nebraska primary and called the victory a repudiation of the Johnson policy in Vietnam and of Vice President Hubert Humphrey. At the end of May, Eugene McCarthy won the Oregon primary. After the loss, a Kennedy campaign aide paraphrased Robert Kennedy—"Oregon, a fine state"—but Kennedy was said to have commented, "It just doesn't have enough poor people, black people, or working people." [34]

Robert Kennedy was attempting to build a presidency on this new Democratic coalition of solely the poor, minorities, and working people. Meanwhile, working- and middle-class whites, especially men, were turning away from Democrats. For decades thereafter, liberals naively followed Robert Kennedy's actions in Oregon. But it was his actions in the Indiana primary that provided the better lesson. RFK's pollster John F. Kraft warned Kennedy in Indiana that he was going to win the black vote but was having trouble with blue-collar whites. Kennedy adjusted the emphasis of his campaign from fighting poverty to law and order.[35] "The best move lies close to the worst," Norman Mailer once wrote.[36]

Breaking with the liberal mores of the time, RFK "saw no incompatibility between racial justice and the rule of law," Arthur Schlesinger Jr. wrote in *Robert Kennedy and His Times*. Although *The New York Times* reported that, under "the malign influence" of some staffers, RFK sounded a conservative anthem in Indiana, he was in tune with what the new school of liberalism was not. "As for the blue-collar whites, they too felt government had forgotten them," Schlesinger explained. "In later years, after intellectuals discovered their existence and gave them the awful name of 'ethnics,' Kennedy's effort to keep the black and white working class at peace with each other in Indiana no longer seemed sinister."[37]

Doing John F. Kennedy's dirty work, as well as his stint as attorney general, left Robert Kennedy both combative and practical. Once, discussing Che Guevara, RFK said that had he not been born rich, he would have been a revolutionary.[38] But RFK was born rich, white, and remarkably advantaged in the world of politics. Che Guevara was from privilege as well. Yet Robert Kennedy, the intrinsic romantic, was also far too much of a brute realist to place the movement before the election. In the end, RFK may have been able to win the White House, if only because of the potential of the times he embodied. But after winning the California primary on June 5, Robert Kennedy was shot in Los Angeles, and with him the liberal political era died.

After the assassination, John Updike commented that God might have withdrawn His blessing from America.[39] By election day, 67 percent of white men and 62 percent of white women did *not* vote Democratic. White men had been more loyal Democratic voters than white women through the 1950s, and this made their move to the Republicans in the Nixon years more of an electoral blow.[40]

Richard Nixon won on the first wave of defections to the Republican Party. He earned a rare second chance at the presidency after frontrunner George Romney said he was brainwashed into supporting the Vietnam War. Nixon later edged out Nelson Rockefeller and a young Ronald Reagan, with Strom Thurmond's help. And as Nixon stood before the Republican convention in Miami, his political career revived, he captured the times as well.

"As we look at America, we see cities enveloped in smoke and flame. We hear sirens in the night. We see Americans dying on distant battlefields abroad. We see Americans hating each other; fighting each other; killing each other at home," Nixon said. "And as we see and hear these things, millions of Americans cry out in anguish: Did we come all this way for this? Did American boys die in Normandy and Korea and in Valley Forge for this?" Nixon asked, pausing, urging America to "listen" to "another voice."

"It is a quiet voice in the tumult of the shouting. It is the voice of the great majority of Americans, the forgotten Americans, the nonshouters, the non-demonstrators. They're not racists or sick; they're not guilty of the crime that plagues the land; they are black, they are white," and he added, "They're decent people; they work and they save and they pay their taxes and they care."[41]

These were Nixon's people. Like Johnson, Nixon felt a tension with the Northeastern establishment. Presidential historian Stephen Hess, who worked in the Nixon administration, recalls, "a bitterness if not antagonism to the Kennedys. They were the rich kids who also got it easy," Hess tells me. "Daddy could buy them a presidency. And there was always some of that in Nixon."

Immediately following the Republican convention, Nixon gained 14 percentage points in the polls.[42] The party of Woodrow Wilson, of FDR, of Truman, of JFK, and of Johnson seemed enfeebled a few weeks later. And the Democrats' undoing came from within.

DEMOCRATIC PERMISSIVENESS AND DECLINE

By late August of 1968, the Democratic Party had lost its two great hopes with the name of Kennedy, saw their president undone by Vietnam, and their King murdered. While Hubert Humphrey won the nomination with little contention on the convention floor, in the Chicago streets outside there was turmoil.

Pushed by Johnson and backed by Humphrey, the Democratic platform committee rejected the plank calling for the United States to unilaterally withdraw from Vietnam. The antiwar delegates put on black armbands and sang the Civil Rights anthem "We Shall Overcome." All they were overcoming was their own electability. The rejection of the so-called peace plank was one of the last victories of the decreasingly influential centrist Democrats. Rule changes diminished the unions' and party bosses' influence in 1968, and with them went the pragmatism that had often won white male voters to their side. Outside on the streets, thousands of protesters, primarily young and a different sort of Democrat, were to be met by the whole of the city's police force. A few days of minor confrontations turned to chaos the night Humphrey was nominated for president.

"They were a generation that would try every idea, every drug, every action," Norman Mailer wrote at the time. "They were young men who were not going to Vietnam. So they would show every lover of war in Vietnam that the reason they did not go was not for lack of the courage to fight."[43]

The fight began when demonstrators took down the American flag in Grant Park. Soon police fired tear gas. Young marchers scattered, screaming "pigs!" The activists regrouped, only for the police to unexpectedly charge, armed with billy clubs and mace, attacking both radicals and pacifists, photographers and passersby.[44]

The "demonstrators were afterward delighted to have been manhandled before the public eye," Mailer wrote, "Yes, the rebels thought they had a great victory."[45] It was a shortsighted tactic.

"The problems in Chicago, the convention turned everybody off. Labor didn't subscribe to it in any way," recalls W. J. Usery, who after serving as a Navy welder during World War II became a labor union official, eventually working for the Kennedy and Johnson administrations as a trade liaison. He too, like so many white men, left the Democratic Party during this period. "To a lot of labor, many of these people were too far to the left," Usery adds over lunch as he takes a bite from his club sandwich. "A liberal as we think of it—I don't know many labor leaders who were. They *never* were."

As the Democratic Party moved left, the loyalty of blue-collar whites became increasingly strained. "Working people felt 'Why take my money and give it to people who don't work,'" Usery recalls, fiddling with a toothpick. "There was a strong feeling about people who were going out demonstrating for issues that I don't subscribe to," he pauses, straightens his navy blue sports jacket and scoots forward. With white hair, thick lips, large ears, and a steely stare, Usery has the face of a bulldog. "It was a difficult time," he continues, rubbing his hand on the table. "All of the legislation that was signed in the Johnson administration; we had a hell of a lot to swallow. Equal rights, equal opportunity, all these things were good. But there was so much change going on," he says. "I'm not saying they were right, but there was a lot of people that saw it as difficult."

Those very same people were all but lost to the Democratic Party after Chicago. "The labor movement, in most of my years, were World War II veterans, people who had come out of a war," Usery says, and the antiwar activists burning the flag, storming the streets of Chicago, were everything the veterans were coming to despise on the home front.

Hubert Humphrey came away from the convention with only a four-point bounce in the polls, ten short of Nixon's.[46] Democrats were badly burned by the week's events. The television images seemed to capture the very problem of the times. The reasons behind the protests and the police response were not the issue to most Americans. The upheaval was the issue.

"A working-class father who may have sacrificed for years in order to send his son to college cannot remotely comprehend why middle-class youths cry that 'the system' is rotten," read *Time* that year. "To him, they are all spoiled brats, profane, obnoxious, unwashed, promiscuous, to whom everything has been offered and from whom nothing has been demanded."[47]

At the very moment that white men saw a surge in crime in their cities, saw adjacent neighborhoods burn in the night, saw national guardsmen stream past their doorsteps, past the yard where their children played and the store where their wives shopped, Democrats seemed utterly incapable of keeping the peace, even among themselves. The call for strength by white men was a direct response to their desire for stability and safety. And even if many whites did not see crime increase significantly on their block, the troubles appeared relentlessly in their morning newspaper and on television.

The disorder emboldened the George Wallace's 1968 third-party candidacy, as he began appeasing the darker sides of white discontent. Chicago had badly damaged Humphrey's chances. When Humphrey served as mayor of Minneapolis in the late 1940s he was one of the most steadfast anticrime mayors in America. Two decades later, after the Chicago convention, Humphrey was seen as a man without the personal constitution to enforce order. The new liberals he represented did not distinguish between police brutality and the need for stern policing, between fighting crime and fighting blacks.

"With half of women in America uptight about law and order what was the liberal response?" Richard Scammon and Ben Wattenberg asked in *The Real Majority*. "Law and order, [the liberals] said, 'is a code word for racism.' In other words, 'lady, you're not really afraid of being mugged; you're a bigot.'" The rhetoric had real consequences. Two months prior to the election, when pollsters asked "Which candidate do you feel could do the best job in handling law and order?" Humphrey came in third behind Nixon and Wallace.[48]

To the white workingman, the Democrat looked, or truly became, ineffectual by his own sympathies for diverging constituencies. Democrats now sought a Balkanized coalition. Concurrently, the populist demagoguery of Nixon and Wallace, especially Wallace, rose with the pertinence of the law-and-order issue. Because, unlike liberals, conservatives bluntly stated that *it was an issue.*

"Where were the Democrats on crime? We were kind of apologetic, you know, 'well, gee whiz,'" 1988 Democratic nominee Michael Dukakis recalls. "You can't be apologetic on crime. People are entitled to live in safe neighborhoods."

Inside Dukakis's Boston office, he's short, quick-spoken, speaking of "Baah-ston" and ignoring the "r" in his words. Dukakis still has a working-class de-meanor. But in 1988, Dukakis was portrayed as part of the liberal elite.

"In the name of tolerance, did liberals tolerate crime?" I ask him.

"We did a lousy job helping people to understand the difference," he re-sponds, placing his elbows on the desk. "It's one thing to treat people fairly no matter who they are or where they come from, no matter the color of their skin. It's another thing not to take seriously the fact that crime in neighborhoods and cities is up and people are getting terrorized and folks don't want to come out of the house and all that stuff, there's got to be a response to that. Clinton under-stood that."

The Nixon and Humphrey race, and the times it embodied, shaped the next four decades of presidential politics. In 1968, George W. Bush was in his last year at Yale. He was beginning to loathe the intellectual elite. In later years this feeling helped him understand anti-intellectualism in American life. Karl Rove was also in college then; by 1969, Rove's father had abandoned his mother, and his mother soon after "withdrew" from life.[49] Rove's understanding of the power of cultural upheaval was visceral thereafter. That same year, Al Gore graduated from Harvard and soon after enlisted in the army. Hillary Clinton graduated from Wellesley, where she was senior class president and embodied a new age of feminism. By 1970, as Rudolph Giuliani became a U.S. Attorney, John Kerry had returned home from Vietnam a hero and soon stood against the war he came to see as ignoble. Bill Clinton was attending Yale Law School, where he met Hillary. By 1972 he had traveled down to Texas to work on George McGovern's behalf, only to learn the limits of dogmatic liberal idealism. A year later, when Barack Obama was not yet a teenager, John McCain returned from Vietnam, after more than five years as a prisoner of war.

The politics of modern presidential campaigns never has freed itself from the late 1960s and early 1970s. But it was Democrats who were damaged most by this paradigm. From then on they have been seen as a party disconnected from the mainstream and unwilling, or too weak, to defend what most within the mainstream care about. The White Male Gap was the result, and it began with Humphrey's defeat. Democrats relinquished the masculine to Republicans. The GOP was stern on law and order and strong on national security. By the close of the Chicago convention, the liberal party appeared to be the permissive parents, afraid to discipline their own youth. Average Americans wanted discipline, though. They wanted a stricter nation. Chicago captured the desire for a call to order. Despite the police brutality during the unrest—where mostly white students were on the receiving end of beatings—the public backed Mayor Daley and his police.

When voters were asked whether "Mayor Daley was right the way he used police against demonstrators," 66 percent of Americans said yes, while only 20 percent disagreed.[50] "When the kids met the cops, they were perceived as challenging the very fabric of the social order," Scammon and Wattenberg wrote.[51] For the 73 percent of America who were not white collar, they might have thought of the 1968 protest as, "those student punks are beating up *our* children, or *our* husbands, or *our* fathers."[52]

Democrats were listening to the unrest, but as presidential writer Theodore White wrote about the 1960 race, "All predictions of a Kennedy sweep based on crowd response ignored an enormous political truth: that quiet people vote, too."[53] Nixon knew this truth far better by 1968.

In the end, it was not any one issue. From rising crime to riots in the streets, from uneasy race relations to the antiwar movement and the self-indulgence of the new youth culture, many white Americans were sick of it. While most of the nation's editorial pages supported Johnson in 1964, they overwhelmingly favored Nixon in 1968.[54]

"It's beatniks, it's hippies, it's draft card burners. It's demonstrators. It's blacks. It's high taxation," columnist James Reston wrote after the Chicago convention. "It's easy sex and dope and kids running away from home. It's uncertainty, fear, madness, murder—all these appearing day after day on television and in the newspapers, adding up to a feeling that something is deeply wrong and must be changed."[55]

It was enough to end the Democratic era. The new political left fractured with destabilized times, split by their intraparty squabbling and uncompromising idealism. It came to be too much for the diverging interests of the Roosevelt coalition. The stresses exceeded the ties that bind in 1968. At times during the campaign, Humphrey was reduced to tears, drowned out by the young liberal activists.

"Humphrey was neutralized by the fact that he was Lyndon Johnson's vice president," historian Stephen Hess recalls. "He couldn't reject the administration at which he was vice president."

Despite Humphrey's pioneering stance for civil rights, the new left had moved on to the next issue, and their vision was most myopic. Humphrey was no Cold War Democrat, nor was he a dove. He was a man caught between two factions. To Johnson, Humphrey "was still a boy, better than most liberals, but too prone to talk instead of act, not a person that other men would respect in a room when it got down to the hard cutting."[56] To the political left, Humphrey was Johnson's boy—he was going to carry on Johnson's war. He was the real enemy because he was a wolf in sheep's clothing, and the dogmatic liberal crowds booed him for it, unyieldingly. "What about Nixon?" Humphrey meekly asked one unfriendly leftist audience.[57] The answer came on Election Day, and most powerfully from Schlesinger's "vital center."

American whites, this "silent majority," spoke loudly from behind the poll curtain. Nixon won 43.4 percent of the vote to Humphrey's 42.7 percent, with Wallace's American Independent Party winning 13.5 percent. Strikingly, Wallace won 66 percent of Alabama and 64 percent of Mississippi but fell as low as 34 percent in border states such as Tennessee. The Wallace vote likely would have split about 70 to 30 in Nixon's favor, had the Alabamian not run as a third-party candidate.[58] Most clearly, four years after Johnson's resounding victory, a strong majority of Americans voted against the Democratic candidate. "In the 1968 presidential election, the American people rejected not only Lyndon Johnson and Hubert Humphrey," wrote Stan Greenberg in *Middle Class Dreams*, "but also a social contract premised on the needs of the most disadvantaged rather than on the needs of the people generally."[59]

It was a GOP victory without the blue-blooded Northeastern Republican establishment. The Democrats won Connecticut, Pennsylvania, Massachusetts, and New York. As Nixon's former advisor Kevin Phillips observed, "For the first time since the founding of the Republican Party in 1854, a Republican president had been elected over the opposition of the principal residential citadels of Megapolitan money, media and fashion."[60]

Despite Wallace's winning many whites, Nixon still won the white vote in 1968, and he won more women than men. But more white men voted conservative, either for Nixon or Wallace, than voted liberal. Only about 33 percent of men and 39 percent of women in the white middle-income bracket supported Humphrey. Wallace won about 20 percent of white men (37 in the South and 14 percent elsewhere) and 12 percent of white women (33 percent in the South and 6 percent elsewhere).[61] From Wallace in 1968 to George W. Bush, southern white women were significantly more conservative than white women in the rest of the nation, in most elections years, while southern white men had more in common with fellows outside Dixie. In total, the candidate of rejection, Wallace, won nearly 10 million votes and, as expected, five states in the Deep South, but the Peripheral South was still not with him. Where race relations were concerned, Dixie was not of one political persuasion.[62] Misunderstanding this fact of the South undercut a half century of Democratic politics. Liberals saw Wallace only for his worst face, his racism. But it was the boxer, the populist, that spoke to whites as well. It was a Southern quality. It was a quality Americans still sought, even if liberals did not.

III

SOUTHERN MAN

Former Virginia Governor Mark Warner looks like the kind of man who could program C++ and also do ten pull-ups. He stands well over 6 feet tall, has a long face, blond hair, a thin upper lip, and a small double-lined crease between his green eyes. Warner's office sits off the Potomac and beside a lighthouse. The former governor was a serious presidential contender for the Democratic Party in 2008, but he withdrew, leaving John Edwards as the only top contender from Dixie. There has not been a nonsouthern Democratic president since 1960, and that year John F. Kennedy needed Lyndon Johnson to win Texas.

"The best predictor of the future is the past," Warner says on a hot August day in 2006. "Nah," he adds, waving his hand, "It's more than just the South. An awful lot of Missouri looks like south-side Virginia. It's saying to people outside major metropolitan areas that you've got a future in twenty-first century America."

In 1972, 24 percent of the white male vote came from the South. By 2004, it had increased to 27 percent. Today, about three out of four southern white men vote Republican in presidential contests, and the South's population continues to increase.[1] Jimmy Carter, Bill Clinton, and Al Gore were all from the South, yet in the seven presidential elections since 1980, Democrats have won a total of only eight southern states (seven by Clinton alone).

"It's fair to say that John Kerry would have been president had he won Ohio. He still would have lost the popular vote by 3 million votes," Democratic demographer Mark Gersh says. "You cannot be noncompetitive in one region of the country as large as the South and hope to win regularly. You'll win occasionally."

Warner and Gersh believe that focusing on the South will also translate to a broad rural appeal, where Democrats are weakest. The census counts nearly 60 million rural Americans, though they wield an outsized influence over presidential outcomes. One Wyoming resident counts as 72 Californians in the electoral college.[2]

"Some of the folks who helped me when I ran for governor," Warner says, "they like to say it was all about the NASCAR race and the bluegrass bands." He shakes his head in denial—"those are optics. You've got to have somebody who believes what they are doing in offering hope for these rural communities."

"NASCAR dad" was always a poor descriptor for southern or rural white men. Only 38 percent of NASCAR's fans live in the South.[3] Among whites, 36 percent of men say they like NASCAR, compared to 29 percent of women. But for those white fans who like the sport "very much," 4 percent more women than men favored Bush.[4] While the nomenclature was inaccurate, rural white men remain a constituency not beyond Democratic appeals.

"There is this enormous opening. White guys around America are willing to take a fresh look," Warner says, "but they are only going to take a fresh look at somebody who is not just about blaming Bush, blaming America for all the problems."

Standing on the wooden pier behind his home in Lake Providence, Louisiana, Wayne Nolan tosses fish food from buckets into the water. Catfish and bass sputter up. He looks down and says that sometimes things are just the way they are. He sticks out his barrel chest and talks low. Nolan is a veteran. He wears a bandana and has a thick mustache that looks like a frown. "[Bush] has just done what he had to do," he says. It's August of 2004 in the period between the two presidential conventions and CBS News has sent me on a cross-country drive to document how Americans are deciding their vote. I am driving from Portland, Maine, to Portland, Oregon, dipping as far south as New Orleans.

A pipe fitter at Northrop Grumman, Nolan picks up the metal buckets, the handles digging into his thick hands; as fish surface, he tosses in more feed and sets down the empty pails. The plant he works at is 25 miles south of the lake where he lives and where he takes disabled veterans fishing.

Nolan can't stand people who "put [Bush] down for what he's done," he says. "If he had done nothing, they'd put him down worse." He's the commander in chief—Nolan juts out his chest—and the president "did what he had to do."

Sitting with Mark Warner, I describe a man like Nolan. "The first thing is whether you walk up to the guy and try to make the case, or whether you walk by him. I think in a lot of ways the Democratic Party has walked by that guy," Warner says. He sits forward, excited, hits my arm like my old coach. Though in a month he'll bow out of the 2008 presidential race, he believes he comprehends something most Democrats do not.

"In the '60s, we were against the establishment. We were against 'the man.' The caricature of that was a white guy in the suit. But what somewhere in that period was lost," Warner hesitates, taps his thumb against his index finger, "was also the Democrats' ability to be the advocate for folks in Appalachia, blue-collar families white or black," he says. "What's the old Bob Dylan song? The whole song was about the enormous connection between the struggle of poor whites and poor blacks."

"Only a Pawn in Their Game" is the Dylan song Warner was trying to recollect. "A South politician preaches to the poor white man 'You got more than the blacks, don't complain,' Dylan sings. The song hit American airwaves the year Lyndon Johnson signed the Voting Rights Act, marking the end to the segregated South. But long before LBJ, southerners were never liberal. In the 1930s it was southern Democrats who joined Republicans to challenge Franklin Roosevelt. The Republicanization of the states on the periphery of the Deep South correlated far more to the gradual liberalization of Democrats than race.

"I somewhat disagree with this so-called southern strategy. If you go to the South now, you will find a whole lot more Republicans than there used to be, but also a whole lot less racially prejudiced whites," Harvard political philosopher Harvey Mansfield says. "Conservatism deserves some credit for that. I think what a lot of white southerners saw is that black folks aren't so bad, but liberals are."

Racism is inextricably linked to the shift in southern politics, but it does not explain why southerners voted Republican before liberals took up the civil rights cause, or why they continued to become Republican through the Reagan era. To reduce the southern defection to racial issues is to miss all that is *also* conservative about the South.

The region has a strong emphasis on individualism and a historical skepticism of big government, despite the fact that the South has the highest poverty rate in the nation as well as the most rapidly increasing number of

Americans without health insurance.[5] Yet southern conservatism is not rooted in libertarianism.

The military is most visible and most respected in the South. Southerners register the highest levels of life satisfaction, fully 60 percent, compared to 43 percent of nonsoutherners, which explains their cultural apprehension about reform. The South has the lowest level of unionization in the nation. It has the highest level of gun ownership: 46 percent of southerners compared to 40 percent nationally; among white men, 62 percent own guns in the South compared to 52 percent outside the South. Not surprisingly, the South also has the highest level of church attendance, and ultimately it was the South's Protestant religiosity that was responsible for the first significant Republican southern inroads under Herbert Hoover. Seven out of ten of the largest megachurches in America are located in the South or Midwest, while nearly half of all social conservatives live in the South.[6]

"But," Mark Warner says, "look at how the national media views people who are NASCAR fans. Look at the shows that supposedly represented rural America over the last forty of fifty years. They are *Hee Haw, Green Acres, Beverly Hillbillies*," Warner continues. "It's rural America viewed as Hicks-ville, a place that you can't wait to get out of. You know, wide swaths of those people don't want to leave."

A similar perception gap occurred within the Democratic Party. As the Deep South left the party over race and the peripheral South left over values, the urban Northeast and the West Coast came to dominate the party's culture.

"The more we've lost ground in the South," Democratic Leadership Council president Bruce Reed says, "the fewer southern Democratic voices there are at the table to counter the other voices that say southern white males don't matter."

The Deep South had changed drastically by 1968. Humphrey won only 5 to 10 percent of the white Deep South vote, in contrast to the region's loyalty to Democrat Al Smith in 1928.[7] Moreover, in Dixie, Democrats won only about one quarter of white southern voters in 1968. Since Eisenhower defeated Stevenson in 1952, Democrats had won at least half of southern whites.[8] The South was no longer friendly territory for Democrats after 1968. The majority of the Confederate states were now with the party of Lincoln, and black Americans—aware that Democrats were now their champions for equality—abandoned the party that had won their freedom.

Yet, the rise of the Republican Party did *not* begin over racial politics, though it did begin in the South. The "southern Flip," when Democrats below the Mason-Dixon line switched parties, is often traced to South Carolina Governor Strom Thurmond in 1948. Thurmond's defection from the party of Harry Truman demonstrated that the Deep South could be sliced from Democrats. With a promise to defend segregation, Thurmond's Dixiecrats won four states in the Deep South, including Alabama and Mississippi.

But the first substantive Republican inroads into the loyally Democratic South had occurred two decades earlier. Hoover won the presidency for the Republicans in 1928 on values issues, portraying the Democratic New York Governor Al Smith as a cultural outsider. Smith was branded with the taint of the slick urban political machine of Tammany Hall; he was Catholic and against prohibition. The portrayal allowed Hoover to reach much of the Protestant South, and he won in a landslide. It was the first widespread Republican victory in Dixie since Reconstruction. The party of Lincoln won five southern states in the peripheral South, including states like Florida, Tennessee, and Texas, on cultural issues. In total, nearly half the southern vote left the Democrats based on a cultural populist appeal in 1928.

There was a common conception that liberalism didn't "hold on to traditional values, the good ones," Harvey Mansfield says. "[Southerners] began to make a distinction between Southern tradition in regard to race and in regard to other things, in regards to honor and moral behavior and religion."

The religiosity of the South has long placed it at odds with secular intellectualism. There remains a conservative conviction, rooted in the challenge of the Enlightenment, that intellectualism breeds atheism and atheism breeds immorality. It is the secular intellectual who challenged biblical inerrancy, a core belief of Pentecostalism.

The antebellum masculine icon—a gentleman but also a warrior—rubbed against the post-1968 emergence of dovish liberalism. One study in which male students from different regions were unknowingly directed into a physically confrontational situation found that southern white men were more likely to start a fight if they felt their integrity or reputation were threatened. Researchers found that white men from the South subscribe to a "culture of honor" at a level that far exceeds that of men from any other region of the country.[9]

A 1992 survey of rural men found that southerners were more likely than midwesterners to validate violence as well. Southern men, for example, were more likely to approve of shooting a man who sexually assaulted someone's daughter or of fighting a man who made advances on his girlfriend. Twice as many southerners say they own guns for protection rather than hunting, in comparison to gun owners from the midwest. More Southerners also say that if a confidant called them a liar, it would likely disrupt the friendship.[10]

"We [Democrats] pay the biggest price for being seen as not as tough on national security," Bruce Reed says. "That's the principle reason, the major systemic reason, that we started losing white men to begin with. In the South we started losing white men earlier over race, but in a lot of places where race wasn't a factor, we were losing white males because Republicans were the party of strength and Democrats weren't."

CULTURAL POPULISM, FROM DIXIE TO THE NATION

At one point during the 1928 campaign, the evangelist John Straton connected Al Smith with the liberalized vices of the city. He said over his radio broadcast that Smith stood for "Card playing, cocktail drinking, poodle dogs, divorces, novels, stuffy rooms, dancing, evolution, Clarence Darrow, overeating, nude art, prizefighting, actors, greyhound racing, and modernism."[11]

Almost eighty years later, as the Iowa caucuses neared, Howard Dean was the front runner for the 2004 Democratic nomination. In some of the first salvos of attack advertising, a conservative tax-cutting group ran a commercial denouncing Dean. In the ad, a white couple was asked what they thought of Howard Dean's plan to raise taxes on working families. The man replied that Dean should: "Take his tax-hiking, government-expanding, latte-drinking, sushi-eating, Volvo-driving, *New York Times*–reading," and the wife chimed in, "body-piercing, Hollywood-loving, Left-wing freak show back to Vermont, where it belongs."

A year after George W. Bush won reelection, Gary Bauer is laughing as I read him the commercial's script. "That one sentence," the social conservative leader tells me, sitting in his Virginia office, his red tie the only color in the small sterile conference room, "summarizes the cultural problem for the Democratic Party. It's something that they've got to address."

Bauer leans forward. Boyish looking, almost impish, he has a small frame. Bauer is in a black blazer with gray pinstripes. His hair is lacquered back. The one-time head of the influential, socially conservative Family Research Council, Bauer also served as Reagan's chief domestic policy advisor.

"I do think that a sort of populism is at work and it's a populism by the way that Republican elites have had their own difficulty feeling comfortable with," Bauer adds. "There are elements of the Republican Party that still prefer the country club without all of these newcomers, even if that means that they lost a lot of elections. I refer to a lot of these new folks as K-mart Republicans. You are not going to see them at the local country club, but these are voters that increasingly feel that the party of Reagan is increasingly a place where they are comfortable."

Grover Norquist was the point man for much of this coalition. The conservative speaks as if his mind is moving too fast for his body. His sports coat is around his chair. His tie is loose on the neck. Short, with a full beard, he is shuffling papers as he chats. Between 2001 and 2006, the White House log recorded that Norquist made at least 97 visits, including a half dozen with President Bush.[12] His true influence, though, is felt every Wednesday at his weekly strategy meetings over chips and coffee, where men such as Karl Rove organized a movement.

"Who's in the room?" Norquist rhetorically asks me. "Gun owners: don't take my guns. Taxpayers: don't raise my taxes. Property owners: don't take my property. Small businessmen: don't regulate or tax my small business. Self-employed people: same thing. Investors: same issue. And then all the communities of faith: Evangelical Protestants, conservative Catholics, Orthodox Jews, Muslims, and Mormons. People often think about conservatives in three parts: foreign policy conservatives, economic conservatives, and social conservatives. You can describe them that way. It's just not useful for purposes of thinking about people's politics." Norquist quickens his speech. "The reason they're all in the room together is the Baptist, the Orthodox Jew, the Mormon, the gun owner, the small businessman all want to be left alone on their most important issue."

To argue that the Republican coalition is held together by this one idea is far-fetched to most Washington insiders. "I don't see a lot of intellectual consistency," political analyst Charlie Cook says. It was, after all, a conservative White House in 2004 that ordered the federal government to interfere with California's resolution to legalize marijuana for medical use. Social conservatives argue for states rights but many also push for a constitutional amendment banning same-sex marriage. But the contradictions do not necessarily disprove the contention.

"The Republican Party has stopped repelling southerners, stopped repelling Catholics," Norquist continues, "and has a coherent economic theory, well, world theory, that says: you are going to be left alone to go to church. You are going to be left alone with your money. So all of the various parts of this coalition that don't have to sleep with each other, that don't have to go to dinner with each other, they don't have to hang out, they don't have to live in the same neighborhood, they don't have to like each other. They just have to show up and vote on the same day for the same party."

In 1968, the practical was addressed along with the prejudiced by Richard Nixon. His use of the law-and-order rhetoric branded all blacks with urban disorder, though never in explicit terms. Northern ghetto nihilism and police brutality was unknown to most of white America. The law-and-order rhetoric was bumper sticker populism, but people seek plainspoken explanations, especially when their cities are burning.

To rally the white everyman, Nixon spoke of the "good people" and the "non-demonstrators" versus the "pinkos" and "bums." From Nixon to George W. Bush, conservative cultural populism defined an "other," often said to be elite, consistently responsible for mainstream discontent. The "non-elite" was rallied, as the good people were assured of their goodness. Nixon and the Republicans who followed him demonstrated that while Republicans claim that economic populism produces class warfare, cultural populism similarly appeals to our divisions, to the worst in people.

Alternatively, by assuming that the white man's unease was solely racist, Democrats inferred that the white male plight was no plight at all, but merely the powerful reacting to the loss of their power. But most white men were never powerful.

Instead, most were like the "able-bodied men here who work from early morning until late at night, in ice-cold cellars with a quarter of an inch of water on the floor—men who for six or seven months in the year never see the sunlight from Sunday afternoon till the next Sunday morning—and who cannot earn three hundred dollars in a year," who Upton Sinclair wrote about in *The Jungle* in 1906. The onset of the Industrial Age brought white men from the farms to the cities, from rural manliness to wage slavery. They were to make it within an urban jungle that took men's lungs, limbs, and lives. But a hard day's labor was respected and offered the regular man standing in society. By 1968, the grunt felt like the rejected man. George Wallace reaffirmed the white workingman's value by appealing to the man who "pays his taxes and works for a living and holds the country together."[13]

"What Franklin Roosevelt understood, and what to his great credit Teddy Kennedy understands is, that if you want to have programs to help small groups in society, minorities, but not just racial or ethnic minorities, you have to make those programs beneficial to the middle class," George Will says. "What happened in the 1960s was the middle class became a problem, the middle class became something slightly disdained. And the Democrats set out to say government exists to take resources from the middle class and give it to the excluded, the oppressed, et cetera, in part because they are excluded and they are oppressed because of the sins of the majority."

At the same time that white men began to be portrayed as the sinners—and notably, their white wives and sisters were not—they began leaving Democrats. White male support for Democrats in 1968 was the lowest since tracking began in 1948, and possibly the worst since the nineteenth century. In comparison, the Democrats' poor showing with white women was equivalent to the Eisenhower era. The most precipitous drop among white men was in the middle third of earners, the very "silent majority" Nixon sought.

Democrats won only 36 percent of middle-class white men in 1968, roughly half the support they had won in 1964 and 7 percent less than they had in their previous low, the election of 1956. If George Wallace had not been in the race, it is almost assured Nixon would have earned unprecedented support for a Republican among the white middle class.[14]

"That the Democrats have held the allegiance of most of the 'plain people' has been the critical fact in American presidential politics," wrote Richard Scammon and Ben Wattenberg. "Now, upon the shoals of the Social Issue, there seems to be the possibility of a rupture in that pattern."[15]

The rupture occurred, and the bad news persisted through the turn of the millenium. But racism was only part of it, even in 1968. When Americans were asked to name the most important national problem in 1968, four out of ten said Vietnam, while a third of those polled said race and riots.[16] The upheaval and Vietnam were one in the same. Whether domestic or foreign security, white men went with the tougher party. Masculinity was not an issue; it was *the* issue.

BLUE-COLLAR BACKLASH
Nixon and the
Men He Understood
(1969–1972)

Richard Nixon was watching the Ohio State–Purdue football game on television while more than a quarter-million protesters poured down Pennsylvania Avenue, filling Washington's Mall with a sea of antiwar activists. It was 1969. In February, the final issue of the *Saturday Evening Post* was published, and with it went one of the last vestiges of the 1950s. By the first of March, Mickey Mantle had announced his retirement, and by the end of March Dwight Eisenhower was dead. In Manhattan's Greenwich Village, the gay patrons of the Stonewall Inn refused to let police hassle them any longer, and so began three days of rioting and the modern gay-rights movement. A month later on Chappaquiddick Island, just as he was emerging as the leading Democratic contender to challenge Nixon in 1972, Senator Edward Kennedy's car plunged off a bridge. Though he escaped, his passenger, Mary Jo Kopechne, died. With her death went the last presidential hopes of Joseph Kennedy's sons.

Soon after, the first U.S. troops began to withdraw from South Vietnam, and on July 20, Neil Armstrong became the first person to walk on the moon. In mid-August, more than 400,000 young people gathered for the Woodstock Music festival. By October protesters gathered on the Washington Mall to unite in their declaration, "Hell no, we won't go!" On November 18, the patriarch of what could have been, Joseph Kennedy, died. In early December it seemed as if the counterculture would soon vanish as well: when some 300,000 people gathered to see the Rolling Stones perform in California, Hells Angels beat the concertgoers, killing several, and the idealism of the flower children slowly wilted with the self-inflicted disorder.

And then there was the white workingman. He ate eggs and corned beef hash, and loved his Sundays, more for football than for church. Each weekday, he woke up when it was still dark, dragged himself to work, had lunch with the guys, came home, chatted with his wife over supper, and watched the activism unfold on television. His daughter could not afford to be a hippie; she had to work. He was proud of his son, who luckily returned alive from Vietnam. The son did as his father had done before him, serving his country when his country called. But now his son was being called a "baby killer" by those who had not fulfilled their duty.

This white workingman was not part of any movement. He was said to want to keep down women, minorities, anyone not like him. And those white men doing a little better but still working hard, they were "the man." They were wrong by birth, white and male and simply "not with it." Like a black face in the ghetto, the workingman was the white face in the white neighborhoods (soon the suburbs, then the exurbs as he retreated from urbanized America) just as society seemed to say he was little more than a rerun, a relic, a dusty outlook to be washed away with the endless good of ceaseless progression.

Amid feminism, black power, and gay rights, he was at minimum a bystander, an outsider. At maximum, he was the very face of everything the counterculture was countering. But his gripe was often larger than him. The protesters were challenging the very social contract he had agreed to, surrendered to, when he decided to be a man, get a job, support a family, and attempt to make it in this world. The common man, celebrated in the 1950s for earning his keep, was now a sucker for surrendering to the system. The road his fathers had walked—paved with the belief in vows, duty, and honor—was being condemned by this new generation.

The white workingman was forgotten, a victim of the very bigotry said to be his sin alone. He was portrayed as being frozen in amber, crying out to dominate, to persecute. So he looked for those who did speak up, men who publicly turned against the new liberal tide. Sometimes this push-back was born of racism. But the progressive tide smothered far more than "white male privilege." It nearly drowned the values and outlook of the traditional American man.

As the nation was awash in protest, white men recalled the Apollo landing. They saw the best of America and hoped not to drown in the worst. Nixon understood this perfectly; he found an American tale worth telling, worth holding onto, worth taking to the critics. When liberals cast white workingmen as the antagonists, those same men began to follow the alternatives—the demagogues, the instigators, the false, the stars, and the worthy—because, though the alternatives were conservative and white workingmen were often moderate, they saw men standing up, and their stand was clear. Some of these alternatives were grunts, some were generals. Some were acting, and some were genuine. But they were *at least men*, men who said it was okay to be skeptical, to be a white man, to question some of the progress of the times without undermining its glories.

How could this white workingman not appreciate that Nixon was watching football while those self-righteous "draft dodgers" demanded his attention on the Washington Mall? With their long hair, their drugs, and their lascivious indulgence, a generation of privileged youth who demanded what their country should do for them, now had the nerve to stand beneath the memorials to Abraham Lincoln and George Washington and denounce the nation that Nixon, and all those white men like him, believed in and had risked death to uphold.

In 1969, *Newsday* detailed the family backgrounds of 400 men from Long Island who died in Vietnam. "As a group," *Newsday* found, "Long Island's war dead have been overwhelmingly white, working-class men. Their parents were typically blue collar or clerical workers, mailmen, factory workers, building tradesmen, and so on."[1]

That same year, a *Washington Post* headline read, "Working Americans Are Rediscovered." Harvard and MIT set out "to learn what makes him tick." An advisor to New York City Mayor John Lindsay said, "We're trying to find out what is bothering them" because "we never had contact with those [working class white] neighborhoods until last year."[2] But the working class knew exactly what was bothering them.

As protesters gathered nationally in mid-October of 1969 for a morato-rium on the Vietnam War, and the green lawns beneath the Capitol were crammed with the largest antiwar rally in American history, the early signs of the white blowback appeared. Mayor Lindsay ordered flags flown at half-staff, "as a patriotic tribute to the dead in Vietnam" to mark the day of protest. Many Americans, mostly white, mostly working class, mostly disgusted by the ac-tivists, saw little that was patriotic in Lindsay's actions. Representing the white working- and middle-class borough of Staten Island, New York, Republican state senator John Marchi, who ran against Lindsay for the mayoralty in 1969, called Lindsay's actions "a dagger in the back of American servicemen."[3] Police officers and fire fighters drove with their headlights on to demonstrate their discontent with Lindsay lowering the flag.

The following day, the New York Mets made baseball history. They had begun the season with a miserable start, turned it around, overtook the Cubs, swept the Braves, and made it to the World Series to face a team of future hall of famers, the Baltimore Orioles. The day after the antiwar march in Washington, the Mets, with few stars and no giants, won the World Series. By Monday morn-ing at work, it was the Mets—not those "damn protesters"—most men wanted to talk about, if only because it was a relief to talk about a victory, a bunch of aver-age Joes who accomplished something phenomenal.

The same year, *New York* magazine published an article titled "The Revolt of the White Lower Middle Class," by Pete Hamill, that described the disdain felt by working-class white men for the emerging welfare state. One white iron-worker told Hamill, "They take the money outta my paycheck and they just turn it over to some lazy son of a bitch who won't work. I gotta carry him on my back. You know what I am? I'm a sucker." Hamill wrote that "usually the working-class white man is a veteran. He remembers coming back from the Korean War to discover the GI Bill only gave him $110 a month out of which he had to pay his own tuition; so he did not go to college because he could not afford it. Then he reads about protesting blacks . . . that they are being paid up to $200 a month to go to school, with tuition free, and he starts going a little wild. . . . The working-class white man is actually in revolt against taxes, joyless work, the double stan-dards and short memories of professional politicians and what he considers the debasement of the American dream."[4] In the White House, Richard Nixon read the article and scribbled a note to his staff, stating, "This is very disturbing. What can be done about it?"[5]

What came back on April 16, 1970, was a confidential Department of Labor report by Jerome M. Rosow, the assistant secretary of labor for policy. Titled "The Problem of the Blue-Collar Worker," only about 25 copies were ever circulated. When a copy leaked to the *Wall Street Journal*, that paper's headline read: "Secret Report Tells Nixon How to Help White Workingmen and Win Their Vote." "Income needs for a growing family rise faster than are normally provided by advancement," the report read, and it was these workingmen who viewed their jobs as "dead ends." "Since 1965," it continued, "money wages have advanced 20 percent but real earning measured in true purchasing power remained almost static." The report stated that, "economic insecurity" was "compounded by the fact that blue-collar workers are often the first to feel the effects of an increase in unemployment . . . [and] are more dependent on sheer physical health for their livelihood. . . . These people are most exposed to the poor and the welfare recipients. Often their wages are only a notch or so above the liberal states' welfare payments." The confidential report found that "the blue-collar worker increasingly feels that his work has no 'status' in the eyes of society, the media, or even his own children," adding that these white men feel like "forgotten people." In a telling paragraph, the report stated that the blue-collar white male's "only spokesmen seem to be union leaders . . . they are overripe for a political response to the pressing needs they feel so keenly."[6]

The events of the day overtook the report's influence. Nixon announced he was sending troops into Cambodia, expanding the war in Vietnam. Student protests resurged on campuses nationwide. After several days of unrest at Ohio's Kent State University, National Guardsmen released a volley of gunfire, killing four students and severely injuring others.

Four days later, in Manhattan's Financial District, hundreds of college students gathered to demand the immediate withdrawal of U.S. troops from Vietnam. All over the city, American flags were at half-staff to memorialize the slain Kent State students. As the hour neared noon, the very blue-collar men in the Department of Labor report—who for years felt rejected, forgotten, but did not complain, or riot to charges of "baby killer" or burn American flags—began streaming into the streets, intent on breaking up the antiwar march. White men, many wearing overalls, some with brown or orange or yellow hardhats, their work boots resounding through the streets, their calloused fists clasped, came from four directions. They moved in on the white activists, many of whom were richer and better educated than them. Chanting "Love it, leave it" and "All the way, U.S.A," a few hundred construction workers broke the police lines. Activists attempted to take refuge in the lunch-hour crowds. But the construction workers sought them out and attacked activists with their hardhats and their fists, even pummeling one man with a wrench. The chanting attracted more construction workers, who made their way to a federal building and forcefully outflanked police in order to place American flags at full-staff beside the statue of George Washington. It was the spot where America's first president had been sworn into office.

Near City Hall, a 29-year-old Wall Street lawyer, who was a Democratic candidate for the state senate, was beaten to screams of "kill the Commie bastards." Running through the streets, yelling, holding American flags up high, workers stormed City Hall, cowing policemen stationed to protect the mayor's office. They forced city officials to raise the flag to full-staff. As the flag was raised, the men sang the Star Spangled Banner. When policemen kept their helmets on, one construction worker demanded that they take the helmets off out of respect. Many of the officers did.[7]

The Hardhat Riot was like an ax in a plank of wood. From then on, the Democratic divisions were vivid in every splinter and, as the plank became more and more broken, the riots symbolized that the Democratic coalition was burning apart, its divisions now incandescent in the worst way. FDR liberals exchanged fisticuffs with activist liberals. Just as militant blacks with afros came to be the caricature of all blacks, the hardhat rioters became the stereotype of white workingmen. When *All in the Family* premiered in 1971, the white workingman was reduced to the character of Archie Bunker, an uneducated bigot. While the new breed of liberal sympathized with hundreds of black riots, to many on the left these rioting white men were proof that the white workingman was the enemy of progress. From that day forward, the white male angst was seen as blowback from a disempowered group. The problem for the new breed of dogmatic liberals—who accepted this line of thought as true by virtue of it being true to them—was that the Democratic coalition depended upon the very white men they antagonized and left behind.

Only a couple of weeks after the hardhatters stormed the streets, Nixon invited the labor unions who were behind the riots to the White House. The president donned a hardhat and proclaimed his support for the men who beat up the activists. Nixon was honoring, in his own words, those "labor leaders and people from middle America who still have character and guts and a bit of patriotism."[8]

"They had very little tolerance for what they saw was a university-driven antiwar movement that they saw as unpatriotic," Charlie Cook says of both Nixon and the white working class. Nixon's onetime advisor, Kevin Phillips, once observed that "knowing who hates who" was a key to electoral success.[9]

By the end of the month, about 100,000 people had peacefully demonstrated in New York City's Financial District to show their support for U.S. policy in Vietnam and Cambodia. The "silent majority," as Nixon termed them, was finding its voice. The very wording, the "silent majority," brought to mind the archetypal American man, the "strong silent type." Nixon's populism was consistently rhetorically shrewd. When some of Nixon's southern white conservative nominees to the Supreme Court were denied, he called it an "act of regional discrimination."[10]

That year, *Time* chose "Middle Americans" as Man and Woman of the Year. "They flew the colors of assertive patriotism," the article read. "In the bumper-sticker dialogue of the freeways, they answered 'Make Love Not War,' with 'Honor America' or 'Spiro is My Hero.'" Their raised voice in 1969 was due to "the American dream" becoming "no longer the dream as advertised." "They feared" that "their grip on the country" was waning. "No one celebrated them; intellectuals dismissed their lore as banality. Pornography, dissent and drugs seemed to wash over them in waves, bearing some of their children away." They "felt ignored," as "angry minorities dominated the headlines and the government's domestic action. If not ignored, they have been treated with condescension."[11]

Vice President Spiro Agnew became Middle Americans' most vocal champion by 1969. The "Spiro is my Hero" bumper stickers were inspired by his brash antiliberal rhetoric. He had a self-assured smile, slicked back hair, a pudgy rectangular face, and a large nose giving him the look of a man who scuffled as a boy. It was Agnew who declared, "It's time for America's silent majority to stand up for its rights."[12] He was relentless: "Ultraliberalism today translates into a whimpering isolationism in foreign policy, a mulish obstructionism in domestic policy, and a pusillanimous pussyfooting on the critical issue of law and order."[13]

"Pusillanimous" was the precise pejorative Agnew intended. The word derives from the Latin for *pusillus*, meaning "very small" or "petty," and *animus*, meaning "spirit." The modern ear heard "wimp," "pussy," "coward," and every other connotation associated with those boys who could not, or would not, fight back in the playground.

Pat Buchanan picked the fights in politics. An advisor to Nixon in 1971, he suggested Nixon separate the majority from the radicals and unapologetically seek "the larger half."[14] Nixon did exactly that. He railed against the "bureaucratic elite."[15] He characterized the coming 1972 election as "square America" versus "radical America."[16] It was the dynamic that built a Republican majority.

"Democrats define themselves" in terms of "haves versus the have-nots," Republican strategist Frank Luntz says. "Republicans define themselves as mainstream versus extreme."

V

THE BREAKUP OF THE FDR COALITION AND THE FALSE DAWN OF CARTER (1972–1979)

In Arthur Miller's acclaimed 1949 play *Death of a Salesman*, an aging white sales-man named Willy Loman loses control of his life. His sales were once unparal-leled but at the very point he should be retiring, he works harder, sells less, and soon he is fired by a man young enough to be his son. The audience watches as Willy's life falls apart, and in time, he comes to the conclusion that he is "worth more dead than alive." Willy kills himself. But his life insurance doesn't cover suicide. Even in death, Willy fails to provide for his family.

The play was an early allegory on the workingman's efforts to attain the American dream. As a boy, Miller saw his father ruined by the Great Depression. It was the New Deal's Federal Theatre Project that gave Miller his start. In 1972, Miller, an active delegate in the Democratic Party, commented: "The traditional Dem[ocratic] Party no longer exists. We've been taken over."[1]

When convention rules were amended in 1968 to add quotas designed to bring more women and minorities into the party, George McGovern chaired the committee. So it was fitting that McGovern came to be the Democratic nominee of 1972. A man thoroughly of the old Democratic sort, he was a preacher's son, a decorated pilot from the Second World War, and worked arduously for public works projects on behalf of South Dakota's farmers. But in due course he became the face of the new liberalism, and with that position came his defeat.

Nixon was not upbeat at first about his prospects in 1972. The Vietnam War was going badly. But all those Democrats he feared—Edward Kennedy, Edmund Muskie, and Hubert Humphrey—soon fell from contention. The front-runner since 1969 had been Kennedy, but his candidacy died in Chappaquiddick. After the ultraright *Manchester Union-Leader* attacked Muskie's wife during the New Hampshire primary for drinking and allegedly asking reporters about dirty jokes, cameras caught Muskie nearly sobbing in her defense. One Democratic National Committee official observed that while Nixon was in China meeting with the leadership of the communist party, Muskie was crying about his wife in New Hampshire.[2] Alabama Governor George Wallace returned to the Democratic ticket, winning several impressive primary victories in the peripheral states of the South, only to be shot. Left paralyzed below the waist, he too soon withdrew from the race.[3]

Only McGovern remained a viable candidate. An outspoken critic of the Vietnam War, McGovern called for the withdrawal of all troops within 90 days of his inauguration. McGovern was the all-American man representing the marginalized, from feminists to civil rights and antiwar activists. Fully eight out of ten delegates were attending their first convention, and so the pragmatism born of wisdom and the wisdom born of age were drowned in the tide of youth. As *Time* described it, "Party leaders sweeping down Collins Avenue in their rented air-conditioned limousines could pass up a sandaled, T-shirted hitchhiker only at their peril; they never knew whether he might be a key delegate."[4]

Fully 94 percent of Americans in one 1969 poll said they would "in general" like "college administrators [to] take a stronger stand on student disorders."[5] Yet, as Americans watched the Democratic convention on television, the very same faces of college activism represented this new Democratic Party. One older Democratic delegate quipped that the convention looked like the "cast of *Hair*."[6] The platform called for an "immediate total withdrawal of all Americans from Southeast Asia." It reduced defense spending, supported amnesty for those who avoided the draft, put forward a ban on handguns, advocated school busing to achieve desegregation, and advocated the ratification of the Equal Rights Amendment. In one section titled, "The Right to be Different," the platform listed the rights of every possible subgroup in America, from youth to American Indians, notably excluding only the white workingman. Challenging the mainstream mores of the day, the platform stated, "Americans should be free to make their own choice of life-styles and private habits." In total, the platform had 92 mentions of "right" or "rights," and 2 mentions of "wrong" or "wrongs."[7] So it was for the Democratic Party through the beginning of the twenty-first century.

Democrats came to advocate for the rights of so many divergent groups that it was no longer clear if they believed in any great Right. If equality was that Right, the means by which it was gauged became increasingly ambiguous. McGovern was at the helm of the sinking ship in 1972. For the first time in years the AFL-CIO did not support the Democratic candidate. "The Democrats were perceived so far to the left, [labor] wanted to be in the center," W. J. Usery, a former labor leader, recalls. "We wanted a strong president. We wanted a forceful president."

Nixon exploited the schism between blue-collar whites and the new school of liberalism. He pushed for a congressional moratorium mandating the "immediate halt to all new busing orders by federal courts."[8] Nixon's surrogates constantly characterized McGovern as the "candidate of the three A's: acid, abortion, amnesty." Some chanted, "Hanoi needs McGovern and Fonda," referencing the leftist Hollywood actress's controversial trip to North Vietnam during the war.[9]

By Election Day 1972, what was likely the world's oldest political party was never so disempowered. Barely 25 years after the *Wall Street Journal* wrote about the American public's terrible view of conservatism, less than a decade after Johnson routed Goldwater with a nearly unprecedented Democratic majority, came the Democrats' worst defeat since its inception as a party in the early days of Jefferson and Jackson.

Nixon won 61 percent of the vote, essentially tying the two great twentieth-century Democratic victories, Johnson's in 1964 and FDR's in 1936. McGovern won 38 percent of the vote, 1 percent *less* than the support the ultraconservative Goldwater received in 1964; he won the electoral votes of the District of Columbia and one state, the firmly liberal Massachusetts. Among whites, Nixon won two-thirds of the vote.[10] The gender gap was meager, but the effect of the White Male Gap was titanic. McGovern was too permissive, too weak, for white America.

"Look at who [Nixon] was running against—a decent man, but arguably the most liberal Democratic candidate since Williams Jennings Bryan," Democratic demographer Mark Gersh recalls. "When Nixon called those students who were demonstrating at Kent State bums, when the workers in New York City beat up Vietnam demonstrators, that was all playing into the hand of Republicans. These were working class people."

Strikingly, Nixon won 58 percent of white labor union members.[11] The Republican won about seven out of ten whites in the lowest- and middle-income brackets, about the same number of men as women. He won 76 percent of southern white men. The father of southern Baptist leader Richard Land was one. A yellow-dog Texas Democrat, he "hated Nixon," Land says, lifting his eyebrows in emphasis. "But he couldn't vote for McGovern," Land adds. "My dad's a World War II veteran and that wouldn't go." McGovern lost, even among younger voters, despite the vocal activism of college students. For those whites between 17 and 34, Nixon won 62 percent of men and 58 percent of women.[12]

"The late '60s and early '70s was when the counterculture or youth culture dominated, America was no less conservative," Republican pollster Frank Luntz, who was ten in 1972, points out. "In fact that's the reason Richard Nixon beat George McGovern in every state except one—because young people were getting all the publicity," he adds, "but they were a small segment of the population. [The year] 1972 was basically the American people saying to this counterculture, '*get a job*'." Nixon's "silent majority" was real.

Roughly three out of ten whites supported McGovern, the lowest level of support for a Democrat in the second half of the twentieth century. Eventually, white women returned to Democrats; white men did not.

"Democrats should be very concerned," Usery says, reflecting on 1972 as the year that lost the white workingman. "It's very easy to look back at Nixon's reelection campaign because I know, I *knew*, very few labor leaders that were willing to go to the Democratic side. That's when things changed. Nixon opened the door to the working class. I think he did a masterful job and if there hadn't been Watergate, what would his second administration have been? Ever since, the Democrats are losing the working class. And the working class is losing too."

NIXON'S FALL

America watched Nixon's presidency unravel shortly after he had stood larger than nearly every president in American history. "Liberals had never liked Nixon, even though from an operational standpoint he was one of them," H. W. Brands wrote, "and when his hubris brought him low, they piled on with glee. This may have been emotionally satisfying, but it was politically myopic."[13] Liberal schadenfreude was indeed shortsighted, as Nixon's downfall proved to be liberalism's as well. Trust in government plummeted soon after, and with it Wilson's credo that government should promote good was trumped by the Jeffersonian concept that government need only prevent bad. In 1964, six out of ten Americans trusted the federal government to do the right thing most of the time. When Newt Gingrich led the Republican ascendancy in Congress, only two out of ten Americans held the same trust in government.[14]

Though Nixon campaigned as a conservative in 1968, he governed as a liberal moderate. He created two massive new agencies, the Environmental Protection Agency and the Occupational Safety and Health Administration. He passed the Clean Air Act. Social spending under Nixon even surpassed defense spending.[15] The voting age was lowered from 21 to 18. And at one point, Nixon even pushed for national health insurance. He was a Republican administering at the dusk of the liberal state.

Nixon's hawkish reputation allowed him to implement arms limitation agreements with the Soviet Union and push his New China policy, in which he departed from U.S. policy by visiting China and backing its bid to join the United Nations. Punch for punch, Nixon's legacy leaves him the most underrated president of the past century. His downfall was so precipitous, so ugly, and so unnecessary, that it has washed out his accomplishments.

After five agents of Nixon's reelection committee were arrested breaking into the DNC headquarters in the Watergate office building, Nixon disavowed any link. The man who had been so up-front with the American people in his 1952 Checkers' speech, who said "the people have got to have confidence in the men who run for that office and might obtain it" and had won voters with his candid humility, was duplicitous and evasive in 1974, leading to the worst presidential scandal in U.S. history. For the first time, a president was forced to resign.

The Republican Party was left in dire condition. Three months later, 50 new Democrats with an average age of 40 won congressional seats. They represented the new species of dogmatic liberal. The majority of their backing came from the middle and upper classes—not working-class whites.[16]

"If there is a role for the Republican Party, it is to be the party of the working class, not the welfare class," Patrick Buchanan said in 1975. "It is to be champion of the cause of producers and taxpayers, of the private sector threatened by the government sector, of the millions who carry most of the cost of government and share least in its beneficence."[17]

For Gerald Ford, the heir to Nixon's presidency, his unexpected decision one month after he assumed the presidency to end "America's long national nightmare" by pardoning the undone president, mired him in Nixon's corruption. Though in time, the nightmare proved to be Nixon's and not the Republicans'.

THE PEANUT FARMER WHO BECAME PRESIDENT

In the year of the U.S. bicentennial anniversary, the man who turned it around for Democrats, however temporarily, was a God-fearing rural evangelical, the first president to have been born and raised in the Deep South since the Civil War. Watergate made the race far more about the man than the movement behind him. Carter's certitude was for this reason less of a prayer than plausible. The one-term Georgia governor was such an unlikely candidate that when he told his mother he intended to run for president, she asked, "President of what?"[18]

In a time of public financing, before campaign war chests cowed outside challengers, Carter tenaciously spent two years campaigning across America, so low on money that he often stayed with friends. While his wide smile was memorable, part of what helped Carter reach people was the authenticity of his faith. Ford was also an evangelical Protestant. But it was Carter who was a born-again southern Baptist.

"When I got in the campaign I was very determined not to ever mention my religious faith," Carter recalls. "But toward the middle of the summer, after the general election started—I think I put this in my book—I was in the backyard of a devout North Carolina couple. They didn't know. They knew I was from Georgia. They supported me because they had a little fundraiser now. They asked me if I was a born-again Christian and I said yes because to me that was like breathing. I had used that phrase since I was three years old. And the northern press was there—finally, *finally* I was able to get them to come to some of my meetings, and it was top headlines all over the nation, that there's this weirdo coming out of somewhere that thinks he has been anointed by God and he has heavenly visions and he's going to operate our country as though he is looking at a crystal ball and he's a magician," Carter pauses, leaning back, touching his face with his index finger. "I couldn't believe it," he says. "So from then on I tried to avoid it as much as I could, but once you open a Pandora's box of a quick phrase and the press grabs it, there's nothing you can do about it."

Carter made every attempt to temper his religiosity during the remainder of the primaries, while still emphasizing his outsider rural status. Carter was to be

Jimmy Stewart with a drawl. But unlike Stewart's famous character, Carter was shrewd. The Georgian was playing to win. Primaries were now a contest in political endurance; the party bosses had been defrocked. Carter did well in Iowa, won New Hampshire, defeated George Wallace in Florida, stumbled in Massachusetts, and when the primary in Pennsylvania arrived, Washington's Senator Henry "Scoop" Jackson made a last effort to oppose the Georgian. The long-term future of the Democratic Party depended on the primary face-off between Jackson and Carter.

Jackson was of the strong and silent mold, clean cut, with an easy smile. When he spoke, he was prone to reflective pauses. Jackson was a Cold War anti-communist, who had been JFK's selection as chairman of the DNC in 1960. But unlike Kennedy, he was a public opponent of McCarthy's notorious 1950s hearings. Jackson was no orator. Like Johnson, he was a man of the Senate who never understood the thematic component to presidential contests. Carter did—his commercials pictured him on his farm, a man raised by the land. But what undid Jackson's last-ditch effort was visible four years earlier, when he first ran for the nomination.

During the 1972 primary race, Jackson was accused of racism by leading Democrats for his opposition to mandated busing, despite Jackson's strong record on civil rights.[19] In calling Jackson a racist for opposing mandated busing, this new dogmatic liberalism was branding all those like-minded middle- and lower-class whites racists as well. Busing was intended to bring poor black children to better white suburban schools, but to many whites, it brought the vice of the inner city to their children. For middle-class white women, whose support for Democrats reached a low point in 1972, the education of their children was not a matter of racial cohesion, but motherhood. As for many of their husbands who worked to escape urban blight and move their families to better neighborhoods, there was little tolerance for calling their effort "white flight" or racism. Once more, as with their service in Vietnam, these men were denounced for doing their duty. "Forced busing" may have looked black and white but it was fundamentally about economic class.

By 1976, the busing issue had become a microcosm of the battle between dogmatic liberalism and pragmatic liberalism, embodied, however imperfectly, in the contest between those supporting Carter and those supporting Jackson. The accusations from some liberals that opposition to busing was racist ignored the polling of the day. Only 3 percent of white parents in the North and 15 percent of white parents in the South still objected to sending their children to integrated schools. In contrast, Gallup polling found that between 1974 and 1978, about 70 to 85 percent of whites were opposed to busing. One study found that half of blacks were as well.[20] But to the puritans of the new wave of liberalism, opposition to busing was racist because of the color of the issue.

After Jackson's victories in Massachusetts and New York in 1976, a win in Pennsylvania might have assured his nomination. Big Labor backed Jackson. He was against arms control agreements with the Soviet Union. He criticized Carter for proposing cuts in the defense budget and for promoting national health care. But he was nailed to the Vietnam War he supported and the old Democratic tradition he personified. As Peter Beinart put it, "In every area, the party had moved to the opposite direction: becoming more dovish, more culturally liberal, and more skeptical of big government."[21] Jackson lost. One of the last classically liberal Democrats was no longer a presidential contender, and with Jackson went the white men who in four years would leave Carter as well.

By Election Day Carter had closed the White Male Gap based fundamentally on the man Americans knew in 1976. In comparison to Humphrey in 1968, Carter won 8 percent more white women and 14 percent more white men. Overall, whites made up about 90 percent of voters.

Carter's greatest gains among white men came from the middle- and lower-third income brackets. He won fully 63 percent of white male union members, a 24 percent gain since 1968. The improvement with union members was larger than the improvement the Georgian made among southern voters over the same period.[22]

Once more, southern white women shifted with the white male population overall. Southern women voted Democratic at a rate 20 percent higher than in 1968, whereas white women not from the South increased their Democratic support by only 6 percent. White men backed Carter by the same increase in the South, but increased their support by 10 percent outside the South. As with white female support for George Wallace in 1968, it appears the white southern regional worldview more significantly separates white women than white men from the rest of the nation.[23]

Carter never could have won the presidency without strong minority support. But notably, in an election year in which the southerner pronounced his intention to end discrimination on the basis of race or gender, Carter's improvement with white working- and middle-class men made his presidency. It was the last time Democrats are estimated to have won more votes of white men than of white women, 47 to 46 percent, respectively. Though Carter still narrowly lost white men to Ford, 47 to 52 percent, it was the last time a Democrat contended for the white male vote. Since Carter's 1976 victory, no Democrat has earned more than 38 percent of white men.[24]

The 1976 race increasingly became solely a contest of character. There was nothing known of Carter before the election. He successfully portrayed himself within the mold of traditional American manhood. Carter had served in the military and showed another sense of duty by returning to his family farm, sacrificing ambition to save it from collapse. He was soft spoken but self assured, a man of few words, with little doubt that when he spoke, he was honest.

His campaign slogan, "Jimmy Carter, a leader for a change," was an effort to sell him as a good man worth following. To further heighten his image as the stern father, in one ad Carter spoke of the millions of Americans "chronically" on welfare and said for those that can work, his administration will offer work, and "if they don't take it when it's offered to them, I wouldn't pay them any more benefits."

The advertising worked. Carter won 27 percent of the voting conservative white men. In comparison, Michael Dukakis and Bill Clinton won only about 13 percent of these same voters.[25] But Carter's gains soon tumbled with his presidency.

"Carter was misunderstood," William Pollack says. "He was caring, thoughtful, in ways that were perceived as not masculine, tough, and strong enough." In the basement office of his suburban Boston home, Pollack adds, "I think some white men voted for [Carter] because they thought they would get a nuclear sub commander but instead they got the preacher who their wife drags them to Sunday lessons with." Although in 1976, Carter may have attempted to deemphasize his Christianity, at the core of his Deep South rural persona was the Christian man. This irenic soul was welcomed in the era of Watergate.

That welcome lasted until his inauguration. Carter stood before thousands at the Capitol Plaza beneath a clear winter's sky, quoting the Jewish profit Micah, almost despondently humble. He emphasized his desire to "be worthy of you," speaking of how "your strength can compensate for my weakness, and your wisdom can help to minimize my mistakes." He asked the country to learn, laugh, and play together, requesting "full faith in our country."

His was a presidency that asked for faith, but exhibited few reasons to have it. After the address, Carter decided not to take the presidential limousine back to the White House and walk the mile and a half down Pennsylvania Avenue hand in hand with his wife and daughter. He was to be the president of the people. But over the following four years, Carter did not lead as Americans hoped. In the end, it was not the preacher in Carter that undid his presidency, but the sermon he chose and the way in which he decided to shepherd.

The president who won by narrowing the White Male Gap was soon undone by it. With the arms treaty SALT II, the handover of the Panama Canal, the inability to combat the energy crisis, stagflation, and the Americans held hostage in Iran, the country looked enfeebled, a nation shaped by events instead of shaping them.

The coming decade called for thematic leadership, and as the president lost his grip over an array of issues and the commander in chief looked more like a secretary of state, many wondered where the fight was in this Navy man. Americans asked for leadership, and the answer came in 1980. How Reagan got there, how Carter's lost his pulpit, was an outgrowth of the emerging gender divergence between Republicans and Democrats, one unseen before the 1970s. In a time when popular culture said that being a man was no longer a noble personal ideal but an ignoble personal failing, Carter was the "new man" of the feminist movement; he understood people's problems. But Americans do not want presidents who sympathize with the cold, but commanders in chief who lead them out of the winter. And from over the horizon rode in the Western man who came to represent the everyman. Ronald Reagan was the nation's great reach back to 1950s certainty—a yearning for something simpler, nobler, and indeed paternal. The traditional man was brought before America, and the politics of culture became the politics of manhood. The 1970s man ran against the 1950s man. One sensitized, one strong; one feminine, one masculine. And as the first decade of the liberated woman emerged, the Democrats became her party. The 1980s was a decade in which white men began to find their manhood in one party alone. And though the politics of masculinity have always been inseparable from the making of the president, only one party heeded the lessons of Jackson, Roosevelt, Eisenhower, and Kennedy. Ronald Reagan defeated far more than a one-term president in 1980. He defeated the counterculture itself.

THE MEASURE
OF THE MAN
The Politics of Personal Manhood

Norman Mailer limps forward, bellows "Hello," and shoves his grip into mine. It's the end of summer in Provincetown. Tall green hedges surround his red brick home. He sits down in a rattan chair beside his patio's sliding doors, facing the Atlantic. Beneath the whirl of the ceiling fan sunlight streams in, highlighting the crevices of his round, wrinkled, unshaven face. Mailer pushes up the sleeves of his denim shirt, ruffling the notes stuffed into its breast pockets, his thin gray chest hair pushing through his v-neck undershirt. He sits in navy blue sweat pants and fleece slippers looking at me, squinting. Mailer is 83 and still pushing on.

Mailer made his name with two superior novels: written at age 25, his World War II tome *The Naked and the Dead* was inspired by his experiences as a grunt during the war; the other was written at about twice that age—in 1968—the story of the 1967 peace demonstrations in Washington, titled *The Armies of the Night*. But the novelist's best work told the tales of presidential campaigns, the wars of attrition, from Kennedy to Clinton. Mailer found the character in the candidate and captured the time in the character, and he did it before anyone else. For a half century, Mailer was the dominant voice of white masculinity. *American Studies* author Louis Menard once called him the "last man of the 1950s."[1] Mailer's voice is still precisely that. It's as if he watched on television what followed Eisenhower, DiMaggio, and Kennedy, and while the world turned to color, Mailer remained in black and white. He is a proud anachronism, contributing to and contorting the times, asserting his relevancy, but never leaving the mid-century that molded his manhood, and America's as well.

"They talk male talk!" Mailer blurts out, explaining why he believes white men shifted to the Republican Party. "And the Democrats, who now owe so much to their need to try to make up for the loss by trying to get the female vote, no longer talk male talk because it outrages the women, those who are up high in the party."

Four distinct creases appear across Mailer's face. Two oval bags puff under each of his eyes, like tired half circles. From his nostrils down to the cleft of his chin, two other lines are shaped like lightning bolts. He thinks like lightning—quickly, in rapid blinks of thought, and then he watches what burns.

"The irony is that most of those [Republicans] are pretty soft also, for totally different reasons. They have had their lips at the hindquarters of the corporation for decades. And they are without honor too," Mailer says. "But they have learned a secret that the way to get the male vote is to pretend you are a repository of male honor."

In 1982, a comedy album lampooning Reagan soared up the charts. Johnny Carson began telling more jokes about the president. But David Gergen, then White House communications director, believed it was not a problem as long as Reagan's "strong masculinity and charm" held up.[2]

"Ronald Reagan seemed to be regarded by certain members of his inner circle not as the powerful and utterly original leader that he was, but as a sort of supreme anchorman," observed former Reagan chief of staff Donald Regan. "Each Presidential action" was scripted "as a one-minute or two-minute spot on the evening network news, or a picture on page one."[3]

The scripting didn't matter to Reagan. He had his big ideas and if the script expressed them, he was pleased to follow it. The great Oxford don of political thought, Isaiah Berlin, said there were two kinds of politicians, foxes and hedgehogs, referencing a line by the Greek poet Archilochus: "The fox knows many things, but the hedgehog knows one big thing."[4] Those politicians whose mental acuity focused on many things—like Johnson, like Carter, like Bill Clinton—held a remarkable capacity to grasp the finite, although at pivotal times their vision got lost in the details. Reagan was focused on the big thing. In time, it was his inattention to details that betrayed his vision. But in January of 1981, the vision was enough. It was intensely American and intensely male.

It was also more than visual. His clear phrasing, his nerve, his willingness to speak in the language of right and wrong, of good and evil were all the makings of the man. Representative John Murtha, a Democratic hawk, recalls that he and Reagan may not always have agreed but "we always knew exactly where he stood." Murtha pauses and stiffens his lip because that is all he feels he needs to say.

Masculinity is "very much overlooked" in discussions of the American presidency, Reagan's chief strategist, Richard Wirthlin, tells me, "and very important in Reagan's case." The 1980 campaign plan, authored by Wirthlin, emphasized that Gallup polling repeatedly found that "strong leadership" remains "the most important thing a president must be able to do." The strategy was to accentuate the candidate's strengths, and make him appear even stronger, clearer, more of a man. Wirthlin succeeded not only with Reagan but with Republicanism itself.

Reagan spoke the same language white men were raised with, from their comics to their western films. White men wanted men who were clear and bold—Carter was enfeebled, and though Nixon was one of them, he dishonored them dearly. For many white males, masculinity was a matter of conviction, an inward quality of pride that adhered to traditional notions of honor. And from that inward ethos, real men were to venture forth because there was always the potential for a reward worth the risk, and so the risk came to define manhood. The manly president was to stand on the edge of the present. He was to face down the future and lead, and when he faltered, so did we. The nation's masculinity was always wrapped up in his.

"What causes the gender gap?" Wirthin rhetorically says, "Reagan above all *is* a man's man. The way he walks. The way he articulates. The way he appeals in framing issues and stories, he's a man's man."

Though Reagan was divorced and from Hollywood, he met nearly every traditional American archetype of the leading man. He was tall, dark, and handsome. He was the strong silent type. He called a spade a spade. He was clean cut and athletic, for God and against communism. "What Reagan communicated without overtly seeming to," conservative columnist George Will says, "was that the backbone of America hasn't changed. That what always made America still does make America. So there was this element of nostalgia for Reagan, an awfully forward-looking nostalgia for change." Even Reagan's pompadour was reminiscent of a more stable era. As certainty itself seemingly withered, he was certain. Reagan played the western man for so long, the actor became the role.

"In this present crisis," Reagan declared in his first inaugural address, "government is not the solution to our problem; government is the problem." Americans were told government would not save them from economic downturn; Americans must save themselves. After all, Reagan had raised himself up and so he believed others could too.

"The primary leadership function of the American president is to reaffirm constantly the country's highest purposes and the potential for individual efforts to alter the course of the future in a positive direction," Reagan's confidential 1980 campaign plan read.

Democratic strategist Stan Greenberg, reflecting in 2000 about his interviews with white voters who left the Democrats in the 1980s, wrote: "In the Michigan focus groups, it was very clear that these white male voters see the Republicans as the party for men and the Democrats as the party of women. . . . 'Democrats are the party of minorities,'" he quoted one white male interviewee, "'because they concentrate on all minority segments, including women.'" Greenberg quoted another stating that, "Moreover, the Democratic Party, at least since Kennedy, focuses on 'groups and classes of people rather than on the individual.'"[5]

The personal manhood of presidents directly affects the support they earn. No one understood this more than Theodore Roosevelt. His father had told him as a boy, "You have the mind but you have not the body, and without the help of the body the mind cannot go as far as it should. You must *make* your body." Roosevelt looked up at his father with a "half-grin, half-snarl," and dutifully replied, "I'll make my body."[6] Roosevelt expected the same from the nation he later led. He forced himself into the trials of bravery. From war to boxing, he did not shirk from tests of manhood. He believed that American men needed, "the iron qualities that must go with true manhood," and that "if Washington and Lincoln had not had in them the whipcord fiber of moral and mental strength," the nation would not have survived.[7] It was their earned manhood that Roosevelt emulated. He believed that only the "strenuous life" prevented "sissiness."[8] He castigated Central America for its "impotence," declaring the paternal United States would police what he believed the less manly nations could not. He was always the Rough Rider who charged the nation into the twentieth century by sailing America's "great white fleet" around the world.

A century later, a linguist on the political left, George Lakoff, argued that conservatives offered the "strict father" while liberals offered the "nurturant parent." On the conservative side were Ronald Reagan and Arnold Schwarzenegger;

on the liberal side were Jimmy Carter and Oprah Winfrey. But history illustrates that the few flirtations with the nurturant parent have been refuted by the return to the strong father or, though untested, possibly the powerful matriarch.

"While all those advisors and consultants can help position you in some way, at the end of the day what Americans do is take the measure of the candidate," Gary Bauer says. "They may not always be able to put into words why they identify with one and don't with another. It is a central part of the whole process and for a variety of reasons the Republicans have been putting up manly men and the Democrats have been putting up people that fall quite short from that."

It was not always this way. In Franklin D. Roosevelt's day, the paternal side came to the aid of the downtrodden American man. This man was not to be nurtured, but offered a good job, and if he took the good job then better days awaited him. "The New Deals' masculine ideal was the selfless public servant," who found "satisfaction," Roosevelt's attorney general Francis Biddle wrote, "from sinking individual effort into the community itself."[9] Even at the infancy of active state liberalism, there was a stern understanding that, except for the ill and elderly, a man earns the fruits through his labor.

FDR referred to the New Deal as insurance, not handouts. He was the strong father giving America's struggling sons a second chance. His calming voice rallied the nation with his fireside chats, while the crippling effects of his polio were hidden from the public. Yet it was his trial through polio, its onslaught on his masculinity, that enabled the patrician to grasp an enfeebled nation. FDR came to personify the nation's perseverance, through his personal tragedy, through our Great Depression, to our finest hour, the Second World War. As with Theodore Roosevelt before him, it was the struggle in the man that made the man.

At FDR's first inaugural address, he proclaimed, "This great nation will endure as it has endured, will revive and will prosper," adding, "that the only thing we have to fear is fear itself." The nation was to rise as he had.

Two decades later, Joseph Kennedy had the family of his son John photographed in a manner that idealized JFK as the perfect loving father and husband, even as he was having affairs. Americans were apt to see Kennedy playing football or swimming, constantly displaying that he was man enough.

It has been said that presidential campaigns are battles of hope and fear. The politics of masculinity are dependent upon the primal desire to dispel fear and provide hope. In 1960, as John F. Kennedy ran for the presidency, he was concerned with not being "out-manned' by Eisenhower. To defeat Nixon, then the vice president, Kennedy believed he had to defeat Ike's legacy. JFK had proved his manhood in World War II, when a Japanese destroyer split his PT–109 boat, sending Kennedy and crew into the ocean. Kennedy saved a badly burned crewmate. He bit down on the injured man's life preserver strap and swam to a small island with other survivors, where they lived on coconuts for days. Ike may have led D-Day, but Kennedy had a hero's tale. He was the strong young buck ready now to lead the herd. Like FDR, Kennedy was always aware of pain (he suffered from crippling back pain every day), but he did not show it. Like an American man was supposed to do, he quietly bore it.

If Nixon was tough, Kennedy would be tougher. The Russians had sent Sputnik into space; China was communist; Korea was split; ninety miles off U.S. shores Cuba had become communist. The Russians were now referring to themselves as "the greatest power on earth."[10] JFK was to redeem the nation's manhood. Kennedy repeatedly used the alleged missile gap to argue that the Russians had gained the military advantage. Communists were a "clever, relentlessly thrusting force,"[11] and Kennedy was not going to look like a candidate who would take it. Columnist Joseph Alsop memorably referred to Kennedy as "Stevenson with balls."[12] And that was exactly the perception Kennedy intended.

Kennedy was the father who expected the nation to meet his expectations. "The new frontier of which I speak is not a set of promises. It is a set of challenges," Kennedy said in his 1960 convention speech. Kennedy challenged Americans to land on the moon "not because it is easy, but because it is *hard*." From the Peace Corps to the Apollo program, "What Kennedy was selling was a government-backed program of man-making, of federal masculinity insurance," Susan Faludi observed.[13]

Lyndon Johnson attempted to be a guy's guy and by the time he left office, he had ruined it for all guys. He was brash, vulgar, a legislative bully, and displayed a formidable bravado. He often wore his Word War II silver star on his suit lapel, demonstrating his manhood daily. As a senator, Johnson resented Kennedy as a showboater. "Jack was out kissing babies while I was passing bills," he once said. Johnson was the grunt to Kennedy's glamour. He was the workingman, the real man, once even feeling the need to assert that he had "had more women by accident than Kennedy had on purpose."[14] In 1964, when Johnson's vice president, Hubert Humphrey, departed from Johnson's stance on education in a speech given in New York, Johnson told White House reporters, "Boys, I've just reminded Hubert that I've got his balls in my pocket."[15]

Bill Moyers, Johnson's press secretary, recalled that the president was concerned that if he left Vietnam, White House advisors like Robert McNamara might consider him "less of a man" than Kennedy.[16] After the 1966 Christmas bombings of North Vietnam, Johnson said, "I didn't just screw Ho Chi Minh. I cut his pecker off."[17] When a member of his administration expressed concerns about the policy in Vietnam, Johnson said, "Hell, he has to squat to piss."[18]

Johnson's obsession with maintaining his hypermasculinity strongly infused his presidency and inevitably became tied up in the war: He was not going to be the first American president to lose one. He had always wanted to be a great president. Surely, if he was man enough for it, he believed he could will a victory, a fatal flaw George W. Bush emulated decades later. "[Johnson] had always been haunted by the idea that he would be judged as insufficiently manly. . . . He had always unconsciously divided the people around him between men and boys. Men were activists, doers, who conquered business empires, who acted instead of talked," and "boys were the talkers and the writers and the intellectuals," David Halberstam wrote in *The Best and the Brightest.* "Thus the dice were loaded; the advocates of force were by the very nature of Johnson's personality taken more seriously, the doubters were seen by their very doubts to be lesser men. . . . And so they bombed."[19]

Richard Nixon did not command a room like Johnson, and women did not adore him like Kennedy. So he made himself into the quintessential grunt. Nixon was a Willy Loman who made it. But he was always measuring himself against larger men, so he compensated. His fight against communism was intertwined, like Johnson's, with proving his political manhood. As one psychoanalytical study of Nixon described him, the president was constantly "afraid of being acted upon, of being inactive, of being soft, of being thought impotent, of being dependent on anyone else."[20] The threat to America, in Nixon's view, was rooted in manliness itself.

"You know what happened to the Greeks? Homosexuality destroyed them," Nixon once told a White House aide. "Homosexuality, dope, and immorality are the enemies of strong societies." Nixon branded his political foes "faggy," in order to prove he was not.[21] His closest advisor, former advertising executive H. R. Haldeman, observed that Nixon's strategy was to build an image as "a tough, courageous, masculine leader."[22]

During the 1968 campaign, the former executive producer of *The Mike Douglas Show*, Roger Ailes (who decades later headed Fox News), was hired by Nixon to produce one-hour programs to improve Nixon's image by directly reaching the public. At one show in Chicago, Joe McGinniss wrote in *The Selling of the*

President, Ailes noticed the background of Nixon's set and "ordered the curtains removed and three plain, almost stark wooden panels to replace them." Ailes added, "The wood has clear, solid, masculine lines."[23]

Yet it would be a misstatement of history to understand Nixon's masculinity only in its most insecure form. If Nixon was not physically tough, he admired those who were. He was never at ease with the liberal high-minded. He was the son of a blue-collar gas station owner, a good poker player, with his Oldsmobile, mortgage, and a wife who was a "wonderful stenographer." He even loved the movie *Patton.* Nixon's cultural populism was so successful because he had only to speak to those like himself.

By the turn of the century, there was another presidential contender hoping to assert his manhood. Faced with a West Texan who was comfortable in his masculinity and handed out buttons that read "Alpha Males for Bush," Al Gore sought his inner strong man.[24] If Margaret Thatcher had once seen a voice coach to lower her pitch, Gore could secretly hire a feminist to make him more of a man.[25] Best-selling author Naomi Wolf was paid $15,000 a month for such internal advice as, "Gore is a 'Beta male' who needs to take on the 'Alpha male' in the Oval Office [i.e., Clinton] before the public will see him as the top dog."[26]

Four years later, after the 2004 election, Bush was in Chile for an economic summit. As he entered an elegant dinner, Chilean security guards did not allow the president's Secret Service detail inside. A shoving match began. Bush, a few steps ahead, turned back. He walked straight toward the scuffle, reached into the crowd and pulled out his lead agent. Bush straightened his jacket and cuffs and, with his agent in tow, entered the dinner. The video clip was repeatedly shown on Fox and CNN.

This was the image Bush savored. When Russian President Vladimir Putin and his wife visited Bush's 1,600-acre ranch, Putin "rode shotgun" as Bush drove his white Ford F–250 pickup truck. They ate guacamole, beef tenderloin, catfish, and pecan pie.[27] Bush gave the same treatment to the Spanish royal family and British Prime Minister Tony Blair. The image was of a man with a truck, the icon of the modern rural man.

Karl Rove believed Bush's masculine everyman image was vital to his popularity. Rove invited a historian to lecture senior White House officials on the "similarities" between Bush and Andrew Jackson.[28] Both Bush and Jackson pushed for a strong executive branch. Like James Polk and Theodore Roosevelt, both were also not apprehensive about using military might.[29] But it was the cowboy masculinity of Jackson that interested Rove. Jackson carried two bullets in his body, was a duelist, an Indian fighter who once during his presidency attacked an assassin with his cane. Jackson was the nation's first cowboy president, and America still liked cowboys. In 2006, a Harris poll found that John Wayne was the third most popular actor of all time and the only deceased actor to make the top ten.[30] A year later, when Republicans mocked John Edwards for his $400 haircut it was an effort to emasculate Edwards as a false populist, un-Wayne "nancy boy."

"Consider the Democrats since 1972: McGovern, Carter, Mondale, Dukakis, Clinton, Gore, Kerry, and now mold that into one man, one perception of manhood," I ask Bruce Reed, Democratic Leadership Council president, in late 2006. "Now consider the Republicans: Nixon, Ford, Reagan, George H. W. Bush, Dole, George W. Bush, and try to mold them into one man? Do you see two different composites of manhood?"

"You'd have to say that at the polls a 1950s male is likely to beat the 1970s male," Reed replies. "And not all our guys fit that mold exactly but pretty close. Ironically McGovern probably fits it the least but his campaign was only partly about him. It's *Father Knows Best* versus, well I don't know who is the perfect archetype is for the Democrats—"

"The father from *Family Ties?*" I ask.

"Yeah yeah, that's not bad," Reed says. "I don't think it is necessarily a party thing," Reed continues. "It's that voters are looking for certain qualities in the president: strength, and confidence and self assuredness are an important part of that and while open-mindedness and sensitivity are in some parts valuable, [they] are not big winners with the electorate. I think that both Gore and Kerry—well especially Gore, Gore had all the right qualities, he was tough enough, he was confident enough—in some ways Bush got elected by downplaying his [own] masculinity."

"But a Republican downplays his masculinity at times because Republicans are presumed strong. Isn't manhood far more than strength—but self-assurance?"

"To me," Reed replies, "what that suggests is that it's not just the masculinity of the 1950s and the '70s, but it's the worldview that goes with it. That we are never going to be a majority party by seeing the world as half empty. Americans really want the confidence and the optimism of the 1950s even more than they want the culture and values of that period."

"But is it not simply the outlook of the 1950s man, but the ability to appear one of the guys?"

"Being able to relate to the average guy has always been at the heart of any presidential candidate's success," Reed replies. "And if you are not somebody that voters want to have a beer with then they have a hard time voting to bring you into their living rooms. Sometimes, neither side offers much terribly clear in that regard. But if there is a clear difference between likeability and normalness, it's a big advantage. Everybody wants to be part of a gang, as Clinton used to say, part of the club, and Republicans have offered white male voters more of a club they wanted to sign up for."

GOD, MANHOOD, AND MORAL VALUES

A month after Reagan accepted his party's nomination, he went to Dallas to speak before 15,000 social-conservative church leaders. As Reagan took the podium before thousands of ministers, many of them southern Baptists like Carter, he told them, "Well, I know that you *can't* endorse me, but I only brought that up because I want you to know that *I endorse you.*"[1]

"That's when I learned what a master politician Reagan was," recalls Richard Land, the Southern Baptist Convention leader. "Reagan walked out," Land chuckles, shaking his head in awe. "I was sitting there. I was in the front row. And [Reagan] says, I know that you can't endorse me but I'm here to endorse you. I thought this guy's really good, he's *really* good."

ONWARD CHRISTIAN SOLDIER

Richard Wirthlin wrote in the 1980 Reagan campaign plan that "the traditional Republican base is simply not large enough" and it "will be necessary to expand the coalition base." Wirthlin named southern white Protestants as one of the key constituencies that Republicans "must convert" to win. By the time Reagan accepted his party's nomination, he advocated that the biblical story of creation be taught in public schools as an alternative to evolution. He was explicitly anti-abortion. He referred to his campaign as a "crusade." And as he closed his address before delegates, he ended with a silent prayer.

"What was even bigger than that was the perception that Carter further weakened the United States internationally," explains Laura Olson, a professor at Clemson University who specializes in religion and politics. "Part of what fueled the emergence of the Christian Right was anticommunism," she adds, "communism being rightly perceived as godless was very threatening to people of faith."

Jimmy Carter still struggles to understand why conservative Christians turned against him in 1980. "I was surprised, yeah. I saw Pat Robertson and Jerry Falwell, at least those two, as very aggressively attacking me for things that I could not quite understand, like the creation of a Department of Education, this kind of thing, or the SALT II agreement with the Soviet Union or the Panama Canal Treaty. Or giving back the Sinai desert to Egypt," Carter recalls. "Those took upon themselves religious connotations which still escape me."

Religious Christians, evangelicals particularly, opposed the Department of Education because they saw it as furthering the secularization of education. Social conservatives opposed the treaties that handed over the Panama Canal and the Sinai desert, as well as SALT II, because they believed it weakened a morally just American cause. While abortion was critical to the Republican populist outreach, ultimately Reagan's primary appeal came down to his clear masculine stance against communism.

In the hymn sung throughout the rise of the religious right, there was a persistent masculine undertone. And it worked. Democrats have been on the trailing end of the values debate since the devout Carter lost churchgoing voters to Reagan in 1980. In 1976, Carter won the white Baptist vote, 56 to 43 percent. In 1980, Reagan won it 56 to 34 percent. From Reagan to George W. Bush's reelection, Republicans have won religious Christians, the four out of ten voters who attend church at least once a week, by about 20 percent in two-man races, a margin that never reached the size of the White Male Gap.[2] It was no accident of history that the central issues haunting the modern Democratic Party matured in the 1980 election. Manhood and moral values were both born of the same fundamental belief that Democrats no longer represented the character of the classic man. Only one party seemingly stood up for faith, family, and virtue, a belief system born of God and country, and for a world slowly being chopped away by modernity.

Blue-collar whites were always hawkish on security. Yet by 1980, the majority of the nation joined them in this concern. In 1973, one poll found that only

11 percent of Americans said the government should spend more on the military. In 1980, support for military spending rose to 56 percent.[3]

The traditional father stood both for the moral world and the "city on a hill." God and country are inseparable to social conservatives, from John Winthrop to Richard Land, not because they believe Jesus cares most for the United States. But because, in their view, the United States can care most for "the good news" that they believe Jesus brought. The Monroe Doctrine was always a most evangelical concept.

"When the McGovern people took over the party, the Democratic Party went hard left and for many of them, particularly those that were shaped by Vietnam, they see America as part of the problem, not part of the solution," Land says. "Whereas, when the Goldwater people took over the Republican Party they . . . saw America as a force for good in the world, that America is not perfect but on the whole—and it's on the whole that such things must be judged—that America is a force for good and a force for freedom in the world," Land continues. "And I can certainly tell you that among Evangelical Christians that George W. Bush is sounding their trumpet loud and clear when he says that America has a special obligation to be a friend of freedom and defender of liberty."

Bush believed that the "good news" of democracy allowed nations to be born again in freedom. After the September 11 attacks, as dogmatic liberals reflexively pulled back from the use of force, Bush's neoconservatism reflexively relied upon it. The classic liberals were nearly extinct and the conservative realists were silenced.

After World War II, modern conservative forebears like Peter Viereck had emphasized a rationalism that was, at its core, a rebuke of the Nazi and Soviet utopian ideal. William Buckley believed, "conservatism is to a considerable extent the acknowledgment of realities," and the neoconservatives were "surreal."[4] "Bush knows that we are concerned. And he is himself concerned," Buckley tells me in 2006. "The question is, under the circumstances, how does he deport himself."

Roosevelt-style liberals had similar concerns regarding Schlesinger's "doughface progressives." It was telling that at midcentury the Protestant theologian Reinhold Niebuhr joined with Schlesinger to denounce liberal pacifism. World War II changed one of America's greatest theologians: Niebuhr. He broke with American Christian socialists who were against entering the war. Niebuhr believed that the Nazis embodied an evil that had to be opposed by force. After the war, he carried that belief to the fight against communism. "If we should perish, the ruthlessness of the foe would be only the secondary cause of the disaster," Niebuhr wrote. "The primary cause would be that the strength of a giant nation was directed by eyes too blind to see all the hazards."[5]

The midcentury alliance of Niebuhr and Schlesinger foretold why Reagan marked both the onset of the religion gap and the White Male Gap. Both Niebuhr and Schlesinger had been left behind by the dogmatic liberalism that had lost its ability to see the "hazards" after Vietnam. The new breed of post-1968 liberal soon left a vast army of white men open to conservatives' appeal. Republicans defined the masculinity that Franklin D. Roosevelt and John F. Kennedy championed, just as Democrats defined the active state liberalism that Abraham Lincoln first championed. But as dogmatic liberals surrendered the traditional masculine image, conservatives defined it in its most stern terms. Given the choice between the fighter and the pacifist, white males will always go with the fighter, as long as they believe the nation is threatened.

"The conventional analysis is, of course, that the Republicans are peeling off voters that care about abortion and same-sex marriage, and that is a factor," the social conservative leader Gary Bauer tells me. "But I do think that the conventional analysis misses the larger cultural issues as their top-agenda items. [These voters] love America. They get a tear in their eyes when the national anthem is played. They are very comfortable slapping a sticker on their car saying we support the troops, things that, rightly or wrongly, the Democratic Party is seen as being uncomfortable with."

Whether I spoke with Pat Robertson, Jerry Falwell, Bauer, or Land, the view was the same. At the very heart of Reagan's appeal to the religious Christian vote was the patriotism he personified. About 14 percent of white women and 11 percent of white men are social conservatives, the majority of whom support an "assertive foreign policy." More social conservatives have a gun in their home (56 percent) than attend church weekly (53 percent) or attend bible study (51 percent).[6] Social-conservative support for Republicans was contingent not simply on values issues, but on the willingness to defend the nation that embodies them.

"The association of the Republican Party with a tough foreign policy, sort of an America first, and the willingness of Republicans to contemplate, and on occasion use American force in order to reach foreign policy goals," Bauer suspects has created a large portion of the White Male Gap. "And probably the opposite of that is the association of the Democratic Party with soft statements of the public debate, whether it is the antiwar movement, the radical left, the Hollywood crowd. I think that combination has made Republicans the place where male voters are more comfortable."

As televangelist Pat Robertson says, "Males want a muscular foreign policy. They don't want people they see us as wimps surrendering our sovereignty to the United Nations."

Richard Land agrees. "Traditional American males are repulsed by what they think of as the antimilitary attitude of the Democratic Party and it goes back to McGovern," Land continues. "Republicans became Goldwater's party and then Reagan's party. But Goldwater and Nixon didn't make them a majority. Goldwater and Nixon made them viable. It was the addition of the traditional values voters that made them a majority."

THE RISE OF THE VALUES VOTER

Americans after the 1950s looked back to find their better future. Whites as well as blacks consider that decade the nation's most idyllic period.[7] America had saved Europe and the cause of freedom was in its hands. There was one enemy and it stood against God and country. The nation had bled together and now it would succeed together. There was *Life* magazine, Joe DiMaggio, and *Leave It to Beaver*. Women took care of the home, the children, and though their days sometimes felt tedious, there was comfort in the stability. Men had one job for life. Each morning they awoke, rededicated their wartime duty toward capitalism, and went to work proud to be supporting their family. And though sometimes they felt like little more than a cog in a machine, so it was in the army as well—at least they found a sense of accomplishment. Boys saw their fathers return from work. They talked of Chuck Yeager breaking the sound barrier, and the man who broke the four-minute mile. Men reached the summit of Mount Everest. At the close of the era, Kennedy promised a man on the moon: the western expansion would be taken upward; space was to be the new frontier. The progress of mankind could overcome nature itself.

With the assassination of Kennedy and King, it all seemed to fall apart. The outward looking national psyche, a nation assured of its preeminent manhood, was turned inward, and soon it faced its original sin of slavery. But at the same time came the crime, the riots, Vietnam, the relentless rise in premarital sex, teen pregnancy, divorce, the loss of one good job for one good man. Ignoring the "red scare," the racism, the sexism, the homophobia, the anti-Semitism, even the fear of nuclear war—all the demons of that decade—many recalled that 1950s America through rose-colored glasses and yearned for the stability it represented.

To white men in particular, this reach back to the 1950s was most potent. The gap between what was and what was fast becoming was largest for them. The stability was theirs to lose. As it slipped away, Republican cultural populism came to be defined by its recognition of this loss, however imaginary to some. Soon, progress itself was no longer simply good. People began to consider the casualties of progress by the mid-1960s. And in that turn toward memory, instead of expectation, was the bridge for a conservative cultural appeal, an appeal to those things many felt were worth conserving.

The conservative social values movements were at their core an effort to restore semblances of the stability, the community, the gender archetypes, the traditional mores of the ascendant 1950s nation. By the time Nixon won his second term, Phyllis Schlafly had begun the "pro-family" Eagle Forum. The following year, the conservative Heritage Foundation was founded. But it was the Supreme Court that rallied a movement.

Alexis de Tocqueville once observed, "There is hardly a political question in the United States which does not, sooner or later, turn into a judicial one."[8] In 1962, the Court prohibited school prayer. Soon after, it ruled that pornography was legal and that obscenity was subject to contemporary community standards. To social conservatives, the decision was emblematic of liberal moral relativism. But the battle of worldviews soon, at least to a fifth of Americans, involved life and death implications. The political had become the judicial and the judicial gradually upended the political.

The 1973 abortion ruling *Roe v. Wade* bred a new urgency in the budding religious right. At the center of it all was Jerry Falwell and his Moral Majority. These were not the blue-blooded Northeastern Republicans. Like Richard Land's father, Falwell's father had been a yellow-dog Democrat. "If I mentioned the word Republican in my home growing up, I'd probably have gotten a whipping. FDR was our patron saint," Falwell recalls, in an interview a half year before his death.

"But it wasn't until I became a Christian as a college student years later and began studying the Bible, and the Democratic Party from, say '68, the Chicago convention on, began gathering the marginal and radical groups of the country under their tent that I found myself no longer voting Democratic. I'm not really sure whether it was a planned kind of thing or just by osmosis," he continues. "But abortion on demand became one of their major doctrines and as a conserva-

tive evangelical Christian, or as a Roman Catholic who takes the church seriously, that is a deal breaker."

Many evangelicals supported Carter in 1976 because "he said he was born
again and that impressed our people," Falwell says. Yet by 1979, "He made it
clear that he was pro-choice, that he was weak on national defense." In the following years, Falwell organized his Moral Majority.

Reagan won Falwell to his cause from the outset. "We had not been 30 minutes in the room in California with Mr. Reagan, the former governor of California, and we were all convinced that this was *the* guy. Pro-life, unswervingly
committed to the sanctity of human life, and particularly—this was the Cold
War days—we liked his commitment to peace through strength, and his support
for the state of Israel. All those things are buzz words for our people and it's for
that reason that we went to work and registered millions of voters and we at least
helped him to get elected." In total, the Moral Majority spent an estimated $5
million on the election of 1980 and signed up 72,000 ministers and 4 million lay
members to support the Republicans.[9]

The religious right of 1980 was a Christian outgrowth of many of the issues
that pushed white men away from the Democrats in 1968. The turn to moral
order was a turn to traditional manhood. But the religious were silent. They
were an army without the motivation to conscript. They lacked clear antagonists. Two issues changed that.

THE SYMBOLS AND THE SUBSTANCE

"You can't run an entire campaign talking about the future. There has to be a
couple of key components," Reagan's chief strategist, Richard Wirthlin, says.
"One is, you've got to deal with the issues that are salient and a concern for people today and you've got to be able to describe those issues as people are perceiv-
ing them today, in a context that will allow you to push the vision toward
tomorrow. But I've always looked at issues as simply a means to another end.
And that end is, what value or value structures do the issues underpin or create?
Issues are rational. But, I believe, if you want to motivate people to vote, or take
any kind of action, you've got to touch them not only rationally but emotionally.
But in developing the issues you've got to look toward how those issues impinge
upon the values of safety, peace of mind, family, and so on. It took me awhile to
realize that Reagan did that almost naturally."

The Reagan campaign's considerable outreach was based on appealing to the common disenchantment of religious Catholic and Protestant constituencies. Reagan was not an ardent believer in the conservative Christian cause, but he was on their side. And with abortion, as well as other smaller issues, Reagan made it known.

Abortion was the first clarion call for a caucus of churchgoing Christians. Feminists view abortion rights as inseparable from women's liberation. Social conservatives view abortion as murder. Meanwhile, most Americans occupy the middle ground on the issue.

Exit polling demonstrates that for white voters, 21 percent of women and 15 percent of men believe abortion should always be legal; 34 percent of women and 37 percent of men believe abortion should be mostly legal; 27 percent of women and 29 percent of men believe it should be mostly illegal; and 15 percent of white men and women believe abortion should be abolished.[10]

Leading Democrats do not speak of abortion as they once did. "I abhor abortion," Kerry tells me. "We went too far on the abortion issue," Carter says of his Democrats. "We became branded with abortion." Both argue that Democrats must be clear they are not pro-abortion. "I think the Democrats have learned not to get burned so severely in any case on the abortion issue," Carter says, a strong opponent of "late-term abortions." Kerry adds, "I would counsel anybody to try to avoid an abortion." But Land argues that for Democrats to win back the religious Christian voter, "They've got to find some abortions they can't at least live with." Leading Democrats have not.

In the spring of 2007 the Supreme Court upheld the Partial Birth Abortion Ban Act. The law prohibited a gruesome type of abortion administered in the fifth or sixth month of pregnancy. Every leading 2008 Democratic presidential candidate spoke out against the decision, despite a majority of Americans favoring a ban on the rare procedure.

While the pragmatic push to moderate the abortion issue is still pervasive among leading Democrats, the stance is often mistaken for the substance. Gay marriage represented the same dilemma in 2004. That issue alone did not win re-election for George W. Bush, but it did damage the Democrats. The cultural hurricane began when the Massachusetts Supreme Judicial Court, during the Democratic primaries, expanded marriage to same-sex couples. Later that February 2004, San Francisco Mayor Gavin Newsom began handing out marriage licenses to gay and lesbian couples. Cable news saturated America with images of joyous same-sex weddings. Kerry stated his support for civil unions, not same-sex marriage. But it didn't matter. Enough Democrats were advocating gay marriage. Two iconic liberal areas legalized it. By Election Day, eleven states placed constitutional amendments banning gay marriage onto their ballots. All passed—most importantly, in Ohio, where a quarter of the electorate is evangelical (5 percent above the national average). The issue likely increased conservative Christian turnout at the margins, but it is at the margins that most presidencies are won.

One look at the polling reveals how deep the divisions over gay marriage run, placing Democrats in a precarious position. The most loyal Democrats, minority women, are the strongest opponents. Among white and Hispanic voters in 2004, only about 30 percent of women and 20 percent of men supported same-sex marriage. For blacks there is no difference between men and women, only 18 percent supported gay marriage. Roughly four out of ten whites supported civil unions. Black and Hispanic men show similar levels of support, while 10 percent fewer black and Hispanic women supported civil unions. Overall, four out of ten white men and 34 percent of white women oppose legal recognition of any kind. More than half of all black women are against any legal recognition, while 44 percent of black men, 40 percent of Hispanic men, and 38 percent of Hispanic women agree in their opposition. Notably, when asked if they were gay, lesbian, or bisexual, 5 percent of blacks and Hispanics, and 3 percent of whites, answered yes.[11]

Society's apprehensiveness about gay marriage did not prevent it from being a cause true to liberal credo. The majority of Americans in the 1960s thought America was moving too quickly on civil rights—politicians can be out in front of the people. But gay marriage will continue to prove a costly fight.

Sociologist James Davidson Hunter wrote in the early 1990s that issues like gay marriage and abortion are viewed by two fundamental mental archetypes, those who define morality through their adherence to external doctrine and those who define morality in terms of personal rationalization and within a subjective moral framework. But William James said it most critically at the dawn of the twentieth century, when he wrote in the landmark book, *The Varieties of Religious Experience*, that liberal morality is akin to Walt Whitman's view of nature. It recognizes the beauty while ignoring the cruel possibilities of the wild. James called Whitman the "supreme contemporary example" of the "inability to see evil."[12]

"In no other country is the Right defined so much by values rather than class," wrote John Micklethwait and Adrian Wooldridge in *The Right Nation*.[13] Each values issue grew out of an underlying belief system, divided upon, as Richard Land puts it, whether you believe that there "are transcendent moral values or whether you don't, and believe most things are relative and situational."

Leading up to the 1980 election, Theodore White argued that Carter "repeatedly" made one fundamental mistake in dealing with the Iranian hostage crisis. "It is impossible in the rhetoric of liberal American politics, of which Carter is a true expression," he wrote, "to disdain or denounce people of other traditions."[14]

By 1983, Reagan was in Orlando standing beneath a banner that read, "Change your world," denouncing communism to the convention of the National Association of Evangelicals in Orlando, declaring the Soviet Union the "focus of evil in the modern world." Among evangelicals, Reagan was always best at being Reagan. Critics questioned whether the black-and-white rhetoric might escalate tensions. Others deemed it "threat inflation."[15] However, the utility of moral clarity is in this weakness. It brushes broad strokes and therefore paints the big picture. But is it not the big picture that moves men? To many Americans, when Reagan stood up on that podium, he was the man they admired most. The "evil empire" address defined the Reagan presidency. Reagan's staff quipped that it was his "Darth Vader speech."[16] The very name of the defense plan Reagan pushed, "Star Wars," framed his fight in epic proportions (of the George Lucas epic, that is). But the value of words like "evil empire" to social conservatives was fundamentally about the president's willingness to call an evil an evil.

"Reagan was smart enough to know that if we were muscular and strong, the Soviets couldn't keep up with us," Pat Robertson says. A central figure in the Religious Right during the Reagan era, and founder of the Christian Broadcasting Network, Robertson spoke to me at its headquarters in Virginia Beach, Virginia. Moving past pictures of the evangelist with the who's who of Republican establishment, past a sculpture of Jesus' Last Supper, Robertson sits inside his mahogany office, in an armchair beneath an oil painting of the apostle Peter. He describes how Reagan, "started a race so intense, [the Soviets] broke and as a result communism fell. But that's the kind of foreign policy that the white male wants," Robertson says, leaning back in the armchair, his thinning hair neatly parted. "Reagan was willing to call it an evil empire. And everybody was just shocked that he told the truth."

It was the truth as revealed by Reagan. George W. Bush's equivalent use of phrases such as "evil doers," Land says, epitomizes the belief that there are moral absolutes. "Some things are evil, and some things are good and some things are always evil and some things are always good and [religious Christians] are comfortable with that moral clarity," Land says. "People who have drunk deeply from the fountain of postmodernism are not comfortable with that kind of moral clarity."

To leading conservative Christian radio host Frank Pastore, there is a "very simple answer" to the religious right's emphasis on moral clarity. "John 14:6. 'I am the way, the truth, and the light and no one comes to the Father but through me.' That is the core of moral certainty and moral clarity," Pastore tells me at his Los Angeles studio. He is tall, casual, with a half smile that curves only his lower lip. Between 1979 and 1985, Pastore pitched for the Cincinnati Reds and, as with many conservative Christian leaders, his strength is inseparable from his faith. "There is no moral uncertainty in capital T, Truth, issues for us," Pastore says. "Jesus *did* rise from the dead! That's not a sorta, maybe. That's not a *Da Vinci Code* spin. If that didn't happen, then all of this is bogus!"

THE JESUS CATHARSIS

The city George W. Bush lived in, Midland, Texas, experienced the worst oil crisis in a generation during the mid 1980s. It led to bankruptcy, divorce, and suicides. The local men's chapter of community Bible study was originally formed precisely to combat a male crisis. "Men were searching for help," said Skip Hedgepeth, one of those who attended the Midland prayer meetings. "[They were] trying to have an air of confidence for their families that things were going to be okay, and they were themselves looking for help to find out that everything was going to be okay." Midland is white, flat, hot, a land of oil and church. "Hard times have a way of drawing people closer to God," Hedgepeth said. "Out of the struggles we become aware, you know, that we are not in charge of everything."[17]

Bush joined the Bible study group during his own personal low point in the mid-1980s. He was drinking heavily. The oil bust forced him to sell his company. His family was threatening to leave him. To the regular guys who sat around the table with Bush, discussing the Bible, there was camaraderie in their common struggle.

Bush's Bible class was nearly all white men. Roughly four out of ten white women and nearly three out of ten white men attend Bible study or prayer group meetings. And among those who do, more white men vote Republican than women.[18] For those whites struggling to get by, regular church attendance correlates more strongly to men's voting preferences than women's. In 2004, among white men with household incomes less than $30,000, 73 percent of those attending church (or other houses of worship) at least once a week voted for Bush. In comparison, only 43 percent of those attending less than once per week voted for Bush. For white women of the same income bracket, weekly churchgoers supported Bush at 61 percent, while 44 percent of less religious women backed the Republican.[19]

"You've got a really powerful finding here," one of the leading experts on American religiosity, John C. Green, says, "that white male lower-class weekly attendees, they look like rich people, in terms of their Republican vote." Going to church does not make white men Republican. Church helps to focus their plight and also creates community bonds. For this reason, religious Christians vote at about a 10 percent higher rate than those who attend church less than once a week.

Poor white men are often unable to support a family, or even find a spouse, unlike women in the same income bracket, who, studies have shown, tend to marry up. Poor white men, like all poor, see more crime in their neighborhoods, more alcoholism, more divorce. Attending church is a way for white men to recognize forces beyond their control, without feeling as if they are abdicating their manhood. Church validates their journey toward order and honor. When these men hear candidates speak in a morally clear language, in the rhetoric of law and order, of good and evil, it reflects what they yearn for in their world. It is often only the belief in something righteous, whether it is God, country, or both, that pushes men beyond their own mistakes.

"The changes in the economy I think are related to these cultural values questions, and if you deconstruct culture, it's really not that much about gays and abortion," political analyst Anna Greenberg says. "It's very much about kids, cultural pollution, pornography, predators, Internet, movies. And this is not because of the economy but it's related to the economy because people have less control over their lives and this lack of control is deeply unsettling to both men and women."

In the strictest sense of secular liberalism and pure libertarian conservatism, the values divide is best seen as a game of poker. Libertarian conservatives believe that each person is dealt a hand of cards in life and how the man plays the cards defines the player. Liberals believe that the deck is stacked against many Americans and that it is incumbent upon society to even out the hand.

Social conservatives and some libertarians define their worth in part by how they help the poor. Many agree that there is a societal obligation. But they believe that government wastes money and creates dependence, rather than allowing a person to take personal responsibility. The belief in personal responsibility is shared by conservative blocs and white men overall.

Conservative Christian opposition to government programs is rooted in skepticism of man's ability to control passions and temptations, a sense that the apple is always hanging out there waiting to be picked. This belief in innate compulsions is inseparable from Christian conservatives' patriarchal doctrine. Personal responsibility is at the heart of evangelism. Each Christian must act autonomously to be "born again." Richard Land sees the issue in terms of the Christian theological concept of original sin. He speaks to the "fallen sinful nature of man and that man is not going to be terribly productive unless they get to keep a significant portion of what they make." Land adds, "Now we can talk about their obligation personally and I think obligation is to help alleviate the plight of the poor, to take care of their family and take care of others. What you do voluntarily is one thing, when you have confiscatory tax rates that's another."

Neoconservative forefather Irving Kristol has argued that there are two diametrically opposed views of governance. The masculine welfare state provided a limited safety net for the needy and those experiencing hard times. In contrast, the unlimited and burgeoning safety net knitted with indiscriminant compassion was the "feminine-maternalistic" welfare state. "Fathers want their children to grow up to be self-reliant, self-supporting, and able to cope with a recalcitrant world. Mothers want their children to be as completely protected as possible from such a world and to be gratefully attached to them as long as they live."[20]

While liberals generally view morality in terms of how one acts upon the world, social conservatives generally view morality in terms of how one acts in his or her immediate life, within the family above all. Liberals tend to look from the top to the bottom to solve society's ills. Conservatives tend to look from the bottom up. Central to this viewpoint is the family unit. Conservative evangelicals see the family as the bedrock of society; to them, the family is a church in and of itself, with the man at the head.

"This is where I think the gender politics is really important," Anna Greenberg says. "It's not so much that Republicans offer something that offers economic security and an ability to achieve what they perceive as the American dream," she adds. "I do think they are the party of preserving the man's role in the family. When you look at these Christian Right organizations, so much of what they are about is fathers, empowering fathers."

FATHER JESUS AND MANLY CHRISTIANITY

"I'm against sin," Billy Sunday preached. "I'll kick it as long as I've got a foot, and I'll fight it as long as I've got a fist. I'll butt it as long as I've got a head. I'll bite it as long as I've got a tooth. And when I'm old and fistless and footless and toothless, I'll gum it till I go home to Glory and it goes home to perdition!"

William Ashley, known as Billy Sunday, was born in Iowa. He lost his father to the Civil War, became a professional baseball player, and at 23 found Christ.[21] For the first two decades of the twentieth century he may have been the leading evangelist in the nation. He was instrumental in the passage of Prohibition in 1919. While some socialists championed Jesus as the carpenter who wanted to redistribute wealth, to Billy Sunday the Gospels compelled men to see sin as a constant trial of manhood.

Christian evangelical leaders have long concerned themselves with masculinity. At one time, Billy Graham criticized dovish congressmen as, "the pinks, the lavenders, and the reds who have sought refuge beneath the wings of the American eagle."[22] But it was the push for patriarchy that defined modern conservative American Christendom.

There is no greater demonstration of manhood in Christianity than duty to brother and family.[23] In the New Testament, John 15:13 stresses that brotherly loyalty is supreme masculinity. "Greater love hath not man than this, that a man lay down his life for his friends." The Southern Baptist Convention's mission statement reads, "God has ordained the family as the foundational institution of human society." Timothy 3:4–5 upholds the value of "one that ruleth well his own house," because, "if a man know not how to rule his own house, how shall he take care of the church of God?"

Much of the feminist movement centered around the liberation from patriarchy, pitting liberalism on the other side of this Christian archetype. Feminism began to question whether a father was needed to maintain a healthy family, as well as whether men were a necessity in fulfilling female sexual pleasure.

In 2006, the brave Shere Hite, a pioneering feminist sexologist, went on Comedy Central's *Colbert Report*. The show is to some extent a parody of Bill O'Reilly and other conservative commentators.

Hite: The stereotype had been of course and still is, that women have difficulty or women have a problem having orgasm. And the fact is women don't have a problem having orgasm. Women can orgasm very easily by themselves. And so it's society that has a problem accepting that.

Colbert: You see, I think that's a terrible idea. That takes men right out of the picture there. . . . Women have their own orgasms and then suddenly we no longer have a steel industry. The country went to hell in a hand basket after women got to work.

Hite: No, that's not true.

Colbert: It doesn't matter if it is true. It *feels* like it is true.[24]

Colbert's hyperbole was intentional, but the sentiments he touched on are real. Among many men, the liberated woman is welcome. They are pleased to be free of the full burden for supporting their households. For men 25 to 55, half say they are more turned on by "more sexually aggressive women," while a quarter express relief to have "the pressure taken off," and only 17 percent say they are intimidated when a woman makes a pass on them.[25]

Social conservatives don't question that some men enjoy the sexual revolution—they question what it does to men, women, and society. They believe feminism caused family breakdown and family breakdown caused the American moral breakdown. And they have their reasons.

Between the 1960s and 1970s, as the number of women in the labor force rose from 38 to 52 percent, the divorce rate more than doubled. Meanwhile, households with children fell from 49 to 38 percent and there were 1.5 million Americans "cohabitating," a threefold increase.[26]

By the mid-1990s, the evangelical Promise Keepers attracted millions of men with the pledge to restore the nation by restoring the family unit. This was to be accomplished by first restoring men's paternal honor. Stadiums across the nation filled with mostly middle-class, mostly white, males. By October of 1997, more than a half million Christian men marched on the National Mall for the Promise Keepers' cause. It was larger than Martin Luther King's March on Washington in 1963 and the Vietnam Moratorium antiwar march of 1969. It may have been the largest gathering of white men for societal action in U.S. history; tens of thousands of minorities were also present as were black speakers. Six hours of hymns, pledges, and prayers followed. The group's founder, Bill McCartney, a former football coach, preached that "men have not stood strong for their convictions," and that "the reason we see a downward spiral in morality in this nation is because the men of God have not stood together."[27]

Promise Keepers believed that men must submit to Jesus and then "reclaim" their patriarchal family role. The push for these men to be stronger revealed how enfeebled many felt they were. Yet to women's groups, it was little more than a push to undermine their equality. The National Organization for Women (NOW) passed a resolution declaring the Promise Keepers "the greatest danger to women's rights."[28]

As Brad Wilcox wrote in *Soft Patriarchs, New Men*, conservative Protestant leaders feel compelled to "uphold patriarchal authority in order to signal their willingness to submit themselves to the principle of biblical inerrancy."[29] The southern Baptist believes "husband and wife are of equal worth before God, since both are created in God's image," adding that, "a husband is to love his wife as Christ loved the church." The husband "has the God-given responsibility" to provide, protect, and to lead his family, while a "wife is to submit herself graciously to the servant leadership of her husband even as the church willingly submits to the headship of Christ."[30]

Wilcox found that a higher proportion of conservative Protestant men believe in the "male headship" of households than do liberal and secular men. They spank their children slightly more, though liberal Protestants who attend church regularly spank as well. Wilcox also found that conservative Christian men are "more engaged with their children, more affectionate and expressive toward them, more likely to praise and hug both their children and their wives, more likely to know their children's whereabouts, and more likely to supervise their television time." Liberal and moderate Christian men may do somewhat more housework, but Wilcox found they are less affectionate with both their wives and children. He found that conservative men display more gratitude for their wives' work in the household. "Evangelical women feel more appreciated and report more happiness with their marriages" than moderate and liberal Christian women. The more conservative men attend church, Wilcox found, the more these qualities are enhanced.[31]

The moral-values push to strengthen families is not an abstract exercise to those Americans who vote Republican. Of the 13 most impoverished states, only one voted Democratic in 2004.[32] The poor feel the breakdown in family structure most keenly, and single-mother households have the highest level of poverty. Republican states have a higher murder rate, 7.4 per 100,000, compared to 6.1 in the Democratic states. Republican states also have slightly higher teen pregnancy rates. Montana had 60 percent more divorces than New Jersey.[33] But Christian conservatives' emphasis on fatherhood is not solely due to teen pregnancy or divorce. Of the 26 states that had the highest fertility rates, Bush won 25; Kerry won the 16 states with the lowest.[34]

The founder and chairman of the influential socially conservative group Focus on the Family, James Dobson, was originally a child psychologist. Today his radio show commands millions of listeners. Much of his outlook is found in his book on Christian child rearing, *Dare to Discipline*, in which he argues that the dramatic rise in teen pregnancy, crime, and drugs, among many other issues, can be traced back to the "permissive" child-rearing style of the 1950s.

For Dobson, it was not what the 1950s began, but what it wrought. Dobson saw '60s activists as the result of America's shift from traditional mores. Activists were children of baby boomer parents who purchased Dr. Benjamin Spock's *Baby and Child Care*. Published in 1946, it was the "bible of post–World War II parenting," former secretary of labor Robert Reich, a proud counterculture progressive, wrote. The book sold more than 50 million copies. In its first ten years alone, it went through 167 printings.[35] Parents were told to reason with and respect children, listen to counterarguments, keep an open mind, to be rational and flexible.[36]

Dobson's book may have sold less—a million copies—but his beliefs have influenced the whole of social conservatism. "It is naive to believe that a system of reward and punishment does not work with children," he wrote. Dobson argued that parents of young liberals "demanded neither respect nor responsible behavior from [their] children." To Dobson, the counterculture was the result.[37]

THE FAITH CONNECTION:
RELIGION AND THE PATHWAY TO CHARACTER

George W. Bush was the evangelical who stood on the shoulders of Reagan. "Without question," Pat Robertson says, Bush is "the most outspoken evangelical to sit in that office in maybe a hundred years. And I think he is putting into effect initiatives that really transcend Reagan. Reagan talked a good game but I think Bush is delivering." As social conservative Kansas Senator Sam Brownback told me at Tavern on the Green during the 2004 convention, "We got a mole in the White House: George Bush."

When Bush first ran for the presidency in 2000, candidates were asked during the third Republican debate to name their favorite political philosopher. Steve Forbes said John Locke. Alan Keyes answered the Founding Fathers. Bush answered, "Christ, because he changed my life," nodding his head downward conclusively. He shrugged his shoulders forward as if to emphasize, *"yes, it's that simple."* The moderator asked Bush to explain to the public how Christ had changed his heart. Bush paused, blankly looked toward the floor as if he were searching within himself, then said, "If they don't know, it's going to be hard to explain." He then looked upward, again with certitude, saying "When you accept Christ as your savior it changes your heart, it changes your life." Every religious Christian, if not at least seven out of ten Americans, knew exactly what he meant, especially if they were "born again."

Four years later at the third presidential debate, as Bush fought to gain ground after two poor performances, CBS's Bob Schieffer asked about faith and presidential policy decisions. "My faith is a very—it's very personal. I pray for strength. I pray for wisdom. I pray for our troops in harm's way. I pray for my family. I pray for my little girls," Bush humbly replied. "Prayer and religion sustain me," Bush added. "I receive calmness in the storms of the presidency. . . . When I make decisions, I stand on principle, and the principles are derived from who I am."

When the question came to Kerry, whereas Bush immediately said faith "is a big part of my life," Kerry acknowledged Bush's faith and initially hesitated to proclaim his own. When Kerry did respond, he fell far short of the president. "I went to a church school and I was taught that the two greatest commandments are: Love the Lord, your God, with all your mind, your body and your soul, and love your neighbor as yourself." Kerry proceeded to criticize Bush. "I have a difference of opinion about how we live out our sense of our faith," referencing the second chapter of James, as Kerry often did during the race. "I talked about the works and faith without works being dead." Kerry neglected to explain how his faith reflects his moral core. Kerry's reticence to speak about faith in public terms was principled. It was simply not a winning one.

"Historically, there was [a cultural reticence among Democrats to discuss faith]," Kerry tells me in his Senate office. "But I don't think there is anymore. I know, for myself, I talk about it in almost every speech now because I'm *not* going to be put on the defensive. I refuse to have, you know, 80 percent of the teachings left on the wayside while people selectively grab onto what serves their purposes and march with it."

Kerry's inability to speak of his own faith most likely hurt him more with white women than men. Among white women, 76 percent "completely agree" that God exists. Only 58 percent of white males believe the same. When asked if prayer is an important part of their life, 85 percent of white women "completely" or "mostly agree," while 71 percent of white men say the same.[38] In total, 45 percent of white women and 37 percent of white men attend church at least once a week. This explains why "moral values" issues affect white women more than white men, as in the 2004 election.

Kerry struggled throughout the race to speak of his faith. His chief strategist, Tad Devine, tells me in his Georgetown office that Kerry's religious reticence was "a product of his upbringing, not just as a Catholic, just the society and culture that he was brought up with in the Northeast." In part, this comes from a strict interpretation of Matthew, Chapter 22: 21, "Render therefore unto Caesar the things which are Caesar's; and unto God the things that are God's."

Carter also believes there is a "biblical exhortation to separate" religion and state. But he adds that presiding by faith is different than expressing faith. It is a "legitimate expectation on the part of the American people," he says, "to have their leaders espouse deep within their heart, as part of consciousness, moral values that are predicated, at least for my consciousness, on religious faith."

Kerry is religious. And once he becomes comfortable, he talks about the "incredible emotion," the "joy," he felt at his first communion. He spiritedly recalls his days as an altar boy with his eyes tilted upward. But then he looks back at you as if he believes he's said all this before, and he's bewildered that few understand how those years in the church shaped him. He expresses how his faith was challenged while serving in the Vietnam War, the "agnosticism" born of combat. Yet at the point where his humanity may show, he'll rush over it, like it's beyond the net of words. "I'm like everybody, you see your faith tested, you see it sometimes questioned, battered," but voters did not see that in Kerry. And quickly he'll say, "whatever," as if it occurs to him that talking about this accomplishes nothing. So he'll return to the optimism of his boyhood and speak to the "renewal" he experienced after the war, and how it wasn't until he was in his thirties that he really started "massively reading the Bible."

"I don't think that in the race we necessarily allowed a lot of that to become evident," Kerry says. "So my attitude is let it hang out. Be who you are in the fullest sense and I'm not going to stop reaching out proactively to people. In a sense, there is a certain evangelical quality to that maybe, in the sense that maybe you are joyfully and happily prepared to talk about what faith means to you." This is the wisdom of those who lose the presidency. From McGovern to Mondale to Dukakis and to Kerry, these Democrats understood so much about the race only after the race was complete. But Kerry was unique. No issue dogged him more than character. The flip-flop attack worked only because voters were unable to see a moral foundation to his politics. His faith, which is real, could have served him. But unlike Carter, whose ability to authentically speak to his faith "was like breathing," Kerry did not offer a pathway to his character.

In a nation that directly elects its head of state—in comparison to parliamentary democracies like the United Kingdom, Canada, or Germany—the American vote is far more about the personal connection between citizen and candidate. Character plays the central role in the making of a president. Religious faith is not the only pathway for voters to get a sense of a candidate's core character, but it may be the most effective way in one of the most religious nations in the western world.

"The problem for the Democrats—and it was a big problem for the Republicans before 1980—they didn't care about that connection," Republican strategist Frank Luntz says. "Religion is such an instantaneous connection. If we belong to the same church, if we sing the same hymn, if we know the part of scripture that you quote from, that's an immediate connection. That you know it and I know it means that we are roughly the same people." Luntz continues. "People want you to have a sense of faith because that means you have a core, because that means you have a commitment to things that are bigger than you."

Little could matter more to white men. They favor candidates who hold certain values so sacred they would commit political suicide to defend them. "Both Gore and Kerry gave you no sense of what their core values were, what things were values they would fight for until the very end," Democratic analyst Anna Greenberg observes. "You look at Bush, he's defined by having this unchangeable moral fiber."

It was Bush's authentic ability to speak about his faith combined with his everyman demeanor that made his populism so effective. He was Carter, but stronger, a man willing to defend moral absolutes. As Robertson put it, "Whereas George Bush isn't all that charming, he's very forceful in his beliefs."

On his farm northeast of Des Moines, Iowa, in 2004, Tim Baldwin tells me, "I hate abortion, is the first thing. It really sucks." He sits on his John Deere tractor, a middle-aged man in a white t-shirt, with a crooked smile and barbered hair. "I don't think there is anything worse [than abortion], and now because of the terrorists, I want them gone. I want them either put in prison or I want them dead."

Behind him is a horizon of cornfields. Baldwin is a Christian family farmer, a relic of another era, holding on, caring for his 130 acres proudly. "I like the way he's straightforward," Baldwin says of Bush. "He just tells you the way it is."

Baldwin is "not real sure about" Iraq, he explains, smoking a cigarette, squinting, tapping the ash. "But now that we are there, I want them to finish them off. No political pressure. I don't care what any other country says. This is our problem." To Baldwin, John Kerry is "just another liberal." Baldwin shakes his head. "I don't know how a man can think that abortion is immoral yet doesn't want to do anything about it. . . . Then he says how he," meaning Kerry, "would have done things differently in Iraq. Like what?" Baldwin asks. "Let's hear what you would have done differently. Don't blow about it and not give any specifics."

There's a history behind a farmer like Baldwin referring to Kerry as "just another liberal." Democrats are more secular than the nation as a whole. In 1992, fewer than 30 percent of Democratic convention delegates said they attended church weekly, while half of Republican delegates said they did (the national average is 40 percent).[39] One could argue that Republicans are hypermainstream, but the alternative seems to prove more detrimental in building majority coalitions, especially in a nation with more than 1,500 Christian radio stations and at least 200 Christian television channels.[40]

White women are more religious than white men, but more white men believe Democrats are "unfriendly" toward religion (25 percent compared to 18 percent, respectively).[41] This may suggest that because white men feel they have been provoked and alienated for so long by liberals, they are more sensitive to criticism of their values as well.

The perceived liberal antagonism to faith particularly undercuts Democrats' effort to win back poor whites. With income correlated to happiness, the working poor often depend on their faith to spiritually uplift them. Half of Americans with annual incomes exceeding $100,000 say they are "very happy," while only a quarter of people with incomes of $30,000 or less say the same. Equally, 43 percent of Americans who attend services at least once a week are "very happy," compared to 31 percent who attend once a month or less, and 26 percent who attend seldom or not at all.[42]

The leading progressive evangelical in the nation, Jim Wallis, argues that if only one party addresses the "spiritual emptiness" that persists in the nation, that party will win voters. "In the end, shopping doesn't satisfy the deepest needs of the human heart," Wallis quips. "People long for meaning and connection. They long for moral purpose," he adds. "It's not just religion; they long for a moral purpose bigger than themselves. When the Democrats became just the party of rights, the rights party, they've lost something, a moral appeal. There's no longer a common good."

When I ask Wallis why he believes Democrats have lost so many white men, he replies, "They lose them on a sort of values-cultural-personal-identity question," adding, "And the [Democratic] Party seems to be more remote, more elitist; it doesn't connect to them."

After the 2004 election, Robert Reich suggested that "the lesson for Democrats is not to bring religion into politics. Religion must remain a personal matter."[43] By 2005, 71 percent of white women and 64 percent of white men believed that "liberals have gone too far in trying to keep religion out of the schools and the government."[44] Yet when Democrats have spoken in the language of right and wrong and explained their positions through their faith, they have won these white religious Christians, not because of the verse they can quote, but what it says about the man quoting it.

With a buzz cut and small blue eyes, Virginia Governor Tim Kaine looks the part of Democratic religious paragon. In Kaine's 2005 race, he was able to rebuff attempts to paint him as an effete liberal due to his stance against the death penalty. He accomplished this by explaining his position as rooted in his religiously based belief system. "Democrats like policy," Kaine tells me in the winter of 2006. "But I think at the end of the day issues are 30 to 40 percent of a race. The other 60 percent is the perception of [the candidate's] character, their values and judgment. Sometimes people will say, 'boy that's wrong that people are not voting on issues.' No, people know that whatever issue we predict today may not be the issue tomorrow. So, they want to put a person in who they feel comfortable with enough on the issue . . . but they also would feel comfortable dealing with an issue that we are not seeing." Voters, he adds, "want to know you've got a moral yardstick and that it's not just coming out of a pollsters' memo and a speech somebody wrote for you." But he warns, "It has to appear authentic."

The following summer, when I mention to Carter Kaine's belief that 60 percent of being elected is talking sincerely about the values that shape your policy, the former president nods. "Well, I hope that in 2008 we'll have a nominee that can do what Tim Kaine just said, that will naturally be able to express views that will resonate with the people and give them confidence that that person shares my deepest moral values," Carter continues. It was this connection, the bridge of his faith to whites, which was vital to Carter's 1976 victory. He may have lost in 1980 because America did not like how he ran the presidency. But beneath the dark shadows of Watergate, Carter's faith was indivisible from the view that he was a man America could trust. "And it doesn't have to be claiming that I've been anointed by God to be your president or I'm speaking on behalf of the Creator of the world," Carter adds. "But I think just to have a rapport with religious believers is something that—I hope a natural rapport, not artificial, not contrived, not last minute, not predicated on political advantage—I think that's going to be a prerequisite for the next successful Democratic president."

VIII

THE STRATEGIC RISE OF REAGAN AND THE WHITE MALE GAP (1980)

Near the conclusion of Reagan's confidential 1980 campaign plan, chief strategist Richard Wirthlin detailed his intention to "break up" the Democratic coalition. To "target the populist voter," the campaign would work toward the "development of the aspiring American populist theme of 'anti-bigness—big government, big business, big labor.'" They were to deflect questions about Reagan's California governorship, under which spending skyrocketed, by insisting that the issue of the election was Carter's presidency. The populist media messages were to be "simple, direct, and optimistic." They were to focus on "specific" media messages for "blue-collar and labor union members" utilizing "principal themes" that "project a realization that these voters are no longer solely motivated by economic concerns but by larger social issues as well."[1]

In 1960, 44 percent of white men were Democrats. By Election Day 1980, only 31 percent aligned themselves with the blue party. Over the same period, white male independents increased to 43 percent from 25 percent in 1960.[2]

It was no accident that the Republican convention was held in blue-collar Detroit, a bastion of the very workingmen Reagan sought. Ironically, as the conservative party began winning the workingman because of white men's defection from the Democratic Party, Japan surpassed the United States that same year as the largest automobile manufacturer. Just as blue-collar white men found their economic situation increasingly precarious, their wages now stagnant, Democrats lost their votes in far greater numbers.

The Reagan campaign set up a Blue-collar Working Group led in part by W. J. Usery, who was Gerald Ford's secretary of labor after serving as the assistant during the Nixon administration. As the campaign neared its conclusion in October, an unpublished AFL-CIO poll of its 104 unions found that among the membership, 72 percent opposed cuts in defense spending, 65 percent favored a constitutional amendment mandating a balanced federal budget, and 60 percent agreed with Reagan's opposition to the Panama Canal treaty. Some key labor leaders, including an official at the International Union of Bricklayers, joined Usery in an informal agreement to strengthen Reagan's candidacy among the working class, in the last month of the campaign.[3]

"I was pretty active in his campaign," Usery recalls. "In fact I worked very hard at it, but I didn't feel the best about it. I always felt that Gerry Ford would have been reelected had Reagan's people really wanted him to be." On Reagan's behalf, Usery set out to win blue-collar voters. "Working men were concerned about strong leadership for America," Usery says. "And yes, I'm included. I'm tired of giving away everything to the other side. I'm concerned about America, my family, and my job. And this guy is a stronger leader for us."

Wirthlin's populist plan, always rooted in presenting the "stronger leader" that Usery referenced, became the framework for the next quarter-century of Republican presidential strategy. The objective was to "position [Reagan] as a doer, a man of action." The plan stated that the GOP campaign must, "reinforce the already existing perception of Reagan as a strong, decisive leader capable of making tough decisions." But the campaign intended to "downplay" the "down-to-earth image of Reagan in a cowboy hat on the ranch" because the nation "already had cause to regret its endorsement of the good ol' boy" image. The campaign was anxious about attacks on Reagan's intelligence. All the while, they were intent on attacking Carter as "incompetent, indecisive, and a weak leader." Utilizing surrogates, the campaign was to be a direct assault on Carter's manhood by constantly criticizing the strength behind his policies and the decisions, without ever going directly personal. And the attacks were to be relentless. Expecting Carter to do the same, Wirthlin wrote that "perceived timidity is equated with lack of leadership." Throughout, and above all, Reagan was to "solidify a public impression" that he "has concern for the common man and understands the problems facing voters in their daily lives."

However closely he emulated Nixon's strategy, Wirthlin did not look back in detail to Nixon's victories. He was far more concerned about avoiding the radical missteps of Goldwater. Wirthlin wrote of developing strategies to "undercut" Carter's probable tactic of portraying Reagan as "dumb, dangerous, and a distorter of facts," through attempts at "demonizing" Reagan, "i.e., making him out to be Barry Goldwater of the 1980s." In fact, this is the exact strategy Carter attempted.

When Reagan was asked whether he was nervous about debating Carter, the actor turned governor replied, "Not at all. I've been on the same stage with John Wayne."[4] Reagan's masculinity was always tied up with Wayne; they were two men who admired the same myth. When Reagan stood beside Carter, as an estimated 100,000,000 viewers watched the debate, he put it simply: "Are you better off today than you were four years ago?" It was those first words that history remembered, but Regan continued. "Is it easier for you to go and buy things? Is America as respected throughout the world as it was? Do you feel that our security is as safe, that we're as strong as we were four years ago?"[5]

"I think Reagan was the quintessential person, and/or actor, and/or politician, who could portray the positive aspects of the classical white male now in a disenfranchised role," psychologist William Pollack says. "And people just gaggled toward him."

Reagan won blue-collar voters, and with them the American presidency. He was to become the most celebrated Republican president since Theodore Roosevelt. He won 51 percent to Carter's 41 percent, the worst defeat by an incumbent since Franklin D. Roosevelt, Reagan's onetime hero, unseated Herbert Hoover in 1932. In due time, Reagan attempted to dismantle the big government programs FDR built, and succeeded in part (while Reagan's conservatism bred a big government of its own). But on Election Day, conservatism had its day. In the electoral college, Reagan defeated Carter 489 to 49.

Reagan cemented a coalition, and in doing so created the White Male Gap. Whether the voter attended church or did not, was a southern man or of the West, never attended college or was a college graduate—the one constant was Reagan's remarkably consistent appeal to white men.

Reagan won 61 percent of white men to Carter's 32 percent. Carter's white male support fell 15 percentage points between 1976 and 1980, while his white female support fell 7 percent. The 1980 election marked the last year more white men voted than white women, while overall, whites were still about 85 percent of voters. Reagan won a majority of white men in all income brackets.[6] Just as the

South was becoming the largest region in the United States, a Californian won the white male southern vote over a Georgian, 66 to 31 percent.[7] Reagan did not win solely because of white men, but they were now the one group Republicans could not win without.

Although the discussion of the gender gap at the time was solely focused on women, the gender divergence was fundamentally due to the White Male Gap. In 1976, Republicans won 5 percent more white men than did Democrats. By 1980, Republicans won white male voters by a 29 percent margin! And the gains were across the ideological spectrum.[8]

In total, Reagan won a majority of white women, by a margin of 14 percent. Reagan did no better or worse with white women than Ford, while Carter fell 7 percent with white female voters. The fact that the media became obsessed in subsequent years with a nearly fictional portrayal of Reagan's loss of the female vote is dumbfounding.

Reagan wanted to improve with women regardless. But Wirthlin believed there was only so much he could do. He had noticed that more men than women followed Reagan during Reagan's gubernatorial years.

"One of the things that I've always felt as a consultant-strategist, you don't stretch the candidates' perception too far from what it is," Wirthlin says. "The candidate may think it is pretty unfair he isn't always supported by women. If you begin trying to alter either position, image, or perception—or the perceptional assets and liabilities of your candidate—too dramatically, it often . . . [triggers] backlashes. And . . . the amount of campaign resources it takes to change those perceptions is so high."

Neither the reduction of the federal income tax, nor abortion, nor the ERA were within the top four issues selected by voters in 1980. Only 7 percent of white women selected the ERA or abortion as the leading issue that drove their vote.[9] The primary characteristics that voters attributed to their vote were "strong leadership" and "good judgment," while the deficit and economy, at its worst since the Great Depression, was the chief issue on voters' minds.

Only the use of force demonstrated a clear difference in male and female outlook. When asked whether they agreed or disagreed that "we should be more forceful in our dealings with the Soviet Union even if it increases the risk of war," 75 percent of white men agreed, while only 58 percent of white women agreed.[10]

"If you were going to design a party to go after white males I think it would look exactly like the Republican Party," Washington political analyst Charlie

Cook says. "And if you were going to design a party to go after the female vote, I think it would look precisely like the Democratic Party."

By the time Reagan led the Republicans, the paternal party had attained the age of reason. The boy was now a man; Reagan was the standard bearer. And the gender divergence was inseparable from presidential politics. Reagan's campaign stood upon the shoulders of all those Republican men. In Reagan were the lessons of Hoover's cultural populism and of the Whigs long before. Reagan's was the policy of Goldwater, sunny-side-up. He was the telegenic Nixon. His paternal politics were Eisenhower's, and he was the man who would have played the general in the movie.

"So, what's this empty nonsense about Ronald Reagan being just an actor," John Wayne once said. Life was imitating art or art was imitating life—it didn't matter anymore. Reagan was as true in life as he was in film. The actor was the role, but the themes beneath the role defined the part. And both the themes and the actor won 44 of the nation's 50 states in 1980.

MILLETT VERSUS MAILER
Vietnam, Feminism, and White Manhood as Vice

The failure of the Vietnam War resulted in two gendered and divergent lessons. To conservatives, and therefore Republicans, the Vietnam War did not mean that all wars were wrong, nor that male strength was more vice than virtue. It did not mean that a good offense was no longer the best defense. The conservative mind was always skeptical of man's passions. And for this reason it believed in strength, because if this nation softened, if our men softened, other nations and other men would pounce. To conservatives, manhood must be reasserted. The loss of the strong paternal figure was seen as a direct cause of the rise in teen pregnancy and crime. With loose revisionism, some conservatives believed that the Vietnam War had been lost because America was not allowed to unleash its strength; the nation was not allowed to be man enough.

Alternatively, to liberals and therefore Democrats, the Vietnam War symbolized the worst outcomes of hypermasculinity. Henceforth, manhood must be reconsidered, remolded, softened, effeminized, redefined as kinder and gentler. To avoid the terrible war of South Asia, to avoid war and violence and the belligerence that Johnson and Nixon exhibited, the American man must lessen his testosterone. To the dogmatic liberals, the Vietnam War was the outcome of unencumbered patriarchy. Ending one was inseparable from minimizing the other.

"One of the most reliable refuges for beleaguered masculinity, the soldier/protector, fell into such disrepute as the news about Vietnam filtered home," wrote Michael Kimmel in *Manhood in America, A Cultural History.* "Once a paragon of manly virtue, the soldier was now also coming to be perceived as a failed man."[1]

To the feminist movement, the failed man was a consequence of acting like too much of a man. Kate Millett's literary tour de force, *Sexual Politics*, the intellectual anthem of feminism, documented the worst instances of misogynistic writing—among them being Norman Mailer's work. It landed her on the cover of *Time*. She was now at the epicenter of the women's movement. She noted that in Mailer's novel *An American Dream* the victims of the white male character were women and blacks. She concluded that his own character was the embodiment of the white man. "Such are the white male's subjects," she wrote, "the objects of his dominant wrath."[2]

Mailer never saw Millett and the feminist movement coming. "I had not been aware what a powerful movement was building. I couldn't believe it," he recalls. "And then of course, I was being called a macho pig, which outraged me. I used to say to women I'd been arguing with, 'Why don't you all go down to Texas where the real macho pigs are. You are just decimating Democratic male intellectuals in New York,' which is true. Their greatest power was in New York. Feminism conquered New York, certainly in the arts, in culture, long before it took over the rest of the country," he adds. "I was taken off my little pedestal and of course, little pedestals feel very big to the people that are standing on them."

The same year Millett's book came out, 1969, Mailer ran unsuccessfully to be mayor of New York City. It was the height of Mailer's popularity as well as of the controversy that surrounded him. He was in the center of Manhattan's social debates. Two years earlier, Mailer's *Why Are We in Vietnam?* had hit bookstores. As the left took up the antiwar cause, the veteran of the Second World War realized that manhood itself was wrapped up in Lyndon Johnson's bravado. "It came, to name the year, right around 1970," Mailer tells me. "Lyndon Johnson contributed to it enormously in that he empowered the women despite himself, you might say, because Vietnam was such a catastrophe of machismo . . . that you might say it was the downfall of machismo as a winning principle in American life," Mailer continues. "Now if you talk about it statistically you might say that respect for machismo dropped; it was once at 55 percent and it dropped to 45 percent. It didn't turn the country inside out. It changed machismo from a value to a liability."

Mailer's analysis was conservative. In a series of studies on what "a real man" meant, it was found that until the late 1960s the overwhelming answer by Americans was "a good provider for the family." Neither sexual potency nor physical strength nor strength of character—or being "handy around the house"—came close to the provider ethos. The pinnacle of this conception of men, and all that it implied, was exactly 1968! The year Johnson did not run for reelection, 85 to 90 percent of Americans defined a "real man" as a "good provider." By the late 1970s, the provider notion fell to third in the ranking, at 67 percent.[3]

Johnson's war was the result of his bravado, to feminists. And in their eyes, if Johnson's manhood led to Vietnam, the logic went, to take down one the other must fall. Millett viewed LBJ as proof of her thesis. White men were not simply acting "too male," they were warped *because* they were white and male.

This notion was worse than stepping on Mailer's Judaism. Manhood was more universal to Mailer. Like Ernest Hemingway before him, Mailer believed in "honorable manhood." Men not only earned masculinity, it was one of the few things worth earning. "I shared with Papa the notion, arrived at slowly in my case," Mailer wrote, "that even if one dulled one's talent in the punishment of becoming a man, it was more important to be a man than a very good writer, that probably I could not become a very good writer unless I learned first how to keep my nerve, and what is more difficult, learned how to find more of it."[4]

Decades later, poet Robert Bly emphasized that this white male belief, which Mailer personified, led Vietnam-era young men down a failed path. Mailer had fought in the nation's finest effort. But in Vietnam, there was little fine about the fight. Bly spoke of a "male grief" that emerged. Men had been betrayed by their father's sense of manhood. They had been taught to adhere to authority and notions of duty, only to serve in a profoundly ignoble war. But Mailer, as much as he opposed the war, refused to heed feminism; he would not oppose manhood as well.

"The war in Vietnam was really a handmaiden to [feminists'] aims," Mailer says. "A lot of men at that time, particularly in the Democratic Party, had a feeling of 'How could we have gone so far wrong?'" Mailer shakes his head. "It is this ridiculous assumption that war is manly and good, and a good many of us hated the idea. We hated the war in Vietnam. It was so obviously a bad war, compared to a necessary war like the war against Hitler. Put it this way: I think the barriers were broken. There was a great breach in the solidarity of men. A great many serious men, who were proud of their manhood, were now disgusted with their manhood, their machismo, their gung-ho."

When Millett lamented the "privileged white man's general sway of empire, . . . and the many other prerogatives of male elite," she conveniently ignored the white female elite.[5] Rich white women were to be seen as oppressed in the same fashion as poor black men. In time, Millett's condemnation of white manhood, instead of the misogyny in many men, backfired. She, and those who championed her cause like Andrea Dworkin, led to the rantings of Rush Limbaugh; extremes often give birth to extremes.

Driving with Harvard's Elaine Kamarck from Cape Cod back to Cambridge, as we sped along the highway in her Audi convertible, I sat in the passenger seat, asking the quick-witted and quick-spoken political advisor about presidential politics and gender. She shifts into fifth gear, navigating both traffic and forty years of presidential politics.

"Thank you Rush Limbaugh for femi-nazis," she sarcastically says over the traffic. "There is still a feeling that women are taking men's jobs, et cetera. Guess what? They are! The fact of the matter is they are. For every one of me, who used to be a corporate wife [or] an upper-middle-class housewife, I'm taking some guy's job." The former senior campaign advisor to Al Gore, and member of the Clinton administration, drove as assertively as she spoke. "The early feminist movement was often quite hostile to white men and frequently for good reason," Kamarck says, speeding just enough not to go 10 mph over the speed limit, avoiding a ticket.

"In my own lifetime, the acceptance of sexual predation in the Carter campaign in 1980, and its absolute rejection by the Gore campaign of 2000, that's 20 years," she says. "The feminist movement was the biggest social change in the twentieth century because you know why, it affects half the population so therefore it affects everybody," she says. "There were thousands of years of history where men ruled, period, end of sentence. By being male you were automatically assured a better place in the world. I think we always underestimate how profound the feminist revolution is," Kamarck adds. "John White, the chairman of the DNC, when I was 27 years old and went to work there, used to pat me on the ass all the time. He thought I was just wonderful. That was the world."

To be certain, Kamarck embodies the accomplishments of feminism. In politics there have been many, none more vivid than support for the idea of a female president. In 1955, 52 percent of Americans said they would vote for a female and by 2006, 92 percent said yes, provided she was qualified.[6]

The issue was not the victory, but the enemy many feminists chose. Fundamentalist feminists came to commit the very faults that defined their admonishment. Criticism of misogyny became poisoned with misandry. Manhood was branded with the worst consequences of man. Masculinity was the reason for war, for racial subjugation, for spousal abuse. And fundamentally, this was a denunciation of white manhood.

The reduction of gender politics to the politics of power led to the fundamentalist feminist view that any assertion of power was an extension of abusive patriarchy, often seen in solely white male terms. "Mailer," Millett wrote, "is fully aware that the American male is sufficiently vicious, virile and violent."[7] And white men, aware that the recrimination was essentially theirs alone to bear, were listening.

To the most famous white male mind of the literary day, who was proudly masculine and pitted on the other side of feminism, the characterization only made him more combative, more bombastic—the wild boar came out in the "male chauvinist pig." Mailer was to be the man they said men were. He became more Manichean, hoping the good outweighed the bad. But modernity has been rough on Mailer. He punched hard against the times, and the counterculture bum-rushed him. Into the turn of this century, critics called him outmoded and pushed his legacy aside along with all the presumptive "white male chauvinists." Old age has humbled Mailer. He's calmer. He knows it often takes radicals to realize the reasonable. After all, he championed civil rights. He may not view Millett's fight as Huey Newton's, but he recognizes the victories, and as he pushes back the winter of his life, with yet another book, he's pleased to be out of the storm.

"It's not bad," he replies, after I ask him if it is difficult to be on the sidelines. "When you get to my age if you got work that you are still serious about, you have very little left over," he continues. "I'm old enough now to know that I am not going to change the world, so the only thing I can affect is my manuscript."

And so it was this Mailer, who is far quieter, who recognizes women's equality but still resents the feminist movement as embodied in Millett. "One thing about the women's revolution that separates it from all other revolutions, is it has not self destructed," he says. "Like all revolutionaries, they were, you might say, mono-linear in their ideology. There were not two sides to an argument. Therefore, if you wanted to discuss feminism, you were opposed to feminism. This was their logic. And the Democratic politicians realized it quickly so they never said anything against what the women were arguing." Mailer pauses. "And you know," he adds, clearing his throat, "the price to be paid for it is the loss of the Democratic Party."

In 1972, the memoir of Democratic counsel Harry McPherson came out. McPherson had been at the very center of Democratic inner workings throughout the tumultuous years of 1956 to 1969. "Democratic primaries and conventions often rocked with the language of rebuke," he wrote. "Very like, it has occurred to me, the language many wives use in speaking to their husbands, particularly toward the end of marriages. You never think of the children, or of my mother, or of me; only of yourself. Substitute the ignored disadvantaged, the homeless, people trapped downtown. The reaction among husbands, for whom read 'white male voters,' is what is normally provoked by attempts to burden people with a sense of guilt."[8]

The white male guilt was a pervasive force in prosecution. It was not simply emanating from the Black Power Movement but from white women as well. Millett was no sideshow. She was emblematic of the counterculture, and therefore popular culture, in a time when intellectuals and writers were fashionable; to be sure, the debate sometimes was reduced to pleasing the stylish mental aesthetics of youthful contrarians.

Not Millett, though. She was a true believer, a revolutionary. She was to be Tom Paine. In her feminism, the American assertion of power was the white male rapist standing over a victimized world. Millett wrote that colonialism and racism were "somewhat analogous" to patriarchy, as both had the "rule of force to rely upon." In Millett's view, Ward Cleaver's marriage to June was analogous to the English domination of India or the French colonization of North Africa.

To feminists, the sentiment long heard from men—at least since sixth century B.C. Athenian leader Themistocles said, "I govern Athenians, my wife governs me"—was the great paternal ruse. Women had been convinced that running the family was enough power. To Millett, wives were oppressed slaves conned into saying thank you.

"Patriarchal force also relies on a form of violence," she wrote, "particularly sexual in character and realized most completely in the act of rape." Rape was not perverted manhood but "realized" manhood. Patriarchy was akin to the "variety of cruelties and barbarities," a reference to foot-binding in China and the veiled burqa in Islam.[9]

To Millett and the feminism that followed her, the strong father was by definition the worst outcome of strength. As the blanket of liberalism embraced the feminist cause, it was only a small intellectual step to see American foreign policy, like the father, as abusive. White men were now defined by the worst instances of their manhood, and the nation was defined by the worst instances of its power. American use of force would henceforth be defined by Vietnam. The noble fight of World War II was conveniently pushed aside. The new breed of liberal saw the nation and white manhood in the same way white men believed their worst girlfriends reacted to them: harping on their vices while forgetting their virtues. Dogmatic liberals now defined the United States as imperialistic until otherwise proven innocent. The White Male Gap increasingly split along this fault line. Was the traditional man more good than bad? Was the American nation more of a force for good or a force for bad? One man was certain of the answer.

THE PECULIAR AMERICAN CONSERVATISM, PATRIOTISM, AND THE CLASSIC MALE (1981–1984)

To Ronald Reagan, America was good. Reagan refuted the denunciation of traditional mores, of manhood, of the American nation. In Reagan's view, a white American man did not owe all others his constant contrition. He did not have to go through life paying interest on older white men's brutalities in generations past and on mistakes of the nearer present. This white man was not perfect and neither was his nation. But white men believed in the modern day that America tried to do the right thing more often than not. And if he went wrong, like the nation at times, it was not the mistakes that defined the man. It was not the way he fell, but how he rose back up.

Reagan spoke to the nation the way a father encourages a son. Even as wages were stagnant, as debt skyrocketed, as crime persisted, as AIDS, gangs, drugs, and teen pregnancy upended American life, Reagan saw America for its better angels. To conservatives, he was proof that the good old things are *still* good, and that whatever the nation became it was to be moderated by the best of what it was. White men saw themselves in this nation's better past but felt branded by its worst mistakes. With Reagan, they sought existential absolution. Reagan is one battle feminism lost.

In every chapter of America's story there were signs that the radicalism within the counterculture was doomed to the "dustbin of history," to borrow a phrase from a radical, Leon Trotsky. Socialism never did win the hearts and minds of the mass of men in the United States; Trotsky discovered one explanation for its lack of American followers when he stayed briefly with his family in a low-rent apartment in New York City's East Bronx, which he called the "workers district," in 1917. It was, he wrote in astonishment, "equipped with all sorts of conveniences that we Europeans were quite unused to: electric lights, gas cooking range, bath, telephone, automatic service elevator and even a chute for the garbage."[1] It was not simply the American quality of life that explained why Socialist Eugene Debs never earned more than a few hundred thousand votes in any of his presidential runs. The defeatism of socialism was its undoing stateside. Americans believed, and still do, that present circumstances do not dictate future prospects. U.S. radicals lacked a great structural antagonist—there was no aristocracy or state religion. The United States was born of revolution, but it was a revolution that pitted reformers and patriots against royalty. In contrast, the French Revolution was an attempt at remaking the world. Institutions were to be destroyed, from the crown to the Catholic church. Jacobins invented a religion to replace Christianity, while in the United States the new republic's motto was "In God we trust." Though most of the Founding Fathers were not as fearful of the "tyranny of the majority" as John Adams, the division of government reflected a conservative skepticism of human virtue. "If men were angels, no government would be necessary," James Madison famously wrote.[2] That "all men are created equal" was extended so slowly to all white men, then blacks, and finally women exhibited the conservatism beneath the American progressive creed.

The Constitution itself kept the nation forever looking back. The past justified the American present. Much of the new government was based on its cultural ancestors, from the natural law of British philosopher John Locke, to the empiricism of the Scottish philosopher David Hume, to English common law, and to the structural emulation of the two houses of Parliament in the U.S. Congress. In fact, English common law was essentially the law of the land until the mid-nineteenth century. Herbert Croly was the architect who designed the intellectual blueprints for active state liberalism. But he justified this liberalism not with new thinkers, but with a new take on Jefferson and Hamilton. Even progressives justified the future through the past in the United States. When popular sentiment veered leftward, the very nature of the electoral college ensured

the political debate was more conservative than the populace by structurally elevating the electoral voice of rural and therefore conservative states.

From the Puritans of John Winthrop's day to Thomas Jefferson and later
Andrew Jackson, distrust in centralized government was inseparable from the
American idea. But this conservatism was uniquely American, and therefore
tepid and liberalized in the larger sense. Not even Adams was a Royalist. However much leading Puritan Winthrop shaped American mores, his oligarchy lost
out to a liberal belief in the people. As George Will puts it, "American conservatism is most distinctly un-Burkean." Edmund Burke influenced the American
nation's skepticism for the passions of men and, later, the emergence of modern
conservatism, but his belief that the mass of men are both incapable of reason
and sheepish in action was antithetical to the liberalized American idea.[3] Born
of this break from European conservatism, an American conservatism came to
reflect the land that bore our optimism, and therefore, was progressively influenced. The belief that beyond the Appalachians any man could reinvent himself
is rooted in the American mind. This optimism was central to the Puritans' belief that this new world could be a land where humanity could be born again.
The Founding Fathers viewed the republic's constitutional liberty as the best
chance for realizing mankind's highest potential. "America is another word for
Opportunity," wrote Ralph Waldo Emerson during the Civil War. "Our whole
history appears like a last effort of the Divine Providence in behalf of the
human race."[4]

But it is indeed a progressive optimism that reaches backward to find its future. U.S. court decisions derive their credence from history. Judicial fights over
religion in the public sphere debate the relevance of Jefferson's doctrine in a wall
separating church and state. The *Roe v. Wade* abortion ruling referenced Greek
and Roman practice. Thomas Paine's credo that the living owe the dead nothing
lost out to Madison's belief that man needs institutional structure. Paine has lost
his popularity while Adams has been redeemed. American radicals, if they are to
progress with the populace, Frenchman Alexis de Tocqueville observed, "are
obliged to profess an ostensible respect for Christian morality and equity."[5]
From the nation's religiosity to the oceans that nurtured its adolescence, the
American historical moderation paved the way for the conservative movement
Reagan championed.

"When you consider how safely removed the United States voting public
has been from the kind of radicalism that happened in Germany, Italy, and
France and to a certain extent in Great Britain," William F. Buckley says, "the

contrast is pretty vivid and it seems to be saying to us, don't worry about truly radical movements, they don't truly make much headway in America."

Reagan earned his early conservative merits by challenging the countercul-ture. As governor of California, he took a hard-line stance against the antiwar protesters at the University of California at Berkeley, by lowering funding of higher education. Reagan became the first president to stand against the ERA. While many leftists saw his cold war build-up as a fallacy of phallic nature, his-tory proved it was Reagan's *continuation* of the Truman and Kennedy doctrine of strength—a then liberal doctrine that the appearance of overwhelming force kept opposing forces at bay—that *contributed* to the downfall of the Soviet Union. But before Stalin's empire fell, as the calendar turned to 1981, this new president symbolized far more than a stance against communism. Reagan's as-cension challenged the conclusions of Kate Millett's feminism; he was larger than the manhood he represented.

It was not Reagan who won the day, but the new conservative populism he embodied. Unlike the Tories of England or the Gaullists of France, this Ameri-can conservatism was not lodged in the past; it relished the past only to frame the future. So it was apropos that the nation's oldest president was its most opti-mistic in decades. His can-do spirit, which would have been terribly trite if it had not been so sincere, was born in the films that made him and in the westward ex-pansion that made the nation. The rugged individualism of Reagan showed little mercy for those who were not fit enough for the rebirth of this invigorated social Darwinism. This was the distance from the state of nature that Republican capi-talism desired.

"Tough love, that manly specialty, is often hard to distinguish from indiffer-ence," as Harvey Mansfield, the author of *Manliness*, puts it. And white men, now more a victim of active state liberalism than a beneficiary, liked Reagan for this as well. The free market imperative was upon us. Americans went with the man who spoke of a smaller government and less taxes since he campaigned on Gold-water's behalf. The pundits said the election was a referendum on Carter. In part that was true. But no truer than Roosevelt was a referendum on Hoover or, more recently, than Carter was a referendum on Ford's pardon of Nixon. Carter won because he was an outsider, a humble rural Christian moderate Democrat. Un-popular presidents do not lose merely by consequence of public discontent (ergo George W. Bush's defeat of John Kerry). Certainly, Carter's inability to curtail the poor economy was crucial to Reagan's election. But when voters went with Reagan, they knew he represented a different social contract.

The New Deal was done. "What populism and progressivism, the New Freedom and the New Deal, meant in terms of political philosophy was the final repudiation of laissez faire and the explicit recognition of government as a social welfare agency," wrote Henry Steele Commager midcentury. "The pernicious notion that there was some inevitable conflict between man and the state had long embarrassed American politics."[6] Thirty years later, with Reagan, came the return of the American notion that there was a "conflict between man and the state." The Republicans chose, and the public elected, the man that sided against the state, who seemed American in every way a man could seem American.

"The forthright appeal to patriotism, loyalty, common defense, is done and said by people who are confident that they are speaking in accents that appeal more naturally to the right than to the left," William Buckley says, discussing the conservative populist appeal. "The identification of particular candidates with, you might call it, pro-American spirit, reflected such differences." And like Gary Bauer, Buckley believes this ability to speak in terms of national pride was pivotal to the Republican Party's emergence as a majoritarian movement, though Buckley is far too conservative to use the word movement. But that's exactly what 1980 meant to American history.

Public displays of patriotism—and the national pride these displays represent—resonate with American whites because they are exceptionally patriotic. As recently as 2005, seven out of ten white men display the flag and 66 percent of white women do as well. Notably, the vast majority of minorities who supported Kerry show significantly less inclination than whites to brandish the flag (44 percent of women and 47 of men), while those minorities who voted Republican displayed the flag at roughly the same level as whites who backed the GOP.[7] This might suggest that those minorities who support the Republican Party feel part of the country in a way that most minorities do not.

About three out of four whites in the United States, and about half of all minorities, say they are "extremely" proud to be an American. In one 1998 study, twenty-three countries were asked how much pride they had in ten specific areas of achievement, from sports to arts to the economy. The United States ranked second to Ireland in "pride in specific achievements," second to Austria in "general national pride," but first among the twenty-three countries when both measures were merged.[8] "The Lord looks after drunks, children, and the U.S.A.," goes the old saying. Many folks still want to believe it.

"There was absolutely no question that [a patriotic appeal] was part of our strategy to cut into the New Deal coalition," recalls Richard Wirthlin about Reagan's campaign. "You can cut into a coalition by going after the components of the coalition: blue collar, southern protestant, building born-again Christians as a wedge group. But there is a more reasonable way to look at coalitions and that is building support for your candidate that cross-cuts coalitions by selecting themes or thematic positioning that will give [the public] entrée to them." No theme has since proven to have more electoral resonance than patriotism.

For the first time, the inaugural was held on the west side of the Capitol. Reagan faced the Washington monument and, past the tower of white marble, was the Potomac and beyond. At the water's edge stood the nation he intended to embody: America's new leading man faced forever westward. He began his presidency facing west and he would be buried with his coffin facing the setting sun a quarter century later, under the presidency of George W. Bush, the conservative son who continued and nearly imploded the Republican ascendancy. So it was scripted that clear day in 1980 for Reagan to be the man Carter was not.

"The economic ills we suffer have come upon us over several decades. They will not go away in days, weeks, or months, but they *will* go away," Reagan said during his inaugural address. "They will go away because we as Americans have the capacity now, as we've had in the past, to do whatever needs to be done." Reagan spoke on behalf of those who defined conservative populism. "We hear much of special interest groups," he later said. "Our concern must be for a special interest group that has been too long neglected," and he went on to list police, truck drivers, industrialists, professionals, and shopkeepers, the people who were Nixon's "silent majority." As Carter sat listening behind Reagan, it seemed that the Democratic Party—what was liberal, what was now progressive—was to remain caught in the past, fixated on conserving a failed dogmatic liberalism, focused on so many ideas that America no longer saw the big idea liberalism championed.[9]

Those most patriotic, those most disquieted by the post-Vietnam Democratic Party and the counterculture, welcomed the title of Reagan Democrats because now a movement welcomed them! The Reagan Revolution, as the hyperbole of the day termed it, was no revolution at all—it was a movement. The great modern Republican push into majority status was to be brought about by the white men who joined this conservative camp. The future was here, and the common man for the first time, in a long time, was not living in spite of the future but was again joined with it.

The same day, as if scripted from the one-time actor's films, the hostages were freed in Iran.

THE LEFT'S LESSONS UNLEARNED

The White Male Gap went unseen or ignored. It should have been the chief concern of every liberal in America. When Democrats ditched the "forgotten man," as Roosevelt termed the workingman decades before, Democrats lost their past and their future. Democrats lost the ability to pass any progressive legislation, to win universal health care, to defend defined benefits that fell away, because the new generation of dogmatic liberal was all or nothing. Like all ideologues, they were gamblers. They were still going for broke. And so liberalism itself broke.

At the 1984 Democratic convention in New York City, New York's Governor Mario Cuomo listed every constituency Democrats represented. The divisions, not the commonalities, got the emphasis. The crowd erupted when he referenced Reagan's "macho intransigence." His largest applause line came after he advocated passage of the Equal Rights Amendment. The convention floor responded with the chant "E-R-A, E-R-A, E-R-A." Notably, it was in exactly the same fashion, with similar passion, that Republican delegates chanted "U-S-A, U-S-A, U-S-A" during Reagan's address at the Republican convention. That evening in New York, Cuomo was the liberal champion.

Like Cuomo, civil rights leader Jesse Jackson also went after Reagan's machismo: "I would rather have Roosevelt in a wheelchair than Reagan on a horse." He said his Rainbow Coalition included farmers, American Indians, lesbians, and gays. His was a stirring address. It was simply not an address to Middle America or to the South, where the Democratic Party was the weakest. The first female vice presidential nominee, Geraldine Ferraro, spoke "to those concerned about the strength of American and family values," but then she said she would help "restore those values—love, caring, partnership—by including, and not excluding, those whose beliefs differ from our own."[10] But to the values voters—however lovely the values she mentioned were—they were *not* the values social conservatives believed were threatened by modernity. More so, values voters were not worried about "including" or recognizing everyone's values. They wanted a president to assert that some values were both timeless and absolute.

This misunderstanding dogged Democrats through in the 2004 election. When Ferraro mentioned astronaut Sally Ride, the delegates on the convention floor cheered far louder than they did for the man she had mentioned only a moment prior, John F. Kennedy. By 1984, women made up 53 percent of the Democratic caucus while they were only 43 percent of the Republican caucus.[11] The focus on the female side of the gender gap came less to reflect public opinion than to reflect the Democratic delegates themselves.

Then there was Walter Mondale's most famous, and some might say infamous, declaration, "Let's tell the truth," adding, "Mr. Reagan will raise taxes, and so will I. He won't tell you. *I just did!*" It was a rallying cry for his party from his moral core. Yet at a time when Democrats were hemorrhaging white voters, it was poor politics.

Two decades later, as Mondale looks back, he recalls that his intention was only to be true to his views. He has attended every Democratic convention since he first saw Kennedy win the nomination. His favorite, understandably, was his own. "The night that we nominated Geraldine Ferraro," he tells me, smiling a grandfather's smile, "We went from a really bad situation—we were running against Reagan, which was a hopeless idea—but by the time the convention was over, we were over him, but we didn't sustain it." Seated at the center of the 2004 Democratic convention, Mondale, in a navy blue blazer and a red tie, with trim white hair, publicly wears glasses now. His boyish face has aged, and he keeps a journal at the convention.

"Do you regret any aspect of your convention, of your speech?" I ask him.

"I was coming from 20 to 25 points behind in a satisfied nation," he replies, leaning back. "All I could think of doing was trying to say what I really believed and take some risks, but some tactics were unpopular. But I think I gained a lot of respect from people. I must have done something wrong to come out that way, but that's the way I look at it. When I look back, I was a damn fool to run."

"A damn fool?"

Mondale pauses. "To run against Reagan, yeah."

When Reagan stood before the Republican delegates in 1984, he conveyed the contrast on national security that John F. Kennedy or Franklin Roosevelt never would have allowed to occur.

"None of the four wars in my lifetime came about because we were too strong," Reagan declared. "It's weakness that invites adventurous adversaries to make mistaken judgments." And as the convention floor pulsed, at times overpowering Reagan, forcing him to pause and say "all right," he waited for them to calm. "Ten months ago, we displayed this resolve in a mission to rescue American students on the imprisoned island of Grenada. Democratic candidates have suggested that this could be likened to the Soviet invasion of Afghanistan, the crushing of human rights in Poland or the genocide in Cambodia," Reagan said. "Could you imagine Harry Truman, John Kennedy, Hubert Humphrey, or Scoop Jackson making such a shocking comparison?" The crowd bellowed back, "Nooo!" And there is little doubt that white men watching on television were nodding right along.

In September of 1984, as the race neared its final lap, Reagan was in Waterbury, Connecticut. He recalled that John F. Kennedy had campaigned from a hotel balcony overlooking the town square on the eve of his 1960 victory. "I hope there are some members of his party here today," Reagan told some 25,000 people. "I was a Democrat once, for a large portion of my life. And it's a funny thing about party affiliation, whether you inherited it for generations back in your family. Maybe you embraced it on your own when you were young," Reagan continued. "But it can be a very wrenching thing, I found, to change parties. You feel as though you're abandoning your past. But I tell you truly, the only abandoning I see is that the Democratic leadership has abandoned the good and decent Democrats of the JFK, FDR, and Harry Truman tradition—people who believe in the interests of working people, who are not ashamed or afraid of America standing up for freedom in the world. And if you see it as I do, I have to tell you—join us."[12]

They did. Reagan won 525 electoral votes to Mondale's 13 in 1984. Reagan carried 49 states, losing only Mondale's Minnesota and the District of Columbia. He won 68 percent of white men in 1984, 37 percentage points more than Mondale. Democrats won only three white men for every ten who voted, likely the lowest level of support in the history of their party. Among white women, Reagan won 63 percent, a 27-point margin over Mondale.[13]

One year after Reagan's reelection, Stan Greenberg found that working-class whites near Detroit saw Democrats as "wishy-washy," their leader a "mouse," "lost," the "mother hen," and a "wimp" who "fiddled around." Democrats were "a party that was seen as vacillating, disorderly, and weak."[14] This view prompted the Republican retort to feminism: Reagan was liked not in spite of his manhood, but because of it.

GENDER POLITICS AND
THE PRESIDENTIAL OUTCOME

In Warren, Michigan, a woman said that she admired Reagan because he was like John Wayne.[15] More than a decade later, the sitcom phenomenon *Sex and the City*, which began in 1998 and stretched until the 2004 election, portrayed the ideal attractive white male, Mr. Big, as powerful in every way a man could be, from build to influence to wealth. The message to white men could not have been clearer. These sexually liberated, attractive, intelligent women still liked the classic male.

The exit polling of 1984 raised a larger gender question: If Reagan was the 1950s man, an archetype of the traditional male, like George W. Bush during the last season of *Sex and the City*, why were white men won by this archetype but an equivalent portion of white women not turned off by the machismo?

Anthropologist Helen Fisher, speaking of George W. Bush in 2004, once said: "Bush wants to be seen as masculine because masculinity is associated with assertiveness and competence and judgment and team-playing and a host of traits that men aspire to and women adore."[16]

"To more modern man and emphatic man," William Pollack, the head of Harvard's Center for Men, says, "one of their major complaints is that women say we should be this way, women demand it in the workplace, but when you see a good 30 or 40 percent—this is what men say, there is no data on this—of those women and who they choose as their male partners, assuming they are heterosexual, they often tend to choose the more classical, stereotypical, John Wayne type of men."

In fact, by 2003, when asked whether "women should return to their traditional roles in society," more white women (25 percent) than white men (19 percent) agreed. About three out of four whites, both men and women, believed "too many children are raised in day care centers." By a tally of 38 to 31 percent, more white women *strongly* agree with the criticism of raising children in childcare.[17]

Gender differences are unmistakable in exit polls. Women question the use of nuclear power and chemical additives in food more than men. Women favor a larger active government. Women are also "more cautious" in "embracing change" than men, explains Karlyn Bowman. Men are more "monolithic" and women tend to fall more often on the ideological flanks of the politics. Women are not as well informed about national affairs as men. One study by Harvard and the Kaiser Family Foundation found that in 1996, 71 percent of women and 83 percent of men could correctly identify the Democratic Party's vice presidential nominee.[18]

Yet men, especially white men, tend to decide their vote more on character than issue. Women are more concerned about the risks associated with overt showings of force, as with the Reagan arms build-up. Women vote far more along their class lines, whereas poor white men have voted conservative since the onset of the White Male Gap. Men care more about world affairs. Women care more about domestic affairs: education, health care, and moral values. Although men are more concerned about economic issues, women and men do not show consistent differences in opposing higher taxes. Women more often tell exit pollsters that their reason for voting was a complex issue, while men are more likely to cite attributes like honesty, strength, and clarity of language in the candidate, which directly caused the White Male Gap.

While nurture undoubtedly plays a role, there is strong evidence to believe that many of these differences reflect innate differences between the genders as well. Dr. Louann Brizendine, a Berkeley, Yale, and Harvard neurobiologist, wrote in *The Female Brain* about one of her patients who gave her three-and-a-half-year-old daughter unisex toys, "including a bright red fire truck instead of a doll." One afternoon, "she walked into her daughter's room . . . to find her cuddling the truck in a baby blanket," and consoling "truckie" that it will be alright. "This isn't socialization. This little girl didn't cuddle her 'truckie' because her environment molded her unisex brain. There is no unisex brain."[19]

And then there was the white woman who never crossed a picket line, who was loyal to Doctors Without Borders, and never voted Republican, but was turned off by feminism. Writer Caitlin Flanagan is one. In spring of 2006 she wrote in *Time* that the "Lions of the left," such "as Barbara Ehrenreich, the writers at *Salon* and much of the Upper West Side of Manhattan have made it abundantly clear to me that I ought to start packing my bags. I'm not leaving, but sometimes I wonder: When did I sign up to be the beaten wife of the Democratic Party?" Flanagan added that she was a "happy" member of a traditional family and that, "In the middle of doing the great work of the '60s—civil rights, women's liberation, gay inclusion—we decided to stigmatize the white male.

The union dues–paying, churchgoing, beer-drinking family man got nothing but ridicule and venom from us. So he dumped us. And he took the wife and kids with him." And she concluded, "now here we are, living in a country with a political and economic agenda we deplore, losing election after election and wondering why."[20]

The White Male Gap was rarely limited to men because the politics that won men did not turn off women. Part of the answer was in the female pushback against feminism. In 1985, more than half of the nation's women said given the choice between working or staying home to care for the family, they'd work. By 1991, only 43 percent of women felt the same.[21] In 2006, 52 percent of women who didn't work outside their home said they were "very happy" with their marriages, while only 41 percent of working women felt the same.[22] Flanagan was right. She was America. "We're Here, We're Square, Get Used to It," her column was titled. But, like decades of middle-class whites before her, the collective criticism she personified was ignored. The two parties were now increasingly consumed only with their bases.

ECHO-CHAMBER JOURNALISM AND LIVING WITH THE LIKE-MINDED

In the 1980s, the minority of whites who still lived in cities such as San Francisco, New York, Boston, or Minneapolis were increasingly removed from the vast number of whites moving farther from urban centers. Those who were members of organizations such as NOW and the American Civil Liberties Union knew far less of those who were members of the National Rifle Association or Southern Baptist Convention. America was becoming progressively polarized. Between 1960 and 2005, ideological activist groups of all political persuasions increased sevenfold.[1] Gun owners lived in one world. People who could not understand why someone needed a gun lived in another.

Whites were now far more removed from minorities; unlike the proximity of suburban communities, the new exurban suburbs were 20 or 30 miles from all that is urban. Typically a white man got up early for work, stopped and bought a coffee from Dunkin' Donuts or, in time, Starbucks—and this choice correlated to whether he voted Republican (Dunkin' Donuts) or Democrat (Starbucks)—and then commuted while listening to drive-time radio. He often encountered a confining sense of relentless rush hour traffic, his bumper sticker reading "Mondale Eats Quiche," as he arrived at work by 8 A.M. He sat most of the day in a gray-felt cubicle that kept out real sunlight. He ate lunch with coworkers and left around six o'clock in the evening, returning to a primly cut fertilized lawn, with sidewalks that few walked on. But doors were left unlocked, his children could walk home alone and play in the back woods. The white men and women of the exurbs never encountered urban life face-to-face, for all its culture and, by the 1970s, for all its blight. The exurbanites drove over, drove in, and drove out.

The very societal ills that the Democratic Party believed the federal government had a role in addressing were now increasingly removed from the Republican majority. Even Reagan, whose popularity spanned so many traditional electoral divisions, barely won white men in the large cities in 1980. Against Carter, the last rural president, Reagan won about 62 percent of suburban, small city, and rural white men. His support among white men was 10 percent lower in the largest cities (those with over 250,000 citizens). More intriguing was the change in party identity within four years. Only in the suburbs were more white men registered as Republicans than Democrats in 1980. By 1984, in every region, more white males were registered as Republicans than as Democrats, and the highest Republican registration was in the suburbs.[2] The shift in politics was intertwined with the shift in where people called home.

In time, those becoming more conservative were likely to become more sure and absolute in their conservatism because they were surrounded by like-minded families, often of a similar culture, race, and even Christian denomination. Some drove further out for their country club. Others had teenagers they dropped off at the mall on Saturday morning and picked up in the evening. At neighborhood parties, nearly everyone was white, many were college educated, most were Christian, and many liked Reagan even if they did not vote for him. They wanted lower taxes and knew black people at work, and may even have had a black friend. They loved boats and cabins up north and some were now jogging. They subscribed to the *Wall Street Journal,* even if they only skimmed the headlines, because this was what businessmen did.

The minority of whites, both the extremely poor and the very well-off who joined the condominium boom in cities such as San Francisco, Chicago, or New York, were increasingly socially liberal. They too became more sure and absolute in their liberalism in time because they were surrounded by the like-minded. In the largest cities, they took community transport and had a sense of the metropolitan virtue and vice. A friend, a neighbor, may have come out of the closet. They knew far more minorities in their daily life and witnessed homelessness each day. In doing so, they felt more of a sense of community welfare because they were immersed in a sea of diverse people—the poor just making it, the middle class, the rich, and the really-really rich. And as the coffee shop boom made its way from Seattle to Manhattan in the 1990s, the liberal mind knew only the liberal mind. The *New Yorker* was subscribed to, even if the "Talk of the Town" was skimmed and the only parts of the magazine consistently perused were the cartoons. Because this was what liberal cognoscenti did.

By the summer of 2007, the conservative *Weekly Standard* magazine was advertising an Alaskan cruise with leading editors Bill Kristol and Fred Barnes to "travel with like-minded conservatives." The liberal *Nation* magazine offered a similar cruise with its stars and the like-minded. There are now online dating services for liberals and conservatives to be sure they fall in love with those who reflect their politics.

Congress suffers the same homogeneity—of their own creation. When districts are redrawn, representatives use computer-mapping software to maximize the portion of partisan voters favoring the incumbent. Due to the gerrymandering of congressional districts, at least 90 percent of House seats are noncompetitive every two years. The ratio can soar as high as 98 percent. The effect is a far more polarized Congress. Moderates have become a minority, and the remaining moderation of America is hardly represented in the House, where the partisan vitriol reflects it. "Politics is like sausage," Stephen Colbert once quipped, "no one wants to see it made and eventually it will destroy your heart."[3]

Meanwhile, the demographics speak to an ever more politically bifurcated public. In the 1990s' fastest growing 50 counties, 62 percent of the vote went for George W. Bush in 2000.[4] After the 2004 election, another analysis showed Bush carried 97 of the nation's 100 fastest growing counties. In only 40 of the 100 counties was the percentage of college graduates higher than the national average. This was a young, middle-class, white demographic shift slated to continue through the election of 2008.[5] In 2004, President Bush won 474 of the nation's 573 micropolitan areas, areas with at least 10,000 people but less than 50,000.[6]

Democratic Party demographer Mark Gersh has found that the micropolitan turnout is on the rise, indicating the residents are more civic-minded. In the key state, Ohio, turnout in the micropolitan communities increased from 53 percent in 2000 to 61 percent in 2004; in Florida, it increased from 49 percent to 58 percent. In the third key swing state, Pennsylvania, micropolitan turnout increased from 47 percent to 53 percent between the two elections. While micropolitan areas amount to slightly more than 10 percent of the overall state turnout, their vote is rising faster than the population, suggesting Republicans are taking root organizationally.[7] And though population shifts may seem like the stuff of wonks, the party that ignores the details of demographics will find itself nearer to its electoral demise.

Overall among white males, Bush won 62 percent of the suburban vote (where 49 percent of all white males live). Bush also won 68 percent of the small city or rural vote (where 27 percent of all white males live). Bush lost in large cities with populations over a half million but won 56 percent of big-city white men (where only 9 percent of white males live). Bush lost the urban vote overall (that is, all cities with a population over 50,000), but still won 63 percent of urban white men (24 percent of all white males live in cities over 50,000).[8] The 13 percent gap in Bush support between rural areas and large cities for white men illustrates the influence of demographics. Whites who once left rural environments for the suburbs and cities are now shifting in waves from the suburbs to distant exurban communities that are entirely independent of cities.[9]

"Young families are occupying and settling in areas 40 or 50 miles from cities—whether they are suburbs, exurbs, or micropolitan areas—because they can't afford a house closer in. They like a slightly slower pace. I think [Democrats] fail to understand how culturally conservative they are," Mark Gersh says. "We can't afford to lose two-to-one in the exurbs, three-to-two in the distant suburbs."

Meanwhile, conservatives were able to reach their increasingly expansive base because of a vital change in federal policy under Reagan. As Americans drove alone each morning on their way to work, isolated in their Saab 900, Honda Accord, or their Ford F–150, a common political voice caught their ear.

THE BLITZ ON FAIRNESS

Since the Communications Act of 1937, the fairness doctrine mandated that television and radio stations offer an "equal opportunity" to legally qualified political candidates for any office if the station had allowed their opponents to also use their airwaves. The government's aim was to ensure that private interests didn't use those airwaves to have a one-sided, propagandistic effect on the public. By 1985, President Reagan's FCC issued a report that the doctrine was having a "chilling effect" on free speech. Soon after, the doctrine was terminated.[10]

In its wake came Rush Limbaugh, Sean Hannity, and a myriad of conservatives. By the time George W. Bush was fighting for his reelection, of the 28 radio personalities who revolve in the top-10 positions in talk radio, 15 were political.[11] Of the 15, 10 were conservative; none were liberal. Limbaugh alone is still heard by up to 20 million people every week. His influence has been unquestioned since

Newt Gingrich credited him with playing a pivotal role in the GOP 1994 congressional victory.

The media that Americans consumed was like the neighborhoods they lived in: racially distinct. Blacks were listening to black talk radio. Hispanics were listening to Spanish media. All the while, the bulwarks of the fourth estate—from the *Wall Street Journal* to the *New York Times* and the three networks—felt increasingly lost in the knee-jerk ideologues' paradise of cable, radio, and, by the turn of the century, the blogosphere.

As John Kerry challenged George W. Bush for the presidency, more white men, compared to minorities or women, got their news from radio and the Fox network. Twenty-seven percent of white men said Fox News was their "primary source." CNN netted 20 percent of white male viewers. White female viewers were divided between CNN, local television news, and Fox (about 18 percent) as their "primary source." One-third of white male viewers watched "some" of their news on Fox, while no other network had more than one-fifth of white viewers. Minorities are roughly 50 percent more likely than whites to watch CNN. Slightly more white men read newspapers as their first choice for news than white women. Minority men listen to the radio, use the Internet, and watch Fox more than minority women, suggesting gender is a significant factor in news media preference. CNN clearly influences more minorities and women while Fox influences more whites and men.[12]

"I don't think they had any idea what they were going to unleash," George Will says of the Reagan administration's termination of the fairness doctrine. "It wasn't a cunning farsight, they just didn't like the fairness doctrine because it was government regulation of discourse. I mean, who knew Rush Limbaugh [was coming]?"

Throughout 2006, from the radio to Fox News, many conservative pundits insisted Iraq had weapons of mass destruction despite bipartisan reports concluding otherwise. In the summer of 2004, during a taping of *The O'Reilly Factor*, the subject of weapons of mass destruction and Iraq was raised. The tape played Thomas Kean's comment as the head of the Senate's 9/11 Commission: "There is no evidence that we can find whatsoever that Iraq or Saddam Hussein participated in any way in attacks on the United States, in other words, on 9/11. What we do say, however, is there were contacts. . . ." The liberal writer who was to be the guest recounts that O'Reilly—who was critical early on of how the Iraq war was administered—told his producers, "We can't use that. . . . We need to redo the whole thing." In the new segment, O'Reilly paraphrased Kean, asserting that Kean said, "definitely there was a connection between Saddam and Al-Qaeda." And for the millions of viewers watching, the part about "no link" was left out.[13]

The distortion phenomena becomes Orwellian, as Paul Krugman has pointed out.[14] Commentators rewrite our understanding of "not only the future but the past." The political satirist Stephen Colbert calls it "truthiness." If a person of influence says something long enough, it feels true, and then, that takes on a truth of its own. What comes out on the other end are cynics and ideologues.

The very nature of CNN, FOX, and MSNBC only furthers the bifurcation of views. Cable news networks split the screen. The liberal and conservative combat each other, and the middle ground is lost. Issues are reduced to point and counterpoint, to blue and red. And soon the nature of the argument is all that is recalled, not the point. The viewer is left more polemical. One detailed study found that when people are around the like-minded their viewpoints become more extreme.[15]

As I sit with George Will in his townhouse office in Washington's Georgetown neighborhood, in the late summer of 2006, I bring up a July poll that found that half of the U.S. public believed that Iraq had weapons of mass destruction when the U.S. invaded Iraq and 64 percent still believe that Saddam had strong links with Al-Qaeda.[16]

"Do you think this reflects conservatives often listening to news that reinforces the Bush administration's perspective?" I ask Will.

"Maybe," he replies, "because Fox News is exhibit 'A.' Liberal voters genuinely believe that the *New York Times* and CBS are objective news sources. They believe that, partly because the *New York Times* and CBS see the world the way they do." Will tepidly agrees that echo-chamber journalism is more prevalent on the political right. "I think so," he says. "It tells you that [as each of] the new technologies, cable, satellite, Internet, talk radio became a new technology," Republicans "put them to use."

While conservatives maintain a louder voice on broadcast airwaves, liberals are gaining ground online. About 50 million Americans use the Internet as a news source on a typical day.[17] Liberals use the Internet for news at the highest rate of all nine voting blocs, 37 percent in total. That is 10 percent more than any Republican bloc and 13 percent more than the national average. The margin represents millions of voters. This explains the powerful force of leftists within the blogosphere and warns Democrats against giving too much credence to leftists' disproportionate influence online, while indicating that there remains more potential for fundraising and coalition building online.[18]

Increasingly, Internet blogs are beginning to reflect talk radio. By 2004, more than 8 million Americans had an online journal, a blog, equaling 7 percent of all Internet users. More white women than men had blogs. By 2006, 13 percent had a blog, still more women than men. Of the 120 million U.S. adults who use the Internet, about 27 percent read blogs in 2004. Two years later, the figure rose to 38 percent, while 42 percent of white men read blogs and 36 percent of white women did as well. Approximately one out of ten Americans who are online read political or news blogs. But it's an influential minority, and they slightly favored Kerry over Bush.[19] Most pernicious to bipartisanship, what they read reinforces polarized viewpoints, and that further polarizes the Democratic and Republican bases.

One day after North Korea exploded its first nuclear bomb, what a reader learned, and how seriously a reader took the news, depended on where he or she went online. The conservative Drudge Report had ten top headlines linked to mainstream media articles from all angles. Drudge earns between 180 and 200 million page views a month.[20] That day, on Drudge, the sex scandal involving a disgraced Republican congressman, Mark Foley, was only a slight mention, on the lower-right side. The rightist blogs like Polipundit led with a photo of former Secretary of State Madeleine Albright toasting with Kim Jong Il. Townhall led with North Korea but had several stories on Foley as well.

On the other side of the political spectrum was the Huffington Post. It was topping its news with the Mark Foley scandal. The only news link on North Korea was a small note in the top right, a one-line mention in a tiny font that read: "North Korea Conducts Nuclear Test," and immediately followed by a line referencing Bob Woodward's latest book, "Woodward Book: Bush Asked 'Why Should I Care About North Korea?'" On October 9, 2006, at 6:48 P.M., Atrios had one entry from about 12 hours earlier, where he wrote: "North Korean Nukes. Heckuva job, Bushie—Atrios 6:34 A.M." DailyKos did not mention North Korea.

The liberals who read the Huffington Post were informed about the Republican scandal and likely did not notice that North Korea had tested a nuclear bomb, and vice versa on Drudge. The ideological divide splintered further and people thought as they lived—wholly separate.

The effect on the mainstream media is pervasive. Journalists read blogs both because of the commentary on their work, and because reporters are often the targets of criticism, at times quite vitriolic and personal. Some blogs, like Drudge Report, actually influence editors' news judgment.

"Thirty years ago at dinner time, 80 percent of the TV sets in use were tuned into three people, Rather, Jennings, Brokaw," George Will says. "All three are gone."

THE VALUE OF GRIT

Beneath a granite sky on the western side of the Berlin Wall, Ronald Reagan stood 100 yards from the columns of the Brandenburg Gate. It was June of 1987. Reagan wore a red tie, white shirt, and a crisp blue suit. Two panes of bulletproof glass shielded the back of the president from communist Berlin. An East German guard tower was visible from the podium.

"General Secretary Gorbachev," Reagan said, a third of the way into his speech, "if you seek peace; if you seek prosperity for the Soviet Union and Eastern Europe; if you seek liberalization, come here, to this gate—

"Mr. Gorbachev," he paused momentarily to emphasize the next word, widening his mouth with a radioman's emphasis, "*open* this gate."

The 20,000 Germans below loudly applauded, waving a sea of small American flags. Reagan waited for the applause to calm. "Mr. Gorbachev," the president continued, steadily holding out for the last cheers to subside.

"Mr. Gorbachev, *tear down this wall!*"

The crowd burst into cheers, waving flags, screaming excitedly. The president looked at the audience and before he continued speaking, he waited, staring, fully aware that the moment was his and this was his legacy. In response, the Soviet press agency reported the address was an "openly provocative, warmongering speech." But as Reagan proclaimed "this unalterable belief: *es gibt nur ein Berlin*" (there is only one Berlin)—harking back to Kennedy in 1963, a far younger president who had declared, *"Ich bin ein Berliner"* (I am a citizen of Berlin) in what felt like a far younger nation—history seemed to be on Reagan's side.[1]

Reagan reached back to Kennedy to find his most memorable moral clarity, and thereby, without realizing it, possibly completed the Republican dominance of national security, and with it, the character behind the issue. If human memory is not a book but a collection of anecdotes, Reagan created an anecdote that personified the reason he won the hearts of Americans, always aware that the minds would follow.

Grit is central to the making of a presidency. Grit is the Gibraltar of the man. It represents the unshakable strength of character of a man or woman who places principles above policy and therefore never loses him- or herself in the poor outcomes of policy. It is the characteristic of one who is clear in purpose and believes in maxims that anchor their principles. It is optimism without idealism, pragmatism without defeatism. It is the value that transcends all values. While issues change, the character beneath the decision does not. "God, guns, and gays" may dominate the moral debates of politics, but grit defines the politician.

In July of 1979, President Jimmy Carter appeared on television hoping to soothe a public reeling from both stagflation and the energy crisis. "I want to talk to you right now about a fundamental threat to American democracy," he said in a sedate tone. "The threat is nearly invisible in ordinary ways. It is a crisis of confidence," Carter continued. "I feel your pain," he said, adding, "I need your help" because the strength to solve our problems "will not" come from the White House alone.

As Carter addressed the nation, Reagan's chief strategist, Richard Wirthlin, was lying down on his green shag rug, his children playing in the background. "When Carter made that speech I thought the world just opened up politically for Ronald Reagan," Wirthlin recalls. "There was no doubt in my mind that we could beat him. I just felt the contrast between Carter's saying we are captives of the forces of history and America really isn't able to deal with the problems of the twentieth century was the absolutely perfect straw man for Reagan because he represented such a different perceptional position about America's future and about America's promise. And what I knew, from a lot of research, is that Americans will respond to a positive message about their future. Yes, Americans were discouraged but they want leaders to lead. They want the optimism. They want the strength, the consistency."

Americans want their presidents to be the people they are not. They want them a little nobler, a little more patriotic, a little stronger, and most surely, to have that much more grit in them. "The American voter," Joe McGinniss wrote in *The Selling of the President*, "defends passionately the illusion that the men he chooses to lead him are of finer nature than he."[2]

"There was a consistency in Reagan's persona that came through visually and verbally, which I think was his great asset," Wirthlin recalls. "It wasn't the fact that he was an actor. If you ask me, what is it that gave Reagan such great appeal when he became a candidate, it wasn't his acting ability. It was speeches he was giving to General Electric. He read audiences like you could not believe."

Reagan sometimes wore one contact lens to read the speech and used the other eye to gauge which lines won the crowd.[3] "It goes back to Stevenson," Wirthlin adds, "he had a marvelous ability to deal with very complex issues in eloquent ways. But it goes back to this issue of rationality verses emotional content. Frequently those arguments are cloudy. They are always more nuanced, than more straightforward and perhaps overly simple communication. But it is the simple communication that breaks through the communication clutter."

On the left and right there is a vocal amount of monomaniac ideologues on issues from abortion to taxes to war. However, most Americans are not single-issue voters. The white noise of news often feels overwhelming to voters. Some lack the time, others the initiative to discern the major matters of the day. "Voters will go with the moral quality instead of the intellectual judgment, of which they feel incapable," as Mansfield puts it.

Yet Americans want to trust that the character of a candidate is based in principle and not ideology. Ideologues act out of emotion, which often leads to skewed policy. Principled leaders put convictions above emotion, and therefore place policy more often above partisanship. When an Emory University psychologist performed brain scans on self-described "partisans," the test subjects were able to notice the hypocritical statements of the opposing candidate but not the inconsistencies of the candidates they favored. Ideology, it was determined, showed effects in the brain similar to drug addiction.[4] Their beliefs must be upheld despite reality.

The Founding Fathers believed in being dispassionate when dealing with matters of consequence, to put rationality and reason above personal passions. If a candidate is emotional, that means he is at the mercy of outward influence. But if he is principled, each action will be influenced from his own internal moral core. He can be elected or defeated based on those principles, which are far easier to grasp than policy, and often more vital. The search for the maxims of candidates is the search for the candidates' underlying principles. A statesman who adheres to maxims believes in something larger than the present circumstance, and therefore is less likely to be swayed by present circumstance.

In *Profiles in Courage*, John F. Kennedy expressed the vital criterion that defines a courageous statesman: the willingness to take an unpopular stand, "defying the angry power" of the "constituents who control his future," because circumstance called for the statesman to follow his own conscience.[5] Courage, Robert Kennedy later wrote of his brother, was the virtue that JFK "most admired" because it was "rightly esteemed the first of human qualities because it is the quality which guarantees all others."[6]

In the modern day, when skepticism of institutions pervades the public mind, grit does not merely illustrate political bravery. It proves a politician is a statesman, with motives larger than vanity. In this vein, it evidences a willingness to put nation before self. Voters, especially white men, admire this trait most, as it ascribes itself to someone who will risk popularity to do their duty.

"There is a natural skepticism and suspicion about politicians. What is your motive?" as Virginia's Democratic Governor Tim Kaine puts it. "There is a suspicion that is held about anybody in politics whatever their party is. How do you break though that suspicion? . . . You break through it not by telling them in more detail what you think about this or that issue. I think you break through it by telling them more about who you are as a person."

Writer Joe Klein laments that candidates today are often pushed toward the popular policy by their pollsters, and in distancing themselves from their principles, they lose the public. "The character of a candidate, [pollsters'] believed, would be inferred from the quality of his policies," he wrote.[7]

If voters do not believe a candidate stands for a cause larger than himself, they will question every stand he takes. Alternatively, if they trust the grit in the candidate, many can forgive an unpopular stand.

In the 1960s, there was a common line among musicians. In gauging the quality of a new artist, the question was asked, "Does he have something to say?" Sincerity has always been the hallmark of leadership. "I do not pretend to be a divine man," Malcolm X once said. "I am not educated, nor am I an expert in any particular field—but I am sincere, and my sincerity is my credentials."[8]

"Men who are on the cusp," Norman Mailer says, "move toward the Republicans because the feeling was these Republicans mean what they say." It was true for George W. Bush as it was true for Reagan. Many wanted to hate Reagan— some did—but for most, the man they knew was too well-intentioned to disdain, beccause on the big things he seemed to mean the best. That's not greatness, but goodness. And good was all Reagan really wanted.

"Often the letters we got [in the White House] would begin by criticizing the president on a particular issue," Gary Bauer recalls of his time in the Reagan administration. "But then they would end by saying, President Reagan I just want to let you know that I voted for you in 1980 and I'm going to vote for you again in 1984, because you are a man of principle."

The stature that Reagan enjoyed rested entirely upon his character. When John Adams took over the presidency from George Washington he thought the stature of the office would transfer over to him. He learned otherwise. It is not the office, but the man.

"Whether viewers remember what you're trying to say," columnist Clarence Page once wrote, "they'll always remember how you said it."[9] As George Orwell observed, insincerity is the enemy of clear speech.

In ancient Greece, Sophists argued that contentious and well-argued reasoning could persuade people. Aristotle joined Plato in countering that rhetoric, however reasoned, is only as effective as the character of the person making the argument. "For it is not the case, as some writers of rhetorical treatises lay down in their 'Art,' that the worth of the orator in no way contributes to his powers of persuasion," Aristotle wrote. "On the contrary, moral character, so to say, constitutes the most effective means of proof."[10] Aristotle later wrote that, "Maxims amount to a general declaration of moral principles: so that, if the maxims are sound, they display the speaker as a man of sound moral character."[11]

The White Male Gap widened in nearly every pivotal election on the issue of grit, as white men searched for the better man in the man. Nixon was able to brand the once-tough anticrime mayor Hubert Humphrey as "wishy-washy." Bush was able to brand the thrice-decorated Purple Heart veteran John Kerry as a "flip-flopper." "People will quickly judge your authenticity," John Kerry tells me, having learned the hard way. "You can't force it." But the accusations against Humphrey and Kerry only succeeded because both Democrats' characters seemed malleable. "Wishy washy," as William Pollack puts it, "is the opposite of what the strong male is."

Neither Humphrey nor Kerry seemed larger than the times. Therefore, as with Al Gore in 2000, the essential personal connection was not made. Gore was undone because his veracity was questioned. That was only part of it. Gore did not connect with voters, leaving Americans only with rhetoric to rely upon. Once the rhetoric loses its authenticity, the candidate loses the voters.

The lesson of every presidential race is that policy defines platforms, but character defines the candidate. In March of 2007, an Associated Press–Ipsos poll made headlines nationally after finding that 55 percent of Americans considered integrity and honesty the most important qualities in deciding on a presidential candidate.[12] But exit polling demonstrates it is white men who value character more than any other, in deciding whom to support in presidential contests.

In 2000, voters were asked the reason they supported their candidate. Honesty earned the highest level of support, 31 percent among white men and 20 percent among white women. Among those white men, 89 percent supported Bush, while among those white women, 79 percent supported Bush. Protestants also valued honesty more than Catholics. By 2004, speaking to similar character traits, more white men selected "strong leader" and "has clear stands on the issues," in comparison to white women, as the attribute that most affected their vote. Consistently, whites valued character more than minorities.[13]

"I'm wondering if honesty in the political context might also mean, does what he says he'll do, and that taps into a man of action," Wirthlin says, after I read him the findings. "Americans want to give power or are willing to give power to someone who they believe they can trust to do what they say they'll do. And I think that is a very close cousin of strength, consistency."

This pattern of white men giving more emphasis to clear principles, has existed for decades. In 1980, more white men also selected "strong leader" than white women.[14] "There may be another issue that in a world so full of ambiguities that you and I now live in, having a leader who is able to articulate clearly and strongly, right and wrong, in direct terms, I think would garner extra support," Wirthlin adds. "I don't think a strong leader paints in pastel colors."

STAY THE COURSE

"I think moral clarity is a portion of it. It may really resonate with faith-based voters," Gary Bauer says. "I think that for another segment of the electorate— for lack of a better name—'Joe-six-pack'— . . . it is almost more of a manliness. A man takes a stand, toes the line, doesn't budge even if it gets hot or tough, and it is seen by some of those kinds of voters who may not always be comfortable with politics and moral issues. It is something they can identify with, in contrast to a more feminist or more feminine approach."

Bush's grit won him reelection in 2004. Beneath every issue, every doubt, it was the strength of character that saved him, especially during an unpopular war.

"I think [President Bush] is an honorable man. I think he's done a good job," Bob Keister of Nodine, Minnesota, tells me. "He went into Iraq, but that's an iffy," Keister hesitates and looks toward a long field of corn stalks. "It's going to be tough," this veteran and retired football coach says of the war in 2004. He supported Clinton in 1992 but did not in 1996 ("You know the reasons," he says), and he supported Bush thereafter.

Bush's appeal was not based on the rhetoric of "stay the course," but on the grit that the phrase implied. The phrase is often thought to derive from sailing, the act of maintaining the course of navigation. This would be a weak metaphor, as icebergs force ships to change course. But the phrase's derivation was actually in the capacity for a horse to complete the race. Reagan used the term early in his presidency. Bush was intent on portraying himself as one who would complete the race.

Throughout the 2004 campaign, Bush repeated that America must "stay the course," that we must "take the fight to the terrorists." He said America will not lose this war on terrorism, or the war on the degradation of its culture; that at least "this will not happen on my watch." Bush's masculine swagger, his "bring 'em on" bravado reinforced his rhetoric. But it was the grit in him that won an unpopular incumbent reelection. Kerry broke like many before him.

A slew of great contenders for the presidency imploded because they lost control of their character. Muskie cried. Gary Hart had Donna Rice. Howard Dean screamed. George Allen shouted "macaca." Then there was the failure to inspire while running against men who could: Carter against Reagan, and H. W. Bush as well as Bob Dole against Clinton. And of course, there were the Democrats who failed to convey principles that superseded their politics: Al Gore and John Kerry.

"Attributes matter more than issues," as Frank Luntz puts it. "If I believe in where the candidate stands on the issues, but I have a problem with their character and who they are, the character wins." He adds, "The number one attribute in 2004 was someone who says what they mean and means what they say. John Kerry had the advantage on intelligence but nobody cared. People believed that Kerry would pander. His quote about 'I voted for the $87 billion right up to the point I voted against it' destroyed him."

Americans became convinced of the Democrat's infirmity. Kerry's chief strategist in 2004 acknowledges the failure. "It's incumbent on candidates to explain themselves to voters in very personal terms," Tad Devine says. "They need to get to know who you are, and this is particularly important when seeking the presidency. I think the president is the most personal vote."

THE LESSON OF JOHN MURTHA

A year after the war hero was turned into an equivocator, one of the last Democratic hawks stood before the whole of Washington. He had turned against the war. This was not George McGovern wanting out of Vietnam. McGovern may have been a hero but he was no hawk. This man was more like Kennedy. He was a rerun from another time. But Congressman John Murtha of Pennsylvania is the kind of man that looks best in black and white.

He is from working-class western Pennsylvania, where hunting is still popular. A retired Marine colonel (a rank just short of brigadier general) with a trim haircut, a double chin, and wrinkles wrapping his face, he often displays a kind and modest smile, like a line that is too humble to be a circle. This day, though, Murtha was gruff, emotional, his eyes red, his voice broken and guttural.

Murtha originally joined the Marine Corps at 19, as had three of his brothers, leaving college to fight in Korea. At 33, and despite being married with children, he decided to reenlist for the Vietnam War, in which he earned two Purple Hearts and a Bronze Star. In Congress he was known for decades as a staunch military advocate. Now Murtha stood broad shouldered atop the podium, to oppose a war.

Murtha tells me later that he only stood up there reluctantly. "I go to the hospitals every week and I see these troops that were blown apart," he says. "Well since I was having no impact quietly behind the scenes as I normally do, I felt that I had to do something publicly.

"When I walked into the room every news media in the country was there, and when I talked to the caucus, there was dead silence—they were shocked by what I had to say," Murtha recalls the day. "And I knew it was going to have an impact then."

It was mid-November 2005. More than 2,000 Americans were dead, 23 in the previous week. Murtha stood before the Washington press corps and declared, "I believe we need to turn Iraq over to the Iraqis." He had once been a supporter of the war in Iraq, but, he said, "This is not going as advertised. This is a flawed policy wrapped in an illusion."

At the press conference, a reporter asked Murtha about a recent comment by Vice President Cheney who, in his Spiro Agnew role, had accused Democratic war critics of losing their "backbone." Murtha responded, speaking of his old friend, Cheney, "I like guys who got five deferments and never been there and send people to war and then don't like to hear suggestions."

Shortly after, Ohio's freshman Republican representative, Jean Schmidt, made a fool of herself on the House floor, stating to Murtha "only cowards cut and run." Jeers consumed the hall. The White House put out a statement that it is "baffling that [Murtha] is endorsing the policy positions of Michael Moore and the extreme liberal wing of the Democratic Party."

The *ad hominem* and cultural argument failed to sway the public because Murtha's grit was intact. In fact, the Republican jabs were a gift to the Democrats. They made Murtha the face of the Democratic Party.

"It was pretty hard to criticize me and what we have done for the country and call me unpatriotic, and I think this may have been part of the problem" for the Bush White House, he says. "But the bigger part of the problem was that they had lost confidence in his policy," Murtha adds, leaning on the back two legs of his chair, as we sit in his Capitol office. "It failed because presidential power is only the perception of power. There is no power in the president. The president only has power if the public supports him."

BUSH'S LAST STAND AND WHY WHITE MEN STUCK BY HIM

Bush was on CBS *60 Minutes* shortly after he announced in January 2007 that he was escalating the troop level by 20,000 strong. The New England Patriots had just defeated the San Diego Chargers in the playoffs. The first ad following the game was a Subway commercial that pictured an immense "Biggest, Meatiest, Tastiest" sandwich, with a low voice touting it as so big it leaves the "burliest burger questioning its manhood."

Bush was on CBS to defend his masculine character. The interview was at Laurel Cabin in the woods of Camp David. It has the look of a hunting lodge, where men feel like men. The president sat patiently, holding back his grimace, and acknowledged that not sending more troops sooner "could have been a mistake." "Yeah," the president said, wearing hiking shoes beneath his slacks. But he added, pointedly, "I don't want people blaming our military. We got a bunch of good military people out there doing what we've asked them to do. And the temptation is gonna be to find scapegoats. Well, if the people want a scapegoat, they got one right here in me 'cause it's my decisions."

It couldn't have been better put to men. He was taking the blame, as a leader is obliged to by honor and code. He was willing to be the scapegoat. He knew he had detractors, but the American man still hung onto the ethos of the rugged individualist who is willing to stand alone. And so Bush did.

In the four-star classic *High Noon*, Gary Cooper plays a marshal abandoned by the town and forced to face his enemy alone. An ex-girlfriend of the marshal, who is a strong woman—the film has several—tells off the brash young upstart peace officer, who also will not stand with the marshal. "You're a good-looking boy," she says. "You have big broad shoulders. But he is a man. It takes more than big broad shoulders to make a man." It is the grit that makes the man.

"You know there'll be trouble," the marshal's wife, played by the beautiful Grace Kelly, says early in the film. "Then it's better to have it here," the marshal replies, resolute. The marshal chooses duty over his newlywed wife, who leaves him for risking death to do his duty (she's a Quaker). But by the film's close she returns to her man. High noon comes. The town is empty. The four armed men enter. A man who was sentenced to death but who was spared by juries and the courts, leads the gang. The marshal must stand up to them, even if alone. It's the principle that makes him fight.

"I'm not gonna change my principles," Bush answered CBS News, about his decision to move forward, despite his isolated stand. "I'm not gonna, you know, I'm not gonna try to be popular and change my principles to do so."[15]

Six months before, when the president was on vacation in the summer of 2006, the situation in Iraq was worsening and increasingly appeared to be a civil war. Bush was reading Albert Camus' novel *The Stranger*, the story of a young alienated man who becomes detached from life due to his mother's death, and eventually murders an Arab on a beach. The novel, which takes place in Algiers at the onset of World War II, explores the concept that man must overcome the absurdity of the world, the sad happenstance and sought serendipity. To do this he must fight for order. Men must write their fate, not accept fate.

One of the temptations of the presidency lies in its clearest constitutional powers regarding foreign affairs. Since the time of Thomas Jefferson, ironically a man who also called for a small centralized government, presidents have been acting unilaterally in conflict. There is a reason Nixon went to China as domestic politics worsened. George H. W. Bush did the same. Clinton attempted to win his legacy with the Middle East. Automony is a central virtue to the classic male. A president's best opportunity to prove his autonomy is through diplomatic action and, even more assertively, by means of war.

In a time when white men were told that their manhood was something to be overcome and that those things they previously honored were now antiquated, they saw in Bush a pride in that which they were told to shame. God and country, unwavering purpose and duty, the "long hard slog," as Donald Rumsfeld put it, were all woven into American epics. Amid all the skeptics, all the jaded minds, many white men still believe in those epics. And there is no winning their votes unless a candidate appears to be a true believer as well. Americanism is a most fervent faith.

"If I am going to generalize very broadly about the average male working man," Norman Mailer says: "He's got a life that requires rugged strength. He's got to get into his pickup truck and drive to work during heavy traffic hours. There's never enough money in the family. There could be trouble with the kids. He could have many, many arguments with his wife because when there is not enough money, there is a lot of ugly rubbing of elbows, shoulders, and minds."

It is the requisite of strength in their own lives, as they struggle to always find more strength, that leads men to honor the strength in others. "There is no statesmanship without politics," presidential historian Richard Neustadt once observed.[16] George W. Bush believed sheer force could project his statesmanship, and this left him with only strength, as the purpose to the war seemed increasingly unclear. To so many white men, Bush may have picked one too many fights. He may have been too much of a man, but at least he was a man. Against the grain of public support, he was going to keep on. He now truly was standing alone, as it seemed month by month that one man's determination was another man's inflexibility.

"They decided they'd make him a hero because he never changes his mind, which is one of the cubbyholes of heroism," Mailer says. "And they keep him there, they keep him there resolutely. Now they are in dreadful trouble because he has to change his mind slightly under the sheer burden of facts. It's like he's making love to a woman who weighs 300 pounds and has decided to get on top of him."

That woman is Iraq, and Bush seems determined not to lose this test of endurance. He can now only set the policy and hope and pray, because he does pray daily, that it works out. His war is powerfully unpopular, but he is going to see it through—one last push forward into Baghdad.

"I'm very impressed by Bush's determination and his willingness to risk unpopularity, electoral loss, to do what I think on the whole is right and remains right," Mansfield says. "But disagreeing on his estimate of things you could easily decide he was over-manly . . . that's clearly a danger." Mansfield wrote in *Manliness*, regarding the dialogues of Socrates, "Courage in holding fast, appears to be a virtue to be found in all virtue." Socrates emphasizes that acting "steadfast in a foolish action is not courageous since folly is not noble and courage is noble." Mansfield adds that, "courage seems to require calculation, as to seek the best place to fight, yet utilitarian calculation (as we would say) is the death of courage."

"A man then, as Socrates seems to infer, can be too manly?" I ask Mansfield.

"Surely," he replies. "Manliness is confidence in the face of risk. But it can be a false confidence and it can be very imprudent. A manly man is inclined to sticking to his guns, taking a stand and keeping it. But this may be imprudent. So I think a manly man is always risking that the place where he took his stand may not be the prudent place to be."

GRIT CONTESTED AND COMPROMISED: THE LESSONS OF McCAIN AND CLINTON

Iraq is John McCain's burden to bear into the future. He has stuck by the president while few have. McCain once said that he was "older than dirt," but "I've learned a few things along the way."[17] Aristotle believed wisdom could not be taught but only acquired. McCain's greatest asset for white male voters was that he, like Bob Dole, had done it the "hard way." Yet, also like Dole, his age was his greatest liability.

McCain was the real kind of hero, a poster boy for American masculinity. An Annapolis man, he served as a Navy flyer in Vietnam. After being shot down in 1967, he was taken as a prisoner of war. Both McCain's father and grandfather were four-star admirals. When the Vietcong who kept him captive learned of his father's stature, they offered him release. McCain declined freedom unless his fellow POWs could leave with him. Where Bush used his father's connections to escape service in Vietnam, McCain refused freedom if it meant abandoning his comrades. Five-and-a-half years later he was freed. Television captured him walking off a plane in his Navy dress whites. Eventually, he won Barry Goldwater's Arizona seat in the Senate.

However talented Hillary Clinton and Barack Obama are, they have no such heroic tale. Hillary Clinton has won kudos in the Senate. Obama has captivating verve. He is a talented orator who excelled at Harvard and led the law review. But that is not the making of a president. Not to the American nation, and especially not to white men who still believe in the tests of manhood that have defined men from George Washington to Theodore Roosevelt to John F. Kennedy.

If McCain could energetically convince Americans that his stance in Iraq was out of troop loyalty, his grit would survive him. It was for honor's sake, in this case, and white men are desperate for honor. Life often feels like a long slog of unappreciated small compromises of manhood, to no great end. In a vain culture in which Americans seek validation not in the journey but in the discovery of their own personal greatness, the old traditions of American manhood resonate most with the men who still want to believe that great ends are worth a good life.

"That is why John McCain looks strong," David Broder says in 2006. "People have formed an opinion about his character. It has nothing to do about his policy positions or whether he is a loyal or disloyal Republican. They have made a kind of a basic judgment about his character and," Broder adds, "that is clearly what is powering [his candidacy]." But as McCain cozied up to the religious right he once opposed, as he stood for moderate immigration reform that lost the right and advocated the troop surge in Iraq that by the summer of 2007 had lost the moderates, his character seemed malleable and so his candidacy suffered.

When Hillary Clinton announced her candidacy online, she began with a monologue. She sat on a couch and said, "I'm not just starting a campaign, though, I'm beginning a conversation with you." *Time* named "You" the person of the year in 2006. Everyone was beginning a blog. Everyone was an individual star. The grunt was dead.

"Let's talk, let's chat," she said. But men don't want to have a conversation. Men admire politicians who lead by example; it's the touchdowns that count. At the end of January, Clinton was campaigning in Iowa beneath a blue banner that read: "Let the Conversation Begin." On Comedy Central's *The Daily Show*, Jon Stewart showed a clip, and advised Clinton: "Look, this might not be the most politically correct thing to say, I don't think that slogan is going to help you with men. I think the typical response would be, *Now?* You might as well get on your campaign bus, the 'I think we really need to talk express,' to unveil your new Iraq policy, 'America let's pullover, and just ask for directions.'"[18]

It was a poor beginning to reach men. And it is men who are watching Clinton's stance on Iraq. Should she apologize for her Iraq war vote, she risks substantiating the perception that she is shaped by popularity rather than principles. For this reason, she intends to "stick it out." It is only her grit that is going to win her the White House. She demonstrated strength of character once before when faced with her husband's infidelity. Clinton did "stand by her man," did not abandon him and "leave him out in cold" when the chips were down. American English is littered with clichés such as these, which reveal the culture's emphasis on loyalty. Little could appeal more to the average man, who has also slipped up, than a woman who is strong enough to stick by him. If Clinton explains her war stand correctly, she could bridge the cold image and appear stronger.

It is, after all, only her grit that keeps her a viable candidate. As her lead challengers turned antiwar one by one—first John Edwards, and soon others—she refused to use the "power of the purse" to cut off war funding. No one would ever be able to say she abandoned the troops in the field. Eventually, she too called for a troop pullout. But she refused to force the commander in chief's hand. Until, that is, the spring of 2007. The antiwar base had won her too. Now Clinton voted to cut off funds. But she would still defend her vote. She backed a war and no one could say this woman easily changed her mind.

Clinton only had her grit and she risked that grit as she danced on the war. To be certain, Clinton's candidacy depended on her political manhood not being emasculated. If she is to be America's Margaret Thatcher, she is going to have to be tougher. Conservatives, Tories, Republicans—all have the presumption of strength. Clinton is both a woman and a Democrat, and the presumption is that she cares but is weak. It is her burden to refute. She did not help found a nation and lead her party, as pioneering Israeli female Prime Minister Golda Meir had in 1969. Her hope is to be Queen Elizabeth, beyond the reach of men and stronger than conceptions of women. It is the perception of her character that will decide her fate. But Clinton's vote to cut off funds will test the perception of grit she's struggled to build. As the 2008 campaign progressed, it seemed that the farther McCain and Clinton drifted from their inward strength of character, the farther each moved from attaining the presidency. Grit was always the value beneath all values politics. But 2008, for John McCain and Hillary Clinton, is to be a contest of pure grit.

AGAINST GOD AND COUNTRY

The Perception of the Effete Liberal Elitist (1988)

Throughout the 1988 campaign, the hyper-American Republican candidate _____ (insert George H.W. Bush) lambasted the Democratic pessimistic liberal elitist _____ (insert Michael Dukakis), as a threat to American values, as weak, and as a sedative on the American spirit. Bush followed this unwritten Republican script while Dukakis played his part all too well for his own good.

"The strategic concept was developed way before we knew who the Democratic nominee was," Bush's campaign manager Lee Atwater reflected. "Whoever it was, we had to paint him as a frost belt liberal who is out of the mainstream, and is not in tune with the values of the mainstream voters."[1]

This was an effort to brand Dukakis with the worst perceived inferences of liberalism: from puny, to appeaser, to spendthrift, to someone who subscribes to a culture of Godless permissiveness. Bush went with a strategy rooted in McCarthy, in Nixon, and in Reagan. To be sure, Dukakis gave plenty of ammunition to his opponent, so Bush took aim and fired.

Bush suggested Dukakis was less than a patriot when the Massachusetts governor refused to sign a bill mandating the daily recital of the Pledge of Allegiance in schools. In city after city, Bush associated the "way out in deep left field" American Civil Liberties Union (ACLU) with Michael Dukakis. "Gov. Dukakis says he is a card-carrying member of the ACLU," Bush said in Milwaukee.[2] Illinois Republicans put out a flier that read: "All the murderers and rapists and drug pushers and child molesters in Massachusetts vote for Michael Dukakis." Bush was to be the real American, like all the rest of "you good folks." Later in September, Bush spoke at an old red-brick flag plant in Bloomfield, New Jersey. "The flags you make still inspire Americans, and those who love our values the world over."[3] Bush's appeal to the "kind and gentle" of America was effective in the same respect Bill Clinton could criticize a black female rapper four years later. A liberal was presumed tolerant. A Republican was presumed tough.

The trick is, "looking for opportunities to renew and reinforce the preconceived notions and sort of trigger fairly predictable reactions," political analyst Charlie Cook tells me. "The thing about it is that George Bush is hardly a hard-core conservative. But look at how they attacked Dukakis. They sort of went back to the old playbook. And it almost doesn't matter who the players are in any given season, the playbook is pretty much the same," Cook continues. "And I think certain types of candidates like Dukakis and Kerry play right into it."

Shortly before Bush spoke at the flag factory, Dukakis donned military coveralls over his suit and red tie. He put on a green helmet and got inside a 63-ton M–1 battle tank. Positioned inside the turret, Dukakis gripped the 7.62-millimeter machine gun as he murmured "rat-a-tat." His small frame bobbed out of the tank, like a boy playing war, as he drove the tank in front of the press corps. Camera shutters frantically clicked. After, the band played the theme song from *Patton*.[4]

"The tank," Richard Wirthlin recalls, "has to go down in history as one of the classic political blunders in the world. It goes back to my point. You can't stretch the candidate. You've got to portray who he naturally is."

By October, the Bush campaign had used the misplayed photo opportunity to attack Dukakis both on the stump and in advertising.

"What you see is an image of what you are thinking," Harvard political philosopher Harvey Mansfield says, recalling the tank incident. "It's a way of saving you the trouble of thinking." Dukakis became exactly what he was said to be, precisely because he so transparently attempted to prove otherwise. All politicians would be well advised to heed Polonius' advice to his son, Laertes, in *Hamlet:* "To thine own self be true."

Dukakis regrets many things. Sitting before me in 2006, his black hair now grayer, he squints with his smile, and the skin under his eyes creases. His eyebrows are still bushy and his powerful nose dominates his face. He looks like an immigrant descendant from the wave of ethnic white migration, a good-old Reagan Democrat.

"I ran a lousy campaign," Dukakis recalls inside his office at the now-public Northeastern University in Boston, "largely because I did not understand that you cannot sit there mute while the other guy is trying to define you.

"Here I am the son of Greek immigrants, and they are painting *me* a cultural elitist running against a Yankee Brahmin who went to Milton Academy," he says of the 1988 campaign. "I *let* that happen!" he crinkles his lip, shakes his head. "I had a terrific economic record. My state was having more economic success than any other state in the country. With the benefit of hindsight, in 1988 the first thing I should have done is told people who I was before Bush told them who I was."

MASSACHUSETTS LIBERAL, PART TWO

When I ask John Kerry whether, like many Democrats before him, a form of Republican cultural populism undid his candidacy, he responds: "Sure, absolutely," pausing, "I mean absolutely." His tone stiffens, and he sits up. "They've very successfully churned a new pot around a set of cultural wedge-driven issues that were stirred for the very purpose of shifting people's focus away from things that matter to them to something else which matters to them."

During the 2004 campaign, on a sunny July day, Bush was in short sleeves in Waukesha, a Republican suburb of Milwaukee. "Senator Kerry is rated as the most liberal member of the United States Senate," Bush said. Beyond the president was the green horizon, broken only by a giant American flag draped over a red barn. "And [Kerry] chose a fellow lawyer who is the fourth most liberal member of the United States Senate. Now, in Massachusetts, that's what they call balancing the ticket." Bush paused. The audience burst into laugher, as they had in Duluth and Marquette earlier in his Midwest tour.[5]

The previous week, Bush had been in vice presidential nominee John Edwards's home state of North Carolina. The president said, "The senator from Massachusetts [Kerry] doesn't share their values." Their values? The president explained in Wisconsin, "We stand for institutions like marriage and family, which are the foundations of society," adding, "we stand for a culture of life."[6]

If conservatives stood for family and marriage, then did liberals stand against them? If Bush stood for a culture of life, did Kerry stand for a culture of death? For a candidate mocked for his poor syntax, Bush has managed to run two campaigns of masterful rhetorical branding.

"What the last four presidential elections prove is that there has got to be a cultural debate," the Democratic Leadership Council's Bruce Reed says. "The question is whether we offer a cultural agenda or whether the Republicans decide ours for us."

THE SUBSTANCE BEHIND
THE ELITIST EXAGGERATION

William F. Buckley famously said he would rather have randomly chosen names in the phone book run the nation than the faculty of Harvard. Buckley's comment encapsulated Republican cultural populism. A half century later, Buckley calls it a "wisecrack," and explains that he meant that the "heavy, heavy ideological inclination of the Harvard faculty contrasts with the ideological inclination of people at large," adding that "regular people change their moral habits more slowly than the modernist class."

The heir to Buckley's intellectual influence, George Will, does believe conservative cultural populism pitted the common man in opposition to an intellectual neo-elite noblesse. "It follows from the premise of progressivism born 200 years ago that people are blank slates, therefore they are infinitely malleable, therefore they are infinitely improvable, therefore politics has this great and stately jurisdiction which is to perfect man and society," Will says. "And to perfect society first, before you perfect man and if you get the institutions right, people will follow."

Americans often view intellectuals as a group who love humanity and dislike people. Dogmatic liberals mocked Reagan's mind. They mocked the intellects of both Bush presidents. But in doing so, they mocked the public that elected them. English historian A. J. P. Taylor once observed, "Above all, he who loves liberty must have faith in the people."[7] When dogmatic liberals lost that faith, regular men lost faith in liberalism.

Republicans remain the party of the rich, from tax policy to funding to base support. President Bush won 64 percent of Americans with household incomes exceeding $200,000 a year, and 59 percent of those earning between $100,000 and $200,000. But the claim of elitist is not merely cultural branding.

When the Pew Research Center divided American voters into their belief systems, it found that there were three Democratic blocs: liberals, disadvantaged Democrats, and conservative Democrats. Liberals are opponents of "assertive foreign policy," most apprehensive about the use of force, believe in government's role to assist the poor, and support environmental protection. They are 83 percent white, the wealthiest political bloc (more than 41 percent have over $75,000 in annual household income), well educated, the largest group in urban areas (42 percent), the least religious, and use the Internet to get their news more than all other groups (37 percent). Pew pointed out that "most liberals live a world apart from disadvantaged Democrats and Conservative Democrats."[8] And the middle- and lower-class white male knows this.

The Republican coalition's advantage is not in its base, which totals only 29 percent of voters. (The Democratic base is 41 percent of voters.) The GOP advantage is in the political center, about 23 percent of voters (24 percent of white men and 21 percent of white women) lean strongly Republican.[9]

Liberals wield more influence over the Democratic Party than any similar constituency does over Republicans. Social conservatives may be the largest force among Republicans, but their leaders do not believe they *are* the party, whereas liberals often see the Democratic Party as purely theirs. Part of the reason is a matter of size. Liberals are a fifth of voters but 43 percent of the Democratic base. Social conservatives are 13 percent of voters, and while the largest Republican bloc, they only amount to 29 percent of the base. Notably among whites, roughly 40 percent more social conservatives are women than men. On the other side, roughly 10 percent more liberals are women than men. It leads to the bifurcated politics that year after year damages Democrats most.

Since David Broder first covered the 1960 convention, he says, Democrats have "become a highly educated" party, and "that's the chief criteria. But," he adds, "it's also an economically affluent, elitist assemblage and particularly the unions that are now represented tend to be the teachers, they're not—they're the white-collar people, not the blue-collar people."

THEATER KID POLITICS

It was not simply that Frank Sinatra allegedly arranged a mistress for John F. Kennedy. Nor was it that MCA president Lew Wasserman became a close friend of Lyndon Johnson or that *All in the Family* producer Norman Lear, a leading liberal activist, founded the strict secularist group People for the American Way. It wasn't even that Bill Clinton made celebrities regulars at White House banquets. It was all these things. Despite the popularity of Ronald Reagan and Arnold Schwarzenegger, Hollywood gives its money and, unfortunately for Democrats, its loud opinions to the left. Democrats rely on a triumvirate of organized labor, trial lawyers, and Hollywood to raise enough money to challenge Republicans, who rely on big business. Democrats receive 69 percent of Hollywood's contributions. In comparison, the oil and gas industry gives 74 percent of its contributions to Republicans.[10]

Shortly after Barack Obama announced his candidacy in early 2007, movie moguls Steven Spielberg, David Geffen, and Jeffrey Katzenberg began organizing a meet-and-greet. The moguls' endorsements were discussed as if the Democrat's viability depended upon the affirmation of filmmakers. The problem for Democrats is not in the fundraising. It is the self-aggrandizing rants of Hollywood, as if playing a great person in the movies makes you qualified to inform the public in real life. Oil executives neither speak publicly nor command attention. They donate, influence, but don't publicly rant. When Barbara Streisand, a major fundraiser for Democrats, called for the impeachment of George W. Bush in late October of 2005, the Drudge Report, among others, pounced on the story. As Matt Bai wrote, liberals in Hollywood "sometimes give the impression that they would run the country themselves, and far better, if only this business of making movies weren't so time-consuming."[11]

"The far left is a fusion of academia, Hollywood, and a residue of antiwar feeling that does emanate from the Vietnam War," Democratic demographer and moderate Mark Gersh says. "In Hollywood, people like Barbara Streisand, they are in the dramatic creative arts, that's their profession, so they are more likely to make flamboyant ostentatious, inflammatory statements."

In the hundreds of psychological sessions William Pollack has done with white men, he has noticed that, "based on their past experiences," many often "see [liberals] as a so-called liberated male who doesn't believe in the classic male values. So they see them as an enemy to their values, and they see them as caring more about people who seem to be more in pain than they are—people of color, people of extreme poverty, and women—and they think, 'Huh, they are hypocrites.'"

Inside New York's Radio City Music Hall, in July of 2004, about 6,000 people attended a fundraiser for Democrats. More than seven million dollars was raised for John Kerry's campaign. It should have been a rousing success. Instead, the stars spoke their minds. On stage, John Mellencamp called President Bush "another cheap thug who sacrifices our young." Meryl Streep mocked Bush's faith. Chevy Chase said the president had the intellect of "an egg timer." In her monologue, comedian Whoopi Goldberg used Bush's name as a sexual pun. The event caused days of bad press for Kerry. He became what his worse critics said he was. Bush continuously told crowds while campaigning that Kerry believed the "heart and soul of America" was in Hollywood.

A year after the campaign, Gary Bauer vividly recalls the storm of bad press that followed. "I think if Kerry would have had the courage to go up on stage, put his arm around [Goldberg], and say, 'Whoopi, I really appreciate your support, I love ya, but I'm running for president of the United States and I'm not going to sit here and see that office demeaned with those kinds of jokes. I'm going to ask you to stop,'" he says. "[Kerry] probably would have lost her as a supporter but that would have been a gigantic story!" Instead, that night, Kerry said nothing.

Hillary Clinton wasn't going to make that mistake. In September 2006, she upbraided film producers for depicting the assassination of George W. Bush. "I think it's absolutely outrageous," she said. "That anyone would even attempt to profit on such a horrible scenario makes me sick."[12]

Images have always mattered. The tank photo of Dukakis affirmed every negative perception of the candidate. During the 2004 election, for vacation, Bush was pictured carrying hay bales in Crawford while Kerry took his holiday windsurfing off Nantucket. Republicans turned images of Kerry's snow boarding into an advertisement depicting him waffling. Senior staff urged Kerry to take more "average person" vacations, but as his chief strategist Tad Devine recalls, "Kerry believed to do otherwise would not be true to who he was." It was the wrong occasion to prove one's authenticity.

"You would not find a single American in a poll of a thousand people that said it mattered," Republican strategist Frank Luntz says. "Yet it goes into how [the people] determine who these [candidates] are. You can't get it from numbers. It would take forty minutes of talking to people and someone would say, windsurfing, and the whole room would go, ahhh."

THE "L" WORD AND DOMESTIC STRENGTH: DUKAKIS VERSUS BUSH

"My opponent, the liberal Governor, launched a media blitz in the media, free media, and it seemed like he appeared on every television show except *Wheel of Fortune*. You see, he was afraid that Vanna might turn over the L word."[13] It was a line George H. W. Bush often repeated during the 1988 election.

The liberal pejorative was damaging in 1988 because it brought forth the worst stereotypes during the resurgence of the law-and-order issue. By the late

1980s, public pressure had amassed for more law enforcement and prosecution. There was a two-and-a-half-fold increase in the prison population between 1978 and 1988, despite the rate in crime slowing and even dropping in some years.[14] Attorneys general campaigned on their conviction rates. It was in this time that Rudy Giuliani made his name prosecuting eleven organized crime figures, in the Mafia Commission Trial.

By the second presidential debate in October, Bernard Shaw of CNN began by asking the Massachusetts governor: "Governor, if Kitty Dukakis were raped and murdered, would you favor an irrevocable death penalty for the killer?" Dukakis looked toward the camera and responded in a dry tone: "No, I don't, Bernard. And I think you know that I've opposed the death penalty during all of my life. I don't see any evidence that it's a deterrent, and I think there are better and more effective ways to deal with violent crime."

Dukakis continued speaking about policy and the low crime rate in his state. He never expressed the rage he would first feel, but that justice is not about revenge. He seemed like an intellectual who saw crime in terms of statistics instead of lives. "When you oppose the death penalty you are asked that question a thousand times," Dukakis tells me. "Unfortunately, I answered it as if I was asked it a thousand times."

Lee Atwater's infamous Willie Horton ad campaign only nailed the perception of Dukakis as a weak liberal. Horton was a black convicted murderer who fled from a Massachusetts furlough, raped a white woman, and stabbed her fiancé. Bush repeated the specifics of the case while campaigning. "He was released and he fled, only to terrorize a family and repeatedly rape a woman," the vice president said, changing the words but not the criticism.[15] Atwater—who in July, as Dukakis was considering a running mate, said, "maybe he will put this Willie Horton on the ticket"—used an independent group to fund the airtime for the infamous Horton ad. The voiceover said, "Bush supports the death penalty for first-degree murderers," while stating, "Dukakis not only opposes the death penalty, he allowed first-degree murderers to have weekend passes from prison." Then Horton's face flashed, a grainy image of a black man with an afro and a full beard. His name was flashed in large type, with the story of his crime, and words like "kidnapping," "stabbing" and "raping" jumping out at viewers.[16] Dukakis hardly fought back. He attempted to rebut with a harsh ad, but it was too late. Dukakis was defined.

"The image of a bushy-haired black guy raping a white woman. Who's kidding who?" Dukakis reflects years later. "[Atwater] knew it. And he was decent enough on his deathbed to say, 'I'm sorry.' On the other hand *shame on me* if I let him get away with it," the former Democratic nominee says. "Take a look at my situation. I'm a guy from Boston. I'm running against a guy from Houston. Greater Boston and greater Houston are about the same size in population. The homicide rate in greater Houston is six times the homicide rate in greater Boston. And yet I let the other guy take the crime issue away from me. I mean, shame on me," he embarrassingly chuckles. "Look, I made a decision I wasn't going to respond to the Bush attack campaign. It was a terrible decision. I'd *never* make it again."

Bush won 54 percent of the vote and 426 electoral votes to Dukakis's 112. It was the lowest voter turnout since 1924. Bush won white men by 29 percent and white women by 15 percent. The White Male Gap had outlasted Reagan. It was not simply in the man but clearly in the message. Reagan had won 59 percent of white male union members, Bush won 52 percent (still respectable for a Republican), while Dukakis won a slim majority of white female union members. Bush won more than six out of ten white men who were not college graduates.[17] In every respect, Republicans were now the workingman's party.

The Willie Horton issue may have evoked larger concerns. A quarter of white men and women said "punishing criminals" was the primary reason behind their vote, and not surprisingly they favored Bush. "Dukakis' liberal views" were the "factor" that mattered most to 30 percent of white male voters, while about 25 percent of white women said the same. For those women who selected the category, they leaned Democratic, while for men, they leaned Republican.[18] The liberal pejorative was always particularly potent among white men because they were, from birth, liberalism's modern antagonists.

XIV

THOSE WHO WORK HARD AND PLAY BY THE RULES (1992)

There was always some of Ronald Reagan in Bill Clinton. The one consistent pattern of the Democratic nominees from McGovern to Dukakis was that they were liberals hijacked by their history. In their view, the ills of the day were proof that the Great Society needed only to be greater. They were not pessimists, but they were incapable of vision. Their rhetoric referenced hopes and dreams and a better America, but the words were never the men. If a woman asked these Democratic nominees if she looked fat in a swimsuit, they might say yes and suggest a dietary regime of weight loss, with the latest medical research on saturated fat and sugar substitutes, while offering an overview of the mistakes that led to her current weight gain. Reagan would look at her, smile, and say, "Honey, you look beautiful."

While people desire honest assessments and real solutions, those same people also seek someone in their lives who uplifts them, who says they are capable, or beautiful, or a good man, and that the future *will* be better. Clinton made important policy shifts for Democrats, but his presidency was won on his optimism. Presidents are, after all, the father figures of the American nation. Every race for the presidency is a search for the paternal. The ideal father sees his child not for their weaknesses, but for what he or she can become. Americans want this quality from their president. This was a vital reason that white men left the Democratic Party. They wanted presidents who saw them not for their failings of the past, but for what they could become.

On Election Day, Clinton would not close the White Male Gap. But he began undoing negative perceptions, and in that effort, he made inroads. And those inroads were rooted in disarming traditional Republican cultural populism, challenging the welfare state, economic outreach to the middle class, and an optimism that suited the man. Like Reagan's resonant tone, Clinton's southern cadence had an optimistic temperance. And beneath that drawl was his story. Beneath his story was his tenacity. And beneath his tenacity was the contender.

They called Reagan the Teflon president. It was true for Clinton as well. When marital infidelity dogged his candidacy early in the campaign, he appeared on *60 Minutes* with his wife, became the first presidential nominee to openly admit to marital problems, and succeeded in moving the campaign forward. He won second place in New Hampshire and convinced the media it was a victory. By June, Clinton spoke before Jesse Jackson's Rainbow Coalition and denounced Sister Souljah's racist lyrics. Jackson was infuriated. But it showed Clinton's political acumen. He positioned himself for the general election. It was an action only Clinton could pull off because he was close to the black vote.

By the convention, after supporting the Republican candidate for three elections in a row, the Teamsters union said they were going to endorse Clinton. He had made it. Clinton began his speech with unnecessary self-deprecation. But then he proceeded to capture his campaign in a few direct words. He was running "In the name of all those who do the work and pay the taxes, raise the kids, and play by the rules, in the name of the hard-working Americans who make up our forgotten middle class," he announced. As he continued, he spoke of forcing fathers to pay child support, making sure there was equal funding for women's health issues, and he spoke at length about how he was not pro-abortion, but pro-choice, and would defend *Roe v. Wade*. It was called the "year of the woman" and Clinton was after their votes.

CLINTON'S INABILITY TO CLOSE THE WHITE MALE GAP

Clinton's small government philosophy, his argument to reform welfare, and his optimism won him the White House. It kept Ross Perot's appeal focused on nonaligned voters and disenchanted Republicans, as Perot neutered Bush's attack lines. What 1992 demonstrated was that the only two Democratic presidents in a forty-year period (by 2004) were southerners who were capable of speaking comfortably about faith, who challenged welfare, but also ran in periods when international security issues were off the table.

The cold war was over. The Soviets were no longer a centralized threat to U.S. national security. Although John F. Kennedy had won the presidency by appearing tougher on defense than Richard Nixon, Clinton only had to prove his "draft dodging" did not mean that he was unpatriotic. But to be tough like his idol, Clinton criticized Bush for being soft on China.

"I think the end of the cold war in many ways allowed Bill Clinton to be elected," says Tad Devine. "I mean, it hurt Mike Dukakis when he tried to run against Bush's father."

In October, Texas billionaire Ross Perot returned to the campaign and scuttled Bush's chances for a comeback. Clinton was the greatest Democratic politician since Kennedy, but his election resembled Woodrow Wilson's far more than Kennedy's or Lyndon Johnson's.

Twenty months after George H. W. Bush had his victory in Iraq and soared in the polls, he lost the presidency. Clinton won 43 percent of the vote, Bush 37 percent, and Perot 19 percent. Perot was a third-party force unseen since 1912.

Four out of ten voters "disapproved strongly" with Bush's management of the economy on Election Day, while a quarter more disapproved "somewhat." With no national security issues, no foreign entanglements, and no great cultural debates dominating the day, James Carville was right. It was the economy, stupid. But it was also Perot.[1]

When exit pollsters asked Perot supporters whom they would have voted for had they not supported Perot, voters split their answers. But nearly every other question and fact argued Perot voters would have favored Bush. Roughly two thirds of Perot voters said that they had supported Bush against Dukakis in 1988. More so, approximately three-quarters of Perot voters also said they supported Reagan in 1984.[2] These do not look like Democratic voters.

Bill Clinton won 36 percent of white males and 40 percent of white females. That means for the election in which Democrats championed themselves the "party of women," Clinton won 2 percent *fewer* white women compared to Dukakis and won 1 percent more white men. Essentially, Clinton won the same portion of white men as Democrats had in the two preceding presidential elections.

George Bush won 41 percent of white men and 42 percent of white women. Thus, while Clinton won essentially the same percentage of whites as Dukakis, Bush lost 23 percent of white men and 15 percent of white women! Among whites, Perot won 23 percent of men and 19 percent of women. If you add Bush's 1992 support among whites with Perot's support among whites that year, you get roughly Bush's support in 1988.

Perot's voters clearly came from the Republican camp. To assume Clinton would have won the 1992 presidency without Perot in the race not only ignored all the damage Perot did to Bush during the campaign, but it assumed Clinton would have made significant gains with Perot's voters. But the more a pollster looked, the more it seemed Perot's voters would have leaned toward Bush.[3]

Had Perot not run, "my thesis had always been that Clinton would have lost," Democratic strategist Tad Devine says. "The dynamic of the campaign would have fundamentally changed."

This is *also* the lesson of the Clinton election. His candidacy did not overcome long-term systemic failures. For Democrats in 1992, the White Male Gap was like a cancer that went into remission: Perot's candidacy hid the problem. But for the time being, Democrats had control of Washington. It was their chance to remake the conception of their party.

WAS THE NEW DEMOCRAT THE SAME OLD DOGMATIC LIBERAL?

When conservative writer Kate Walsh O'Beirne was asked about the failure of the political right's ideas in 1992, she responded: "What do you mean that conservative ideas didn't work in the 1992 election? They worked for Clinton."[4]

Nixon ran as a conservative and governed down the center. Clinton campaigned down the center and soon governed on the left. Clinton pushed a liberal platform and Republicans unrelentingly pushed back. Polarized Washington went to war.

Clinton's first great push was to fulfill a campaign promise and order that gays be allowed into the military. But in doing this before welfare reform, he squandered the intangible political capital of the first hundred days of a presidency, and with it went his intention to redefine his party. Instead, he touted an ill-timed, voluminous, and poorly advocated proposal for national health care.

On the first day of his presidency Clinton also canceled the "gag rule," the ban on abortion counseling for federally funded health care clinics. He reversed a ban on abortions in overseas military hospitals and a ban on fetal-tissue research related to stem cells. He pushed for gun control. He raised taxes. The head of the task force to reform health insurance was the First Lady, allowing detractors to dub the program "Hillary care."

Already, by 1993, Clinton was substantiating the negative perceptions he hoped to dispel. Worse for him, his inability to turn his legislation into law gradually emboldened his political enemies.

Meanwhile, those voters who supported Perot had not gone away. "[The 1992 election] told you that anywhere from a fifth to a quarter of Americans were truly fed up with the two-party system and wanted radical change," Perot's director of research Frank Luntz, who later worked for Newt Gingrich, explains. "And then '94 happens."

THE ANGRY WHITE MALE
Kicked Out and
Charged with Abandonment

Perhaps it took the death of Richard Nixon before the Republican majority could fully resurge. In late April of 1994, five presidents and first ladies attended Nixon's funeral in California. Clinton praised Nixon's "wise counsel," referenced his "mistakes," but spoke of the "remarkable journey." Seated before him were Ford, Carter, Reagan, and Bush. Behind the presidents was Newt Gingrich. He was soon to be Icarus, a man who overreached. Gingrich wanted the power of the presidency but hadn't been elected to that office. He led the new majority, but hubris soon undid him as well.

Gingrich was intent on reaching back to Nixon's silent majority to tear down Clinton's Democratic revival. Meanwhile, Clinton was creating more white male disgust. Democrats seemed not simply to be rejecting or ignoring white men, as Reagan declared, but jabbing away at them, issue by issue.

How was a man to understand the Democrats' 1992 declaration that they were the "party of women?" Was this Millet's feminism? Were white men again being portrayed by liberals as more barrier than brother? "Bill Clinton's Administration has, fairly or not, come to symbolize an attack on men and masculinity as 'problems' to be overcome," wrote the *Atlantic's* Steven Stark in 1996.[1] Clinton was now like the feminists whose votes he had won. Two years into his presidency, Bubba was not one of the boys.

If Clinton was the champion for white men as well, what did he mean during his convention speech when he advocated "equal funding" for women's health issues? It was men who needed a leg up in the health crises of the early 1990s.

As of 1991, a woman was 14 percent more likely to die from breast cancer than a man to die from prostate cancer, yet funding for breast cancer research was 660 percent greater than funding for prostate cancer research. The death rate for prostate cancer grew at nearly twice the rate of breast cancer from 1986 to 1991. Black men specifically had the highest rate of prostate cancer in the world. By 1992, heart attacks were the number one cause of death among women, compared to other diseases. But men were still dying of heart attacks at a rate of three to one, compared to women. Men were 90 percent of all AIDS deaths by 1991. Men made up more than eight in ten homeless Americans. As of 1992, at every age cohort, men suffered from a higher level of major cardiovascular diseases. Men were more likely to suffer from mental illness, but women were almost twice as likely to be treated for mental illness.

Suicide was largely a white male problem. About 90 percent of all suicides were among whites, usually college educated, and at least middle class. In 1988, for teenagers age 15 to 19, the suicide rate was 18 out of every 100,000 boys compared to 4 out of every 100,000 girls. For those 20 to 24, it was 26 for men and 4 for women. The drastic increase among older men, mostly white, was nearly unnoticed by the 1990s. In 1970, for those age 25 to 34, the suicide rate per 100,000 people was 20 for men and 9 for women; by 1988, the rate among men increased to 25 and among women decreased to 6.[2] The rate was highest among elderly white men. But it was the age group of 25 to 34 that was most telling of the state of white manhood by the 1990s. While the onset of unaddressed mental illness plays a significant role for this age group, it is also in this stage of a man's life when he is under the most pressure to establish himself. If a man's fundamental worth is judged by his ability to support himself and stand on his own, then what is a man worth who is unable to get good work?

Gender roles were ambiguous by the mid-1990s. Rosie the Riveter now was expected to bring home the bacon and still cook it. While men were told to be sensitive and caring to attract a woman, a man was still expected to be powerful either physically, in work, or in money and influence.

"There has been a confusion about what genuine or real masculinity is about," says William Pollack, the head of Harvard's Center for Men. "Men brought up in a more traditional form of masculinity, the bread winner, the provider, are living in an environment where that is not looked highly upon and

they don't know how to engage in any other form of self. Other men," he continues, "in their 30s, 40s, et cetera have grown up with mixed ideas of what their
masculinity is. They've been told that men should be caring, empathetic, mutual
partners of women, respectful of women in the workplace, but they've still been
given that message, that male or boy code, that they should stand on their own
two feet, fight back, don't be a wimp and show how strong they are," Pollack
adds. "Well, that is a split in the sense of self, and masculinity for men to a large
extent is an essential component of their definition of themselves."

AFFIRMATIVE ACTION AS
"POSITIVE DISCRIMINATION"

Affirmative action made it more difficult for white boys to get into college and for
white men to get work. To white men, affirmative action was a direct assault on
their ability to be men. Consider law school, which has been at the center of the
affirmative action debate. The average LSAT test score in 2003–2004 for whites
and Asians was ten points higher than blacks, 152 to 142, and 6 points higher than
Hispanics (the margin has held steady since at least 1997). White males score the
highest of all test takers, yet many more male than female test takers do not indicate their race/ethnicity. Among men and women, those who do not indicate their
race are the highest scorers. This may suggest a reticence among some talented
white and Asian students to indicate race due to affirmative action.[3]

The University of Michigan Law School, one of the top schools in the nation, utilized an affirmative action system that considered race a significant factor
among several. The Supreme Court had upheld the methodology in 2003. By
2005, after controlling for test scores, grades, residency, and legacy or alumni
connections of an applicant, among men white males had a 10 percent probabil-
ity of admission while Hispanics had a 28 percent chance of admission, and
blacks a 68 percent chance of getting into the law school. Even after affirmative
action was scrutinized between 1994 and 2005, it was clear that race and gender
(not class or any other factor) made law school acceptance significantly more difficult for white and Asian men.[4]

The white male stance on affirmative action was not racist or sexist; it was
practical. It's easy to defend an abstract policy based on an abstract goal of equal
ends. But for a white male in his mid-twenties, when law school directly affects
whether he will get into the top law firms, which directly affects a lifetime of future income, and, in his view, his ability to attract a wife, his stance is wholly

pragmatic. Yet, white men do *not* oppose all forms of affirmative action and white women often share a similar opinion on the matter.

In 2005, when a poll asked, "In order to make up for past discrimination, do you favor or oppose programs that make special efforts to help minorities get ahead?" fully 61 percent of white women favored it and 56 percent of white men did as well. But the support of white men and women increased dramatically when the question focused on those in poverty. "Do you favor or oppose programs that make special efforts to help people get ahead who come from low-income backgrounds, regardless of their gender or ethnicity?" yielded 87 percent of white men saying yes, as did 89 percent of white women.[5]

It's clear that if affirmative action was refocused to assist the poor, and thereby still disproportionably aid minorities, it could garner the support of white America. Adam Smith pointed out that the force behind the Invisible Hand was vanity. Self-love and the potential for success drives people to excel. Altruism guides few. The same is true in politics. Voters vote their interests.

Affirmative action, to white men, stood for a society that said everyone but the white man should get a hand. What began as a presidential decree by Kennedy in 1961 to combat racial bias in hiring was expanded by Johnson, and later Nixon, to women. The white male frustration with the program, which emerged in the 1970s, was captured in the synonymous term for affirmative action: "positive discrimination." It was negative when everyone else was discriminated against but positive when white men were on the receiving end. White men did not miss the inference.

GINGRICH GAINS FROM THE WHITE MALE GAP

A half year after Nixon's funeral, Newt Gingrich led a Republican victory, and won the control of Congress for the first time in four decades. Perot voters returned to voting for Republicans with 65 percent of their support. The victory for Republicans was historic. The White Male Gap was not merely a presidential phenomenon but one for Congress as well. Republicans gained 52 seats in the House, to win a 230-seat majority for the first time in two generations. It was the greatest gain since 1946. In addition, they won 8 Senate seats and 11 governorships. Not one Republican incumbent was defeated. In Texas, the son of a president, George W. Bush, became the governor.[6]

White men won Bush his 1994 gubernatorial race. A majority of women supported the Democratic incumbent Ann Richards, but overall six out of ten men, and *two of three* white men, backed Bush.[7] It was a harbinger of the White Male Gap fovoring Bush later. As Democrats would do in 2000, Richards underestimated Bush, once commenting that he was little more than "some jerk."[8]

The new Texas governor had learned his lesson. It began in West Texas. In 1978, Bush had been defeated in a congressional race by a native Texan who painted him as a privileged Yankee from the Northeast. Christian conservatives even criticized Bush for attending a rally where alcohol had been served.[9] By 1994, Bush was born again as an evangelical Christian, who was now able to campaign as a West Texas family man, advocating that "individuals should be responsible for their actions." The outsider was now the insider. He won in an upset.

It was not long after the 1994 election that the results were credited to, or blamed on, the "angry white male." The "angry white male" was a mountain of conventional wisdom built upon a misunderstanding, a myth, and some tepid white misandry. The misunderstanding revolved around the gender gap, as it had since 1980, that women were the cause and that they had left the Republicans. The myth was that white men's politics was merely anger, the rage of the disempowered dictator. The tepid white misandry was in the unsubstantiated generalizations widely accepted.

White men did favor Republicans over Democrats by a 63 to 37 percent margin. The 37 percent mark was roughly the portion of white males Clinton earned in 1992, and the approximate amount every Democratic candidate won between 1980 and 2004. More striking, the 63 percent was essentially the margin George H. W. Bush earned in 1988, the preceding two-candidate presidential election.[10]

It is true that in terms of the congressional vote, white men went from supporting Republicans at 51 percent in 1992 to 63 percent in 1994, while 49 percent of white women supported Republicans in 1992 and increased their support to 53 percent by 1994. Why this happened is what is misunderstood. The election of 1994, like 2006, was a national off-year election. Usually, these seats, especially in the House, turn on local issues. It was clear no matter how you broke down the election of 1994, the result reflected the 14-year-old White Male Gap. What earned less attention was that Republicans also won a majority of white women, between 53 and 55 percent, depending on the poll. That was approximately the margin of white female support that Bush had earned in 1988.[11]

Almost two-fifths of white Republicans in 1994 said they had been raised in Democratic families.[12] Perot voters in 1992 backed Republican House candidates in 1994 by a two-to-one margin. This was another indication they would have likely leaned to favor Bush in 1992 had Perot not run. Those Perot supporters who voted Republican in 1994 had suffered, since 1979, twice the wage losses as those Perot voters who supported Democrats.[13]

In the end, 1994 represented the year Newt Gingrich, Frank Luntz, and other key Republicans molded the congressional vote to emulate the presidential. That indeed was historic.

HYPOCRISY AND MYTH:
THE ANGER BEHIND THE
"ANGRY WHITE MALE" SLUR

Little could have antagonized white men more than the 1993 *Newsweek* feature titled "White Male Paranoia." The article described how white men were creating a false victimization. To prove it, it noted the most affluent and elite white men:

> It's still a statistical piece of cake being a white man . . . just 39.2 percent of the population, yet they account for 82.5 percent of the Forbes 400 (folks worth at least $265 million), 77 percent of Congress, 92 percent of state governors. . . . So now they want underdog status, too and the moral clout that comes with victimhood?[14]

The victimization issue will be discussed later in this chapter; first "white male privilege" begs addressing. White men at the top were still at the top. The Legacy Principle applied to white men just as it did to white women. Those in the ruling class had a better chance at getting in the best colleges and were provided a social network that put them at a vast advantage in employment.

Consider presidents. John Quincy Adams was the son of John Adams. Benjamin Harrison was the grandson of William Henry Harrison. Franklin D. Roosevelt was related to Theodore Roosevelt, Ulysses S. Grant, and Zachary Taylor. John F. Kennedy's father was a viable presidential contender until he shirked from World War II, and of course, both of the younger brothers of JFK were serious presidential contenders. George W. Bush was the son of George H. W. Bush. And perhaps, most ridiculous, George W. Bush's grandmother was a bridesmaid at Howard Dean's grandmother's wedding.[15] By the 2008 race, the son of former 1968 faltering frontrunner George Romney was contending for the Republican nomination. Romney was contested by the son of two generations of admirals, John McCain. And among Democrats, the wife of a former president was seeking the presidency.

Consider the ultrarich in the early 1990s (the trend was exponentially more staggering by 2006). Between the end of World War II to Richard Nixon's reelection, nonsupervisory workers' real wages increased as the GDP increased. The rising tide did lift all boats. But in 1972 the motorized yachts sailed off and everyone else got stuck in a bog. While GDP output continued to rise, real wages began to decline. Between 1977 and 1989, accounting for inflation, production of all goods and services rose 42 percent. Yet, 60 percent of all the gains in after-tax income went to the richest 1 percent of families. The bottom 80 percent of the population received only 5 percent of the increase.[16] The vast number of white men, who on average have seen the most wage stagflation, are as powerless in the economy as all others.

But the *Newsweek* article was typical. It didn't bother looking at all those who were not at the upper echelon of power. This other white guy *also* wanted inside the "old boy's club." But he didn't come from the right neighborhood, the right culture, the right schools, didn't talk the right way, and he lacked the financial safety net that grants boldness to those who otherwise would be meek. And the troubles were his too. Between 1973 and 1992, the weekly earnings of men in the middle of the wage scale *declined*.[17] The trend reverberated throughout the economy. Between 1973 and 1993, the average American's standard of living rose at a slower rate than in any previous 20-year period since the Civil War.[18]

About half of white male voters had only a high school education by 1994. Their occupational hopes were grim because of the waning industrial economy. For a white male who entered the workforce in 1984 and had only a high school education, his wages would have remained essentially the same ten years later, while those with better educations fared far better. As Michael Zweig put it in *The Working Class Majority:*

> Radical politics of the 1970s and 1980s were increasingly dominated by identity politics . . . in these formulations, white men are either irrelevant or the enemy, and white working class men are stripped of their legitimate standing among those who suffer wrongs in this capitalist society. This type of politics is a recipe for alienation and anger among white men, dividing the working class and creating needless hostility toward the justifiable demands of women and minorities.[19]

It was not that the economic problems for blacks or Hispanics were not worse. They were. But unlike with white men, society understood, validated, and sought to lessen the plight of minorities and women. White men got the tin ear. Worse yet, as with the *Newsweek* article, it was often inferred that white men were racists or misogynists if they opposed programs that discriminated against them.

The *Newsweek* feature began by mentioning the end of the film *Falling Down*, when Michael Douglas asks, "I'm the bad guy?" He had just blown up half of Los Angeles. The film depicted a white man who bottled up his anger and became a psychotic killer. He turned "against a rainbow coalition of Angelenos. It's a cartoon vision of the beleaguered white male in multicultural America," the article explained. Absolutely. That was the point of the film; Douglas was playing the white man's "pseudo victimization." So what does the article do? In the tradition of the mainstream, the reporters and writer created a cartoon of white men by literally re-creating the lunacy of the film, but now reported as fact, summarizing what was bothering white men:

> His cash machine asks if business is to be conducted in English or Spanish. A panhandler pointedly wishes him a pleasant and safe day. He's passed by a car, more luxurious than his own, booming rap music. (He has lately acquired a taste for country music.) He opens a door for a woman who didn't need it opened. . . . Certain public figures begin to get his goat: Spike Lee, Sinead O'Connor, Al Sharpton, Faye Wattleton, and, he hates to admit it—it's so trite—but Hillary Rodham Clinton. . . . People seem to be talking in code—wack? def?—and he's getting sick of feeling obliged to pay attention. He hates the word womyn, and anything with the suffix -centric. He worries that he's becoming a fascist. He has been thinking about buying a gun.

The closing line says it all. Not only is the white male a misogynistic, racist, ethnocentric petty man, but he's getting a gun.[20] The misconception of the gender gap by 1994 verged on astounding. In one CNN story and debate after the election, the narrator, setting the tone for the debate, broke down the white male and female vote, adding, "That means some of the white males who voted for Democrats two years ago have switched parties." The piece continued to incorrectly analyze the election.

"Exit polls show some decided President Clinton wasn't the good old boy he appeared to be during his campaign," the voiceover continued (and no, there was no "good old boy" question in the polling). "Others disliked his wife. But still more white male voters say it came down to money, and they liked the GOP pledge to cut taxes and to reduce programs such as welfare. But some observers say white males are not just worried about their wallets, they also fear losing something white American men have always had: economic and political power."

Here was the common perception of the "angry white male" factoid. He was either a hick who wanted a "good old boy" as president or he was a bigot. The stereotyping was so offensive only because it often came from the very people who preached tolerance and claimed to have an open mind.

This scene is from the November 15, 1994, episode of CNN *Talk Back Live*. Susan Rook is the CNN anchor, with guests Sean Hannity (he was not yet with Fox News, but even in 1994 he was a highly influential conservative talk radio personality), columnist Jeff Katz, another white male, and *Vanity Fair* contributing editor Gail Sheehy, who is also an accomplished author.

> *Sheehy:* Well, I've been talking to a lot of white males who are very angry across the country over the last couple of years in the course of doing some interviewing for my next book. And mainly, what they're angry about is structural problems that are creating lower income for them. *They kind of took advantage or took for granted that they would have a natural advantage as white males* coming into the work force. But today, if you look at over the last 20 years, white males have been losing income or remaining flat in every age group except those over six. . . . They blame it on minorities and women who truly, over the last 20 years, have improved up to 18 percent. . . .
>
> *Hannity:* If you look at the white male, *it's the only group in America that doesn't have a built in excuse-making mechanism if something doesn't go wrong in their lives.* I mean, we have become a society where people have *abdicated their responsibility.* . . .
>
> *Sheehy:* There's an exaggerated sense of disadvantage with regard to women and minorities. And Bill Clinton, I think, has become the poster boy for that for a lot of white males, because he has represented bringing those people into the system, giving them appointments in his administration. He has a brilliant wife who can give a political speech for an hour without a single note and intimidating to everybody . . .

The debate went on for an hour. At one point there was discussion of multiculturalism, prompted by an audience question, and whether that has played a role.

> *Katz:* Just a quick point. Obviously, American culture is not, you know, we're not heirs to Chinese culture to any significant degree or to, you know—we are heirs to European, to Western European, culture.

This was a response to the rising 1990s movement of multiculturalism. History was seen as the refuge of "dead white males." The intention was to downplay the presence of white male faces in history while emphasizing all others. The bad white guys of history, though, were not deemphasized. It was what historian Arthur Schlesinger called the emerging trend of "underdog history." Bertrand Russell called it the "superior virtue of the oppressed."[21]

But to white men it meant that because these guys were white, whatever good they did, the bad was increasingly on America's mind. "It may be too bad that dead white European males have played so large a role in shaping our culture," Schlesinger wrote. "But that's the way it is. One cannot erase history."[22] But Americans could learn only the history that interested them.

This trend was prevalent in middle schools and high schools, but it was most measurable in colleges. While requirements for American history and Western civilization dropped off between the 1970–71 and the 1993–94 academic years, the number of colleges conferring ethnic, cultural, and gender studies degrees rose from 2,579 to 5,435, and by 2003–04, fully 7,181 colleges offered degrees in these areas.[23]

Vanity Fair's Gail Sheehy exemplified the mainstream press coverage at the time. Sheehy's comments that these men voted against the Democrats because Clinton appointed minorities, that it was because he has a "brilliant wife," and that men took for granted that they would have a "natural advantage as white males" was an utterly unsubstantiated analysis entirely indicative of the received wisdom of the day.

It was not because of race and gender that white men felt entitled to the American dream. It was because they felt entirely American. Many white men neither knew what it was like to be different nor allowed themselves to feel distanced from the very American sense of entitlement that many white women, Asian Americans, and Jewish Americans also feel. This is what was misunderstood. White men did not feel entitled because they believed they were superior. On the contrary, this rejected man was coming to believe that his race and gender were a drawback. Every time a white man applied to college or for a job and checked his race and gender in the square, he believed he was going to have to be that much stronger of an applicant to make up for being a white male.

The mistake of much of the analysis of 1994 was the charge that white men were portraying themselves as victims. White men were *not* claiming to be victims. In fact, such a claim was antithetical to the pressure on men to appear powerful, even when not. The real issue by the 1990s was that white men were no longer comfortable being portrayed as the reason everyone else was a victim.

"They have been brought up and indoctrinated with the ideal of what is a heroic, good, and positive ideal, living it out, and then being told that they are the worst piece of crap alive for doing it. What could be worse than that?" William Pollack says. "And any woman who was taught that she should only be feminine, and nice, and lovely, and all of the sudden realizes she can be bright and capable, and someone says you are not a real woman, how would she feel about that? And she probably wouldn't even feel as bad as a woman, because you are not a real woman does not hurt as much to a woman as it is to a man because for men, so much of their own selves equals masculinity, whereas for women there are other parts of themselves by which they define themselves.

"As one mother said, when I said, 'Boys lose their voice,' [she said] 'What do you mean, he's screaming all the time!'" Pollack recalls from his innumerable sessions counseling boys as well as men. "I mean they are unable to articulate what makes them feel disenfranchised, unsupported, what they need in a candidate that will make them feel that their country is working better and their life will go better," he adds. "And so many men rather than just withdrawing have just moved over to the Republican Party because they speak the voice that men can't say and it sounds like something they would want to say."

Rush Limbaugh did not represent white men. But he did capture those who were increasingly aggravated. Limbaugh was bombastic. He exaggerated. He browbeat. But he was entertaining and telling. From the 1990s to the presidential race of 2008, Limbaugh has remained a phenomenon of modern media. When he came on the scene, he weighed over 300 pounds, stood 6 feet, and his voice sounded like it.

"You were 55 or 60 percent more likely to vote for the Republicans if you listened to Limbaugh," Frank Luntz says. "There was something about his attacks on the cultural elites that not only registered, but it caused people to vote and actually caused people to change their minds."

"What was he a metaphor for?" I ask.

"He was a metaphor—and I use bad language and my mother won't get it—he was a metaphor for 'fuck you!'" Luntz stiffens his voice. "Back then. It was legitimately 'Fuck you. I'm tired of Ivy League professors telling me that I'm wrong, not just how to live my life but saying to me that my values, my beliefs, my convictions, my religion is wrong.'"

XVI

THE HARD WAY, AND SOCCER MOMS

Bob Dole carries the war with him every day. His right arm is bent, unmovable, as if forever held in a plaster cast. He holds a pen in his right hand that permanently forms a fist. He wants the arm to seem useful. Dole was raised in a generation of men who must be useful. He is a Kansan in every way a man can be a Kansan. He is humble, plain-spoken, and always in the back of those eyes that seem dark but are light up close is something wide and unceasing, like the Great Plains that weaned him. Dole remembers living through the Depression in the small town of Russell, Kansas. After his teenage years, he joined the Army and served in the Second World War. Near Castel d'Aiano, Italy, at age 20, he attempted to pull a wounded man to safety and was hit by German machine gun fire. His right shoulder and arm were shattered. Nine operations later, his right arm was still paralyzed. But he survived.

Five years passed and though he still had trouble putting on ties, buttoning his collar, doing the daily routine, he felt recovered enough to make use of his life. He went to law school, then to Congress, and over years that turned to decades, he became Senate majority leader. When General Colin Powell decided not to seek the presidency in 1996, the nomination was Dole's to win. He had worked hard, played by all the rules, waited his turn, and his turn had come. But he was 72, and unlike Reagan, Dole seemed his age. He was always a step behind the moment throughout his race for the presidency. But then, he never did race. Like his life, his campaign for the presidency was a sheer act of will. As Dole said at the lowest point of his campaign, finally catching hold of the moment, "I have done it the hard way and I will do it the hard way once again."

Far behind Clinton in the polls by mid-May, with his campaign war chest down to $2 million for the following four months, Dole decided to resign his Senate seat. He was going to focus full time on the presidential campaign. "I do not find this disheartening," Dole said. "This is where I touch the ground, and it is in touching the ground, in moments of difficulty, that I have always found my strength." It was to be his last great push for office. "For little has come to me except the hard way."[1]

It was politically bold and intensely male. The derivation of the "hard way" is in the game of craps, when with the roll of the dice, you attempt to hit your number with the odds most against you.

Bill Clinton was the child of another generation. He was weaned in the counterculture. He was the "new man," declaring to America, "I feel your pain." Dole was the 1950s man. He was to lose the "hard way" but at least it was his way. And that was also part of being a man. Dole attempted to utilize the cultur- ally populist game plan, accusing Clinton of "a devil's bargain in which high taxes force parents to spend more and more time at work and less time at home."[2] It was the same script without a new context. But Clinton was a beta version of Democrat 2.0. He knew the old lines and rebuffed them. At his age, Dole was simply not a man made for the modern thematic presidential race. Clinton was far younger, more vital, and while Dole represented the old and sto- ried tradition of manhood, with national and domestic security off the political radar the strong father seemed no longer necessary.

Clinton won 38 percent of white men in 1996, improving 2 percent over 1992, but essentially staying within the same range as every Democrat since Rea- gan (and as Al Gore and John Kerry in later elections). Clinton improved with the white female vote, winning 48 percent, a significant improvement of 8 per- cent over 1992. White women were again clearly voting Democratic. Perot won 11 percent of white men and 8 percent of white women. From 1992 to 2000, these white men who supported Perot favored the Republican two to one over the Democrat, if not more.[3]

In substantial respects, Clinton won what he sought in 1996. He was after the "soccer moms." In this effort, Clinton's campaign divided moderate voters into Swing One and Swing Two. Swing One voters were white middle-class women and Swing Twos were primarily the elusive white male voters.

"It was easier to get the Swing Ones than the Swing Twos," says Bruce Reed, who before heading the Democratic Leadership Council was an advisor on Clinton's reelection campaign. "Swing One voters were suburban couples, soccer moms to use the stereotype of the time, who were concerned about family issues, and Swing Twos were disproportionately men, mostly white men who were concerned about security, welfare reform, immigration, and crime."

Clinton split moderate white men as Carter had in 1976, but Clinton gained 7 percent more moderate white women than Carter had. The search for the soccer moms paid off.[4]

Whatever the effect of Perot—and excluding the extraordinary political talents of Clinton—it seems that *only* with domestic or foreign security as a minor issue in the election and a major third party candidate in the race, was a Democrat able to win election without significantly closing the White Male Gap. Reelection was a different matter. But by 2000 and 2004, it was clear that absent one or both of those conditions Republicans won.

Clinton was a president book-ended between the cold war and the coming age of terrorism. It was a rare reprieve from war and high crime, when the maternal politics might be the most winnable strategy.

"The '92 election and the '96 election were probably the last elections we are going to have for a while where you could run as this sort of über-governor," says Elaine Kamarck, who worked in the Clinton White House.

THE NATURE OF THE LIE AND
WHY IT OFFENDED WHITE MEN MOST

Then there was the White House intern name Monica Lewinsky. The affair went public in 1996 and deeply damaged Democrats with white men. A president lied to a nation and tried to use syntax to escape the truth. In the profligate times, it was just the sort of banal drama for a nation obsessed with the soap operas of the day. From O. J. to Monica, we watched.

To be exact, 70 million people watched Barbara Walters interview Monica Lewinsky on ABC's *20/20*. Never had a network news program reached so many Americans. ABC insisted companies give record payments for commercials. And those commercials included Victoria's Secret lingerie, a promotion for the film *Cleopatra* that said, "When she was 20, she seduced the most powerful leader in the world," and a Maytag advertisement that seriously stated, "It actually has the power to remove stains."[5]

"Clinton was a huge disappointment, because he seemed to have vitality," Norman Mailer says. "In fact, he had everything but machismo, which was the one trouble with Clinton. You could say there was not a single political idea he was willing to die for." With Clinton's conviction unclear, character attacks were especially pernicious. To white men, the shame was not in the scandal but the reason and how Clinton attempted to weasel out of it. "It depends on what the meaning of the word 'is' is," Clinton notoriously answered in his grand jury testimony, as Ken Starr carefully recorded in his salacious 676-page report.

Eventually Clinton came clean. He told America he answered "questions no American citizen would ever want to answer." But that "I must take complete responsibility for all my actions," and that "I did have a relationship with Miss Lewinsky" that was "wrong" and "constituted a critical lapse in judgment." He explained that "now, this matter is between me, the two people I love most—my wife and our daughter—and our God. I must put it right."[6]

Reagan's speech eleven years earlier, regarding his role in the Iran-Contra arrangement, succeeded where Clinton's did not. "A few months ago, I told the American people I did not trade arms for hostages. My heart and my best intentions still tell me that's true, but the facts and evidence tell me it is not," Reagan said, admitting some culpability for Iran-Contra. Iran-Contra was shown to be part of a larger scheme to create a covert White House military strike force unbeknown to Congress or the American people. It was a constitutional issue! Yet Reagan's admission sounded like a man who had America's best interests in mind. Clinton's admission sounded like a man who had his own interests in mind.

"We are hollow men," T. S. Elliot wrote in 1925 about a world that goes out "not with a bang but a whimper."[7] The two Democratic presidents of the past four decades were unable to revitalize their party to win the presidency for the long term. As with Carter, Clinton revived himself. "I identify with people who get beat up," Clinton said years later.[8] His post-presidential life has brought him praise from Africa to Asia as a champion of the underclasses. But as he left his presidency broken, frail, frustrated, his hair white, with bulbous bags under his eyes, white men recalled the whimper.

POLITICS OF THE COMMON MAN AND GUN CULTURE (2000–2003)

Andrew Jackson was the first modern president to seek the common white man's vote and, in 1840, the first modern campaign was an effort to undo his legacy. In this endeavor, Whig William Henry Harrison was championed as the everyman. His campaign sang of his log cabin. He referred to himself as a humble back-woodsman. But Harrison was from a most distinguished American family, raised on a palatial Virginia estate, and classically educated. His father was a signatory to the Declaration of Independence. It was 1840 and Jackson's heir, President Martin Van Buren, was fighting for reelection.

The Whigs realized that they had no hope of retaking the White House if they continued to be perceived as the privileged party. They were intent on re-orienting the public debate along cultural lines, to transcend class, as Sean Wilentz explains in *The Rise of American Democracy*. The Whigs alleged that "Democratic corruption was spiritual as well as material," Wilentz writes. Davy Crockett became a symbol of the Whigs as leaders "suddenly showed a fondness for the manly." With vivid echoes of the conservative cultural populism of the modern day, the Whig Horace Greeley said, "Wherever you find a bitter, blas-phemous Atheist and an enemy of Marriage, Morality, and Social Order," it was "one vote for Van Buren."[1]

During barbecues and bonfires, Whigs handed out free hard cider. Harrison paused at one point in a campaign speech to take a swig and whooped Indian calls on the stump.[2] An astonishing eight out of ten eligible voters turned out, and Harrison won.[3]

There was much of Harrison in George W. Bush. The son of a president and the grandson of a senator, Bush nevertheless campaigned as a regular guy, "a plain-spoken fella'," and a Christian man. Americans sought a "straight shooter" who understood why so many were offended by Clinton's conduct. If Reagan was intent on reinvigorating America's manhood, Bush was intent on restoring the moral promise of that manhood.

"There's no question in my mind that Clinton's personal misbehavior was a huge factor in the 2000 election and a huge problem for Gore," says David Broder, sitting in a swivel chair fortified with stacks of books piled three feet high, as reporters stream by his office and the day's *Washington Post* is put to bed. "[Gore] would have had a hell of a lot easier time," had the Lewinsky affair not occurred. "It was a *huge* problem. It set a psychological frame around the whole election choice that would not have been there otherwise," Broder continues. "Over and over again, I heard on the doorstep and in the living room, the people talking in very passionate personal terms about how terrible an experience it had been to try to explain to their children what they were seeing," he adds. "And they wanted an absolute guarantee that that would not happen again. And Bush clearly understood that."

As the Texas governor accepted his party's nomination in Philadelphia, he told Americans, "Our current president embodied the potential of a genera-tion—so many talents, so much charm, such great skill. But in the end, to what end? So much promise to no great purpose." And it was this son of a president, a failed oilman, a recovering alcoholic, who was born again with Christ and with it, intended to regain America's moral purpose. Bush campaigned as the nation's prodigal son.

"Our generation," Bush continued, "has a chance to reclaim some essential values, to show we have grown up before we grow old. But when the moment for leadership came, this administration did not teach our children, it disillusioned them. . . . So when I put my hand on the Bible, I will swear to not only uphold the laws of our land, I will swear to uphold the honor and dignity of the office."

Bush stumped as a man more Main Street than Wall Street, who was a "compassionate conservative," while offering traditional conservative appeals such as an immense new tax cut. But he primarily ran as a "straight shooter" who worked his ranch and was a West Texan.

With the pall of Clinton hanging over him, Gore's forthrightness was beginning to be second guessed. Small misstatements on prescription drugs, or his proposed release of the petroleum reserves, combined with his statement that "during my service in the United States Congress, I took the initiative in creating the Internet," one by one summed to substantiate the perception that Clinton-era Democrats lacked veracity, and therefore grit.[4] At the debates, Gore was caught sighing and passive aggressively rolling his eyes. In one debate, Gore stood up while Bush was still speaking and took a step toward him as if to intimidate Bush. Bush stopped speaking, unflinchingly looked toward Gore, nodded brashly, as if he was saying, "What's up?" like the two men were standing toe-to-toe in a bar. Gore stepped back and Bush looked the stronger man. From the outset of the debates, Bush was intent on conveying his everyman sensibility. "I fully recognize I'm not of Washington," he said, "I'm from Texas." Bush had attended Andover, Yale, and Harvard, but word was put out, early in the campaign, that he never *really* liked those "Northeastern types." And it worked.

THE WHITE MALE GAP AND GORE'S LOSS

Despite serving as vice president during staggering economic growth, low crime, and peacetime, Al Gore won the popular vote by only about 500,000 votes, and lost the electoral college to Bush, 266 to 271 respectively. Ralph Nader earned 2.8 million votes. Had Nader not run, at least New Hampshire and Florida would have gone to Gore and the presidency with them. Nader damaged his larger liberal cause by entering the race. But beneath the 2000 election, as it had been for 20 years, was a coalition without its fourth leg. The White Male Gap had hardly ever damaged Democrats as it had in 2000. The election never should have been so close for Republicans, so close for Nader to make a difference. But Gore was the culmination of every modern Democrat before him. Nader and Perot were fleeting players.

It was the White Male Gap that lost Gore the presidency. Gore lost white females by a margin of 3 percent to Bush. But Gore lost white men by 27 percent! Gore was able to win the popular vote and keep the race so close because he nearly split the white female vote, and did split white women if Jews are included in the white Democratic tally. But the Democrats' inability to win white men was the permanent Democratic error. The Democratic Party without white men was in every sense a minority party.

Perot was out of the race. The effect: Gore's 47 percent of the white female vote was roughly what Clinton won in 1996. Among white men, Gore matched Dukakis with only 35 percent of white men. Overall, Democrats proved their continued inability to make significant gains with white men. In fact, Gore earned 1 percent less white men than Clinton did in 1992.[5]

Democrats were still about 12 points short of the support that Carter earned with white men in 1976. But they won approximately the same portion of white women as Carter had that year.[6] The White Male Gap had never been so vivid. George W. Bush earned two terms in office because Democrats ignored, rejected, or showed only a superficial interest in white men. While much of white men's Democratic affiliation shifted before 1972, between 1972 and 2000, Democrats still lost 15 percent of white men and 7 percent of white women.[7] Gore won only 35 percent of white men with annual household incomes between $30,000 and $75,000. Overall, he lost every income bracket of white men.[8] If a white man graduated from college he was *less* likely to support Democrats, but if a white woman graduated college she was *more* likely to support Democrats. While winning far more men than women, Republicans won every level of education for whites except a noteworthy loss of white women with postgraduate degrees (10 to 12 percent of white female voters). And so it went. Gore even lost white male union members, while winning white female union members.[9]

On Election Day, voters were asked why they supported their candidate. The highest level of support for any one reason was honesty. About one out of three white men said honesty mattered most, while one out of four women said the same. Gore's issues of veracity solidified the cloud of credibility that Clinton's scandals left over the Democratic White House.

"My wife is in the same boat. We are both registered Democrats and we are voting Republican now," David Travis tells me in August 2004, setting a ball on the tee at a golf course outside Phoenix. His club arcs downward like the rapid hand of a clock. Click. The ball sails more than 200 yards along the length of the green fairway. "I think the Monica Lewinsky thing had an effect," he adds. "[Clinton] kind of made a joke of the White House, and the Democratic Party hasn't come out with anything different over the last two elections."

In 2000, slightly more white men said they voted on a personal quality and slightly more white women said they voted on an issue. After the issue of grit, gun rights dogged Gore most among white men.

Rodney Mason is one of those men. It's spring 2005. I am sitting with the North Carolina ferry mate the day after Easter Sunday. Mason voted for Bill Clinton in 1992 and 1996. But Mason could not vote Democratic in 2000. "I'm a hunter and I felt like Gore would have taken the guns," the 43-year-old tells me. "When I get off the boat all I want to do is hunt and fish."

THE GUN CULTURE

The cover of the November 2000 issue of *Field & Stream* magazine, which hit news-stands weeks before Election Day, carried a black and white image of three white woodsmen in front of a cabin. The cover story was the "The Great American Deer Camp," which brought to mind the familial culture of hunting. Beneath the picture, the words in bold type were: "Why Gore Wants Your Guns." Inside the magazine, the headline on that story read, "No Choice at All," with an illustration of Bill Clinton passing the key of a gun cabinet to Gore. The article began by pointing out that after eight years of Clinton, "we have it pretty good. The Dow Jones exceeds 11,000, unemployment is at an all time low, and there's no major war. . . . Things are not bad at all—unless you happen to be a Branch Davidian or a gun owner." It continued, "*we* have had our worst eight years since the republic was founded." It stated that Clinton, whose "sheer gutter shrewdness is unequaled in modern American politics," is committed to gun control. It consistently attacked the honor of Clinton and Gore. After listing the Democrats' support for trigger locks and back-ground checks at gun shows, the article's author added that the reader may decide not to vote, but should Gore win, "open up your gun cabinet and gaze at your firearms for a good long while—so you'll remember what they looked like."

About 10 million Americans read *Field & Stream*. Three out of four of all its readers are white males and they are also middle class—the median income of the average reader is $44,768.[10] It was a powerfully destructive piece of commentary for Gore in terms of the White Male Gap. In contrast, photographs of Bush with his guns appeared in several outdoor magazines. Outside the debate over Gore's veracity, no issue was more relevant to the White Male Gap in 2000 than guns. As the article exemplified, the honesty issue related to honor and honor relates to the gun culture. For this reason, gun control has been a losing issue for the left. And in 2000, Gore knew it.

"It's not as fashionable in party circles to do what you need to do to cut your losses in those areas," Bruce Reed says. "In fact, the pressures in the party go just the opposite."

In 2000, fully 59 percent of southern white men owned guns, compared to 48 percent outside the South. What marred Gore so badly with the gun vote was a stance he took during a primary debate with liberal New Jersey senator Bill Bradley, as they sparred over who had the stricter platform.

In the modern tradition of Democratic primaries, the contests were pushing the mainstream candidate leftward. To push back against Bradley, Gore said handguns should be registered and licensed. The comment haunted Gore throughout the campaign. It was a self-inflicted wound, but one indicative of the effect of primaries on Democrats.

"Gore knew full well that he did not want to make the 2000 election about gun control. He had been elected in Tennessee. That was the last thing he wanted to be a divisive issue," recalls Reed, who served as Clinton's chief domestic policy advisor before heading the Democratic Leadership Council. "But at the primaries Gore was nearly beaten by Bradley who challenged his liberal credentials on every front and one of the big issues was guns. So against his own better political judgment Gore came out for registration or licensing, because Bradley was coming out for far more extreme measures. And it was just never an option for him to approach the election the way Mark Warner would approach the Virginia election a year later by saying to Democrats 'I'm going to be better on guns than the other guy.'" Reed hesitates, sighs. "But that's not our path to power," he regrets.

There is no getting around the gun in American culture. The Second Amendment was an outgrowth of an American psychological need to maintain an individualistic recourse under all circumstances. We are a nation built on the distrust of centralized government. "All men having power ought to be distrusted to a certain degree," said James Madison, no radical himself, at the Constitutional Convention. Checks and balances were to ensure no Caesar could corrupt the republic. The right to bear arms, in part, represented the last recourse of American democracy. But the culture behind the gun is larger than the right. After Gore lost to Bush, many on the left misunderstood this and were often derisive of white men in the process.

"The prestige of white macho has definitely taken a hit, and the resulting sense of loss moves many issues," wrote one *Nation* magazine writer. "Take gun control. Despite the precipitate drop in crime, white men cling ever more tightly to their guns."[11]

Many liberals, often because they live in cities, only see guns in the negative context of crime. To rural America, the gun is emblematic of their way of life.

The call for further gun control is a call for the limitation of their rights as men. In the same respect that abortion rights groups defend nearly all forms of abortion because they are afraid that the criminalization of one form will lead to the criminalization of all forms, gun rights groups defend some guns to defend all guns.

In total, 55 of every 100 white men in America have a gun in the home, with gun ownership in rural homes far exceeding ownership by urban dwellers. In 2000, there was a stark gender difference between white men and women in their position on "stricter gun control legislation." A large majority of white men oppose gun control while a large majority of white women support it.[12] But opponents of gun control are significantly more likely to support Republicans than proponents are to support Democrats.[13] Gun control is not merely unpopular with white men. In January of 2004, as the presidential primaries began, two-thirds of Americans believed that there were "enough" gun laws.[14] Polling such as this, as well as the example of Gore, has led Democrats to stop pushing for further restrictions on guns. Even after the 2007 Virginia Tech massacre, in which 33 people died in the deadliest school shooting in U.S. history, leading Democrats were noticeably silent on the issue. The political cost of gun control has proven too high.

When Charlton Heston declared that to take his gun someone would have to pry it "from my cold, dead hands," he was defending not a weapon but a brotherhood. Hunting remains one of the premier rituals of manhood. Sons hunt with their fathers, as their fathers had before them. Thanksgiving is a time to sojourn in the woods, at a cabin or campsite, where there is the simple camaraderie of being among men only, and the peace of escaping work and responsibilities.

"It's a tradition in my family that my father's father did with all of his friends," says a friend of mine, Nate Moe. Moe grew up in Mondovi, Wisconsin, which has some of the best deer hunting in the nation. "Honest to God, it's the only time my father and I get along. We don't bitch at each other. We only get along. It's the only time I feel like I get his ear without judgment. It's the time he treats me as an equal and not his son. It almost is a primal experience," he adds. "Beyond the action of the hunting, you get to be outside and do something and do something you do not get to do in day-to-day life. It's walking as quietly as you possibly can. It's sitting as quietly as I possibly can. And then it's listening to how loud nature is. It's not like the first time you do something extreme, the first time you have sex or go snow boarding out of bounds," he continues. "When you decide to put your sight on a deer and shoot it," he pauses, "it's exhilarating.

But not more than an ounce of that deer's flesh will go to waste—even the major-ity of that I take to my parents' farm and dispose of it and other animals eat it. It's a big animal. For a nonhunter it's really hard to come to terms with shooting something that is human size but it's cherished—that it is venison brought to the table by the person providing it."

This is the culture gun control groups compete against. In 2000, half the American electorate had a gun in their home. Bush carried those voters at a ratio of six to ten. As part of the National Rifle Association's multi-million-dollar ef-fort to defeat Gore in the 2000 election, it put up billboards in swing states that read "Vote Freedom!"[15] The NRA knew exactly what guns meant to the bulk of those who own them.

By late 2003, as the Iowa caucus neared, Kerry was determined not to make Gore's mistakes. Following a speech in Iowa advocating modest gun control, Kerry also wanted to demonstrate that he supported hunters' rights. The Boston Brahmin exited the barn on the autumn day. He wielded his 12-gauge shotgun and in two shots, blew two pheasants out of the sky. He walked off wearing his orange safety vest, L. L. Bean duck boots, a flannel shirt, and blue jeans, trudging slowly through the cornfield, his shotgun tucked downward.[16] This was the candidate it seemed, way back when, whom the Democrats were going to field.

The NRA dedicated $20 million to reelecting Bush in 2004.[17] On Election Day, 55 percent of white men said they had a gun in the household compared to 45 percent of white women, and they strongly favored Republicans.[18] It is the middle class that has the highest level of gun ownership.

As I speak with Rodney Mason inside the Swan Quarter Ferry, which shuttles passengers to the Outer Banks from the coast of North Carolina, Mason explains that he believes that the Democrats' stance on guns is consis-tent with their general weakness. He remains a registered Democrat but sup-ported President Bush in 2000 and 2004. Metal spoons, ladles, and spatulas are clanking and clapping as the ship rocks in a storm. In his green fatigues, Mason sips a Pepsi.

"I think Bush went over there and done what he should have done," Mason says when I bring up the war in Iraq. "He got Bin Laden, I mean Saddam Hus-sein." Does it even matter if we caught Saddam or Bin Laden, as long as Bush has a bad guy? Mason trusts Republicans on war. His perception of the two par-ties: "The Democrats are more yuppie and the Republicans are more cowboys—shoot 'em up, bang, bang—but *they tell the people straight.* You feel they are standing up for the flag, the military. I think [Republicans] have *backbone*." Mason recalls his father, a port captain, his grandfather, a fisherman, as a storm blankets the Carolinas and hail ricochets off the ship's metal deck. The Democrats Mason sees today are not the same men his father knew. "I would vote Democratic," Mason adds, "if I saw a man with a backbone that would go over there and take care of things."

THE "FEMININE PARTY" IN WARTIME
Bush, Kerry, and Bravado (2004–2007)

After the president's second 150 mph flyby, Bush came in for a landing, relinquishing the controls to another pilot as the Navy S–3B Viking descended from the blue sky. It was May 1, 2003. Bush felt vindicated landing on the hardtop of the aircraft carrier. The U.S. military had pummeled Saddam Hussein's army in less than two months. In the hypermasculine theme of the Bush administration, the president strutted on deck in his green flight suit. Grinning, Bush soon declared, "Major combat operations in Iraq have ended." Above the president, a sign read "Mission Accomplished."

The speech was perhaps Bush's most foolish political mistake, if only because the theatrics were so wholly refuted by reality. That day he reveled in the bravado and blinding overconfidence that defined his administration. "Presidents don't go into war for political profit but they may exploit them, as Bush apparently intends to do," historian Arthur Schlesinger Jr. tells me shortly after. "Of course [Bush] took it to ludicrous extremes when he impersonated Tom Cruise. Eisenhower and Kennedy—Eisenhower was a general, Kennedy was a war hero—neither of them ever put on uniforms when they were president."

Leave it to George W. Bush to put on the uniform. Presidents from Lincoln to Roosevelt had promoted the commander in chief image during wartime. But something was different that day Bush stood on the aircraft carrier. It seemed more grounded in ideology and hubris than the "ground truth." The lessons of history were unheeded.

Yet the white men who believed that American power was still a force for good, even as Iraq went bad, were not ready to give up on their belief. They watched Howard Dean's antiwar candidacy and saw those "weak liberals" opposing yet another war. When the distinction was not made between Afghanistan and Iraq—leading Democrats made this differentiation, but the activist left did not—white men were lost to the Democrats. However gradually, white men, like others, grew to be skeptical of the war, but they trusted the president, because he was the president, and the nation was at war. So they could forgive the showmanship. The image of Bush was both priceless and costly. The bravado succeeded where history would not. He was the flyboy with the grunt's demeanor.

"Nobody would say that Bush in that flight jacket made them like him more," Republican strategist Frank Luntz says, when discussing how men might respond in focus groups. "But man, he fit into that jacket and after 20 minutes you'd hear, they'd say it to you," that the aircraft carrier landing did have a positive effect. "But they are not going to say it on the surface because it isn't on the surface."

For so much of Bush's presidency, it seemed that his manhood was his greatest asset, as well as his greatest liability. This was the same man who stood on top of the World Trade Center ruins at Ground Zero in 2001, intuitively embracing an old firefighter, telling a crowd of ironworkers that he hears them, and soon the terrorists would hear from America. This was the man some Americans would remember—not the flyboy who didn't go to war but the commander in chief.

During my drive across the country in 2004, I encountered a consistent skepticism about the war in Iraq. But there also was a consistent pride in Bush for not bowing to his detractors on the war. "I'll probably vote again for [Bush]," Fred Crenshaw tells me that August, his voice scratched and waning. "I admire him for starting something and trying to stay with it and finish."

Crenshaw lives in the small arid town of Trinidad, Colorado, where the Santa Fe Trail once passed. The 81-year-old veteran of the Second World War jabs his finger at the headline with the name Moqtada al-Sadr across the paper's top fold. Crenshaw has a gaunt, wrinkled face. He wears a white button-down shirt and slacks. "Kerry at times sounds like he's got some good qualifications. I like a man that makes up his mind what he's going to do and sticks to it," he says. "Kerry's been a little, ah, hasn't been quite stable enough in saying and doing what he believes in."

Family photos line the wall behind him, including pictures of relatives who served in Vietnam. "I haven't seen anybody burning flags like they did during Vietnam," he says, his hand trembling. "I had two stepsons who served in Vietnam. Anytime servicemen are involved in a foreign mess, I feel like we ought to stand behind them and not be divided because I don't think that helps their morale. And I think morale is part of winning the war."

He looks toward me and waits, as if he is reaching for the words, reaching further than my lifetime, recalling his service in the war that brought forth the nation's ascendancy. "You know the American people like to win." Crenshaw clears his throat. "They don't like to lose and they don't like to have things drug out."

Shortly after Representative John Murtha demanded American troops be redeployed out of Iraq, he was having a private conversation with the then House Majority leader Tom DeLay. DeLay said Murtha was antiwar. Murtha replied: "You were killing bugs when I was killing Vietcong."

Murtha was possibly the only Democrat left in Congress at the time who could have changed the conversation as he had. It was the mark of Murtha's success that efforts were made to recruit men like him, who had fought and were not doves, for the 2006 midterm election. The biggest problem Murtha saw in Democrats from 1972 to 2004 was not simply an unwillingness to fight wars. The party lacked a sense of masculine fight.

"McGovern was a war hero but he didn't defend himself. Kerry had the same problem, he didn't defend himself. Gore didn't defend himself. For crying out loud!" Murtha blurts.

"Why?" I ask.

"I've thought a lot about that," he replies, steadying himself, "and I think it is because they are trying to appease an element of the Democratic base."

"So many white men like you left the Democrats—why did you stay?"

"As much as I was disgusted with some of the liberal policies," Murtha says, grimacing, wrinkling his cheeks, shaking his head, "I never considered changing parties, no, no. I'm a Henry Jackson Democrat—strong on the military—and yet there are social issues we've got to support," he adds, leaning back on the rear legs of his chair as he often does.

The divergence of views regarding the use of military force rapidly grew after Vietnam. The political right believed in protection as means to safety. The political left believed in security. Security was the state of feeling safe, the state in which precautions are taken to assure that something of value is not taken away. But protection was the *act* of preventing harm, the state of taking precautions in anticipation of harm to ensure safety. It was indeed a classical feminine and masculine divide. And both, in their extremes, had their dangers. Safety did not have to mean Iraq. It could mean Kennedy's and Reagan's strong language in Berlin; it could mean the war in Afghanistan.

"You have to act to make yourself safe, as opposed to security where you put yourself in a position where you don't have to act to make yourself safe, like Social Security," as Mansfield puts it. "Peace to liberals, with the Democrats, became very much both means and end. You mustn't use warlike means to secure peace at the end. Peace must be your policy all along, therefore negotiate, dialogue."

THE WHITE MALE WARRIOR AND IRAQ SYNDROME

After the first gulf war, George H. W. Bush expressed, "I think that Desert Storm lifted the morale of our country and healed in a wonderful way some of the wounds of Vietnam. I'm sure of it."[1] Bush's son saw to it that the wounds were reopened.

"That's one of the sad legacies of the Bush administration," Democratic strategist Mark Gersh says. "We were over [the Vietnam syndrome] and America was proud of its military and proud of its role around the world and this debacle in Iraq has set that back. . . . Who knows how many generations or decades" it will take for the United States to lose what could be called the Iraq Syndrome.

The attitude toward the military is an issue particularly close to white men. The two institutions of government where white men are most disproportionately represented are Congress and the military, although congressional representation has become more diverse over the years. In 1955–57, 96 percent of the

House and Senate combined were white men. Two decades later, in 2006–07, the composition of Congress was 74 percent white males.[2] The largest obstacle to gender and racially equal representation in Congress is the nearly insurmountable incumbency rates of members.

Overall, the proportion of white men in Congress by 2006 was roughly equivalent to the proportion of white men who died in the global war on terrorism. White men are serving in the military from the very top to the front lines. The powerful positions receive the attention but few consider the sacrifice of those other white men.

"You must understand that Americans are a warrior nation," Senator Daniel Patrick Moynihan once told a group of Arab leaders.[3] One 2001 study found that among military officers, 64 percent identify as Republicans while only 8 percent identify as Democrats. Between 1976 and 1996, the percentage of officers identifying themselves as Republicans doubled from 33 to 67 percent.[4]

Today, the military remains a white male institution. Unlike in the corporate world, this cannot be chalked up to discrimination or to class and color advantages. For decades the military has made intense efforts to recruit more women and minorities. It is more likely that it reflects that soldiering captures basic notions of manhood and patriotism. The result is that white men serve and die for this country at a level disproportionate to their percentage of the population.

In the global warfare since September 11, 2001 (which includes the war in Iraq, Afghanistan, and related antiterror operations) about three out of four of all U.S. soldier deaths have been white men—as of early 2007 about 3,400 deaths. Hispanic and black men each represented about 10 percent of deaths. Women amounted to 2 percent of all deaths, though the *New York Times Magazine* still termed Iraq the "women's war" in the spring 2007.[5]

The fatalities in the war were not only falling on white men at a level grossly disproportionate to the population, but their overall service in the military itself reflects the same trend. Fully 58 percent of the military is white male, 13 percent black males, 9 percent white females, and 7 percent Hispanic males. Although only 9 percent of the military, white women are 34 percent of the civilian workforce.[6]

Since the current conflicts began, I have spoken with many young white men who served and survived, some in the Marines, one in the special forces, and some in the Army. One of these men was David Cross. Tenth generation military, his grandfather was an admiral. Nearly 140 years ago a relative of his fought in the Civil War, and before that his family fought wars in Germany.

Cross wipes a table at a Waffle House in Little Rock, Arkansas, where only one couple is dining. "I think I'm going to go for Bush," he explains. "I'm in the military and he's done a lot for us. He's protected us when we needed him the most. We went over [to Iraq] to protect the people and because we thought there were weapons of mass destruction," he says. "The ability to lead Americans," is most important, he says. "Be able to lead through the thick and thin." He believes President Bush does exactly this, using the words "commander in chief" in a blunt tone.

Cross's trim mustache only slightly compensates for his clear boyish face. It is always striking how young these men are, who serve and die and risk death, for an America that they barely know, a nation that has hardly been easy on them but that they still dearly love. Taking a break behind the counter, standing stiff with his navy blue "WH" hat on perfectly straight, the Navy quartermaster explains that he feels "duty bound" by his grandfather to serve in the military. "I guess," he adds, "you can say it's my destiny to be in the military for a while."

Those like Cross shift from being lost boys to having a mission, and suddenly they are men. For those returning without either the mission or the structure, it's more difficult. But they have done something noble, not by innate gift like athletics or academics, but by force of will alone. It grants them an existential worth in a time when many young men, like Cross, feel worthless. This is why as President Bush honored one young man during the 2007 State of the Union address, he noted that the Silver Star recipient, in his green dress uniform and crew cut, was not so long ago pumping gas in Independence, Kentucky. As that young man stood, the chamber rose to its feet, cheering, and the joint chiefs of staff smiled. It was a rare bipartisan moment.

Military service becomes a path for some young struggling white men to gain honor and life direction. Many serve out of pure patriotism. For others, it is all they are truly good at. Ulysses Grant devolved to reclusive drunkenness and depression until the Civil War called him back to duty. For the larger voting public, soldiers symbolize what becomes the politics of war, peace, and patriotism. There may be no issue on which the gender vote is more bifurcated than on issues of war.

As late as January 2007, white men believed troops should remain in Iraq until the situation is stabilized (65 percent), while white women believed the troops should be brought home (54 percent). The explanation is not that white men saw Iraq as imperative to U.S. security. A slim majority of white men believed that the threat of terrorism "does not" depend on success in

Iraq, and 64 percent of white women agreed. More striking, while half of white men supported Bush's plan to send in more troops, seven out of ten white women opposed it.[7] In general, whites were more supportive of the war than minorities.[8]

White men and women began the war in Iraq strongly behind the president. But as the war dragged on, year by year, women were significantly more likely to change their views about the war, while men stuck with the president and the war effort. In July 2003, a few months after the war in Iraq began, as the U.S.-appointed Governing Council met for the first time, the same proportion of white men and women, about three out of four, believed the war was the "right decision." By December 2005, as Iraqis voted for their first full-term government since the war, six out of ten men and half of women still believed it was the correct decision; about the same proportion thought the war was going well. By January 2007, with the war in Iraq continuing longer than America's involvement in the Second World War, 56 percent of white men still believed the United States had made the "right decision" to use military force against Iraq, while 56 percent of white women believed it had been the "wrong decision." The disproportional support for the war among white men was *not* because they had a significantly more rosy view of the conflict than women. Only 42 percent thought the war was going well, compared to 37 percent of women. It was also not a matter of women being more informed, as 10 percent more white men reported reading or hearing "a lot" about the troop surge in January 2007, for example.[9] White men were not only paying the far largest cost for this war, but they were the last voting bloc to stick with the president into 2007.

The explanation transcends Iraq. More white men than white women say that they "completely agree" that they are "very patriotic," and more white women than white men "completely agree" that leaders should make compromises.[10] In 2006, when asked about their greatest concern regarding U.S. policy toward Iran's nuclear program, more white men than women said they feared the United States might "wait too long," and they voted overwhelmingly for Bush in 2004.[11] The results mirrored public opinion throughout the Iran crisis and the cold war. During the 2004 election, slightly more white women expressed concern about another major terror attack.

One academic study, taken as the first Gulf War raged, found that men and women agreed on the interpretation of events leading up to the war and that they supported both the goal of removing Saddam Hussein from Kuwait and

protecting the world's oil supply. However, in all of the industrialized democracies women were "significantly less willing to support military action to accomplish these goals."[12]

CLIPPING THE DOVES' WINGS

Bruce Reed believes that fundamentally, in nearly every election since the 1960s, the White Male Gap is a "function of two" factors. "First that Republicans have an historic advantage as the party of strength," he says. "And second, the Democrats have an historic burden as being seen as the party of big government."

There was no election in 2006 that was more relevant than the race of Joe Lieberman in Connecticut. If Lieberman was not a liberal, neither was Truman, Kennedy, or Johnson. But he had ardently supported President Bush's war in Iraq. It wasn't merely his support, but that he was a cheerleader for the president, that irked dogmatic liberals. But the AFL-CIO supported Lieberman. It was a microcosm of the 1970s, the pragmatists versus the dogmatists, all over again. The hardhats were with Lieberman. Clinton was with Lieberman. But the activist left was not. In keeping with the new demographics of the left wing, activists backed an antiwar candidate who was a millionaire, who defeated Lieberman in the primary upon a wave of support from the left wing, most vocally within the blogosphere. There was intense pressure on Lieberman to drop out of the race by the Democratic establishment. Lieberman stayed in and won the general election. Bush, in a true show of loyalty, led the top leading Republicans in their refusal to campaign for the Republican candidate. Lieberman had stood by them. This was the stuff of grit to white men. Lieberman made some mistakes, such as commenting that antiwar Democrats were undermining the mission. Yet it was telling that Lieberman lost support from Democrats but won in the general election.

On Election Day, in a three-candidate race, Lieberman won 51 percent of white women. What was unusual was that he won 54 percent of white men. More telling, Lieberman won despite 66 percent of voters disapproving of the war in Iraq and 63 percent believing that some or all troops should be withdrawn. Among these voters, he won four out of ten. It was a dangerous harbinger for Democratic electoral ambitions in 2008, should the party veer to the antiwar position, which was occurring by 2007. The antiwar Democrat who challenged Lieberman tellingly won exactly the percentage Democratic presidential candidates win among white men, 36 percent.[13]

"The Korean War destroyed Truman. The Vietnam War destroyed Johnson in 1968. The Iraq War will destroy Bush," Arthur Schlesinger, Jr. tells me, "possibly."

"But looking toward 2008, there has never been an antiwar candidate elected president?" I ask the onetime Kennedy staffer and cold war Democrat, a couple months before his passing.

"No there has not," he replies. But he emphasized at some point the United States was going to have to get out of Iraq. "The way we got out of Vietnam was disgusting. But it was cut and run. If the issue was presidential power, presidential war, preventive war, what Bush did was replace the foreign policy of the United States, which was deterrence, which was the cold war, with preventive war. The Bush doctrine of preventive war will be the issue."

The issue of preventive war remains a thin rope to walk for Democrats. It rarely benefits a party to advocate any aspect of a position that has wedged it away from the American public. It only damaged Republicans when some vocally advocated ejecting illegal immigrants from the nation, thus feeding the stereotype that the Republicans are intolerant.

Within a month of the start of the 2008 race, Hillary Clinton, Barack Obama, Bill Richardson, and most firmly, John Edwards, were all pulled to the antiwar wing as they campaigned for the base. Each offered different timetables for exiting Iraq. Even George McGovern, by mid 2007, tells me warily of his hope that Democrats will end the war in Iraq. But, the 1972 nominee adds, "I'm not sure an antiwar Democrat can win. We haven't proved that yet." It was a haunting warning. The antiwar base was again pushing Democrats leftward. History was to reassert itself. The doves of the left are powerful, and bad war is their feed.

"My biggest worry is not the debate about Iraq, where nobody has the answer but the debate after Iraq. Where, if it goes the way of Vietnam, it will push us away from supporting the use of force for any reason, even a good one," Reed says. "Democrats were right to bring Vietnam to a halt and were punished severely for it. The antiwar tendency can lead to grievous damage, if it morphs into a philosophy as opposed to an understandable reaction to one administration's mistakes."

Fully 65 percent of liberals favor cutting defense, while about 44 percent of the next highest group favoring defense cuts includes more minorities and poor.[14] Liberals today also have the "strongest preference" for diplomacy over military force. Nine out of ten believe the United States relies too much on its military to deal with terrorism, while only half of all Americans agree.[15] For these reasons among others, only 16 percent of white men consider themselves liberals. Republicans will face a phalanx of conservative isolationists after the war, and Democrats the antiwar base. But if history is a roadmap to the future, it will be the Democrats who will have a harder time handling their flank in 2008 and 2012 due to Iraq. The war in Iraq will only empower a leftist movement similar to those that immediately opposed military actions since World War I.

Antiwar meant no war. Americans have long been hesitant to go to war, unless attacked. But once attacked, they rallied. The young white men of America were willing to risk death in its service. As long as honor was tied to war, war could win honor.

But the Philippines, Vietnam, and Iraq were different. The only honor was in the battles that made small heroes, but the wars themselves were increasingly suspect causes. There was a gray area between those who hated all wars and those who hated bad wars.

In questioning the "warrior culture," feminist author Barbara Ehrenreich wrote, "We seem to believe that leadership is expressed, in no small part, by a willingness to cause the deaths of others." Soldiers were reduced to primitive men, in her view, "intoxicated by their own drumbeats and war songs, fascinated by the glint of steel and the prospect of blood."[16] This was the central point of divergence on war between feminists and many men. "All war is hell," William Sherman said. But Americans, from the Civil War to both World Wars, to Afghanistan, saw some wars as a hell that must be waged, in order to put down a larger threat.

Those most visible in their denunciation of the war came out of Hollywood during the 2004 election. To white workingmen, Hollywood represented the apostasy of honor. They were seen as the blowhards, the talkers, the guys who never dared to fight when the bouncer was not present, who hated violence until violence was thrust upon them, and then those men deemed primitive were deemed necessary. As Matt Bai wrote about the Hollywood left's stance on Iraq, "Artists tend to be reflexively pacifist, and one of these days it was just bound to make them look prescient."[17]

"I think [it's] the biggest problem we've had," says Democratic demographer Mark Gersh. "I worked for Walter Mondale. I admire George McGovern. I didn't admire Jimmy Carter. I think we have been nominating candidates, Bill Clinton and Al Gore, who have a sensitivity about America being firm abroad, muscular with the military."

THE LESSONS OF KERRY'S LOSS

If Kierkegaard was right that life is lived forward and understood backward, John Kerry is a man that cannot help but look backward. Outstretched, wearing a navy blue suit, waving his long arms, crossing and uncrossing his lanky legs, staring a penetrating stare, Kerry is emphatic. "As a result partly of this campaign, I'm going to be more proactive because I'm *not* going to have people cast their votes on misconceptions," he asserts, narrowing his eyes, sitting across from me in his Senate office. He leans on his left hand, squishing his fist into his cheek, and waves his right. "I'm *not* going to have people cast their vote on fabrications!"

Before me is a man who had intended one more run. But by January 2007 the hard truth had caught up to him: His chance passed. It was an uneasy thought to Kerry. Kerry was a moment away from his frustration for at least two years after his loss. He resented the very forces that undid his presidential bid. He blames himself for allowing it to happen. Kerry's presidency was undone by a strategy he foresaw.

Shortly before the New Hampshire primary, former Senator Max Cleland sat in his wheelchair beside Kerry. At a small community center, more than 300 people listened as Kerry took hold of the microphone and said he was motivated by what he called the "most craven moment I have ever seen in American politics." Cleland raised his remaining limb, turned his face toward Kerry, wanting this fight as well.

Cleland was unseated in 2002 when his opponent, a Republican from Georgia, Senator Saxby Chambliss—who avoided service in the Vietnam War—put out attack advertising that questioned Cleland's patriotism. Chambliss placed Cleland's face beside pictures of Osama Bin Laden and Saddam Hussein. Cleland, a triple-amputee Vietnam veteran, did not respond. He thought it was beneath him. Chambliss won.

"It is notorious and it is a classic example of slam politics, their willingness to do or say anything for political gain," Cleland tells me after the rally. "They will be running the same kind of slam politics against John as they did against me," Cleland adds. "I'm out here until the last dog dies."

It was Kerry's candidacy that died. In late July 2004, the Democratic National Convention was a pageant of Freudian compensation. Two decades earlier Jeane Kirkpatrick called them "San Francisco Democrats," so Kerry would prove they were not effeminate. The hallways of the convention were covered with pictures of Kerry in uniform. Speaker after speaker reiterated that Kerry had fought in Vietnam. Senator Barack Obama said Democrats represented a new hope, "the hope of a young naval lieutenant bravely patrolling the Mekong Delta." When Kerry stood at the podium, the convention floor was organic

with energy. He declared that he was "reporting for duty." It was the culmination of a lifetime of ambition. Kerry saluted America on national television.
There were 17 mentions of the words "strength" or "strong" and 18 mentions
of the word "values." Kerry spoke powerfully, tapping the podium, a man confident of his place in providence. "I will wage this war," he said, "with the lessons
I learned in war."

It was too much. Americans like their heroes humble. George Washington
had emulated the Roman leader Cincinnatus by returning to his farm after the
war. Thereafter, the nation emulated Washington.

"Kerry overemphasized his military background at the convention," Carter
says, shaking his head. "It is ironic that the people that had accused him have
never been to war."

The night before Kerry spoke to the convention, I was sitting with George
McGovern, wrinkled and thin, his crackled voice nearly drowned by the convention noise. More than three decades after the Democratic Party had nominated
him, McGovern believes Kerry could challenge another wartime Republican
president and win what he could not. "[In Kerry's speech] he has got to show that
he is a man of strength, that he is decisive," McGovern said. "I think we are
going to win this time," he quietly adds. But then McGovern was, if anything,
the candidate of optimists.

Kerry was still fighting McGovern's fight. His momentum during the primary race was built upon an edifice of Purple Hearts. Each medal, each action to
demean those medals, was at its core a battle over Kerry's manhood.

"The Democrats know they have to have somebody that is combative,"
Richard Nixon's advisor Kevin Phillips told me during the Democratic primary
race. "If they aren't combative they reinforce every male view that they are the
feminine party."

What Americans took away from the convention was that Kerry served in
Vietnam, nothing more. Kerry's candidacy was gambled on his war record, and
therefore, his manhood. At the Democratic convention, only 14 percent of
delegates said they left the Republican Party. In comparison, at the Republican
convention, twice that number of delegates, 28 percent, had left the Democratic
Party.[18] In every respect, Kerry had the harder task. Bush had to live up to the
best perceptions of Republicans. Kerry was forced to disprove the worst perceptions of Democrats. In this effort, though overdone, a campaign of strength was
the right bet. But when it came time to fight, to punch back, he and his campaign hesitated.

THE FORESEEN ATTACK: SWIFT BOATS

Kerry wanted to respond when a right-wing group of Swift Boat veterans put out their first round of attack ads in August 2004. "As soon as this stuff came out, he was outraged by it and irate," Kerry's chief strategist, Tad Devine, recalls. "His impulse was very much, 'Let's have a big fight about this.'" But the senior staff pushed back. "We knew that the moment we engage it, it is guaranteed to be a free media story because of the outrageousness of the claims. And we thought, try to hold back, try to hold back, for several days, and while that's going on, the thing builds because it has outlets like Fox and others who are broadcasting it nonstop. But, we were concerned about if it transfers to the mainstream media. Once the big networks and the big newspapers answer this thing in the fray, we know we're going to deal with it for days. And so, we hold back until we get to a point where we see and it is clear that this thing is damaging us. Meanwhile, John's impulse is to fight, fight, fight."

On his lunch break with two fellow air conditioning repairmen, Fred Billings tells me the month the ads first aired, that "when all this ruckus came up about his war experience that's now in the media, I feel like he should stand up and say, this was the way it was in 1968, and this is what we had to do; *we were soldiers*," he says. "Rather than try and backpedal whether what was politically correct now was politically correct in 1968. I think he should say what it is to the voters, and let the chips fall where they may."

Devine regrets that they did not attack the first salvos by Bush, when surrogates began questioning his patriotism for protesting the war. It was "my mistake," he says, though other senior officials gave similar advice. "Obviously [I was] too much lawyer and not enough soldier," Devine continues. "Not that I'm a soldier. I'm a lawyer. That's my problem. I needed to *not* be a lawyer. I needed to appeal to the gut in [Kerry]." He adds, "We should have pleaded guilty to being tough and stayed with it, because really, it was much truer to John."

What happened to Gore happened to Kerry. They were too isolated. Both were once passionate men who found their passion again after their failed presidential bids. They rose within their party, were processed by polling, preserved by advice, and by the time they were packaged for the public, they seemed packaged.

"Comparing Clinton and the draft with Kerry's war record, with [George W.] Bush and the draft," political analyst Charlie Cook says, "I think it shows that a liberal from Massachusetts even with a distinguished record could manage to get hit harder than two people who did everything in their power to avoid the draft, who were from very different backgrounds. It goes back to the stereotypes."

In the end, Kerry lost over the issue of grit. His character was undone by the Swift Boat ads and a comment in October 2003, a year after voting to support the use of force in Iraq. His vote against the $87 billion in supplemental funding for Iraq, and the explanation that, "I actually did vote for the $87 billion before I voted against it," only reinforced prevailing perceptions. It was this indecisive rhetoric that was contrasted with Bush's intent to "take the fight to the enemy." As a commoner, Bush was false. But in terms of masculinity, for its good and bad repercussions, Bush had plenty.

"Democrats are completely confused, and remain so, as to how white middle class men could, in that old-fashioned mode of masculinity, see George Bush, our present George Bush, as being one of them. I mean after all, he comes from a privileged class, went to an elite university, and is adept at passing legislation that will keep the wealthiest .25 percent of the United States citizens from ever paying an inheritance tax," psychologist William Pollack says. "Yet he is seen as one of them. But he reaches out in a kind of folksy way and talks about the kinds of issues so that they feel culturally as if he understands them."

Bush was a president intent on bringing back the nobility of the common man. He championed mediocrity. His populism was both anti-elite, anti-intellectual, and at its essence, against all that implied the regular white workingman was passé.

"We have a cabin up in northern Michigan and I was up there on vacation in the summer of 2004, between the conventions," political writer David Broder recalls. "And Bush came through Traverse City, Michigan during a political swing. The headline across eight columns on the *Traverse City Record Eagle* the day after his visit was a quote from his speech talking about himself, and the quote was, 'a plain-spoken fella.' F-E-L-L-A. I took the paper in to see my wife—who is a yellow dog Democrat—I said if he wins this election, this is the reason, because, I mean, first of all, it seemed like an accurate description of himself. Second—in contrast to John Kerry, whom you have to listen very carefully to parse what the exact meaning of what he was saying, and it might not be the same today as what it was yesterday or tomorrow—that notion, that what you see is what you get, was a very powerful and appealing notion for a country at war."

Only weeks before Election Day 2004, the CBS News/*New York Times* poll found that of those polled, six out of ten Americans believed that Kerry "says what people want to hear," while less than four out of ten believe Kerry "says what he believes." For President Bush the numbers were reversed.[19] This is most notable because it was one of the president's few positive ratings. Bush's approval rating fell below 50 percent overall as Election Day neared, as did his approval on the war in Iraq and the economy. About six out of ten Americans even said they believed the country was on the wrong track.[20] By historical measure, these should have been damning electoral statistics for an incumbent. They weren't. Republicans had Bush's grit to thank.

The true acumen of Karl Rove's strategy was not in his microtargeting. That helped to bring out the Republican base. But Rove never would have rallied the base, if he did not understand that in a time of war, it is strength of character that wins the race.

Bush was perpetually concerned with appearing strong, both mentally and physically. When *Sports Illustrated* asked its readers to name the better athlete, Bush or Kerry, they far and away said Bush, though the managing editor handicapped Kerry as the "much better athlete."[21] By the close of the campaign, Kerry made efforts to win back his manhood. Americans saw footage of Kerry watching the playoffs, beer in hand, on a couch among men, as the Boston Red Sox pulled off the improbable victory over the New York Yankees. Kerry went hunting once more, walking out of an Ohio cornfield with four dead geese. But it was too late. One NRA ad exemplified how Kerry had been sissified. The NRA put out a print advertisement picturing a poodle prancing with a Kerry sweater on, across the top of the page. Beneath the poodle, in large type, was, "That dog don't hunt." In explaining Kerry's gun stance below, it used liberal buzzwords like "Ted Kennedy," "big city," and "Rosie O'Donnell." In bold type it read: "If John Kerry wins, you lose."

Bravado is a quality, either real or imagined, that indicates courage or boldness. In Bush, it felt real. In Kerry, it did not. But it was not entirely Kerry's fault. He inherited a softened party that emerged in 1972 but had roots in 1948 with Henry Wallace and the "doughface progressives," as Arthur Schlesinger called them. In our collective memory, George W. Bush stood on top of that pile at Ground Zero and it won him the election.

Kerry won more votes than any Democrat in history, but Bush won more. The Republican earned the support of over 60 million Americans, winning by a comfortable margin of 3 million votes, or 3 percentage points. Democrats pointed out that if 70,000 more votes would have gone to Kerry in Ohio, they would have won. That was the math of a minority party hoping to eke out a victory. A majority party hoping to win and sustain the White House forms a winning coalition and campaigns with it. In contrast, Democrats have campaigned to Americans and hoped a coalition would follow. On Election Day, there was no mistaking the fact that Bush had done what no Democrat had for a quarter century: Bush won a majority.

Once more, a Republican had won by holding the White Male Gap and splitting or winning white women. It was white women who gave Bush a comfortable margin instead of a slight victory. Bush won 56 percent of white women to Kerry's 44 percent, an improvement for the Republican of 5 percentage points—though still 1 percentage point *less* white female support than his father had earned in 1988. Bush also increased 1 percent among white men in comparison to 2000, earning 63 percent of white men to Kerry's 37 percent.[22]

Overall, Bush won white women by 13 points and white men by 26 points. White women were more liberal, less conservative, and more Democratic by 2004.[23] But the same issues and characteristics that were winning men for Bush, were also winning women. More black women backed Kerry than black men.[24]

Bush won white men in every region.[25] He won white men at every level of education, while Kerry only won white women with postgraduate degrees. Bush again won *every* income bracket of white men. Kerry defeated Bush among white women with annual household incomes under $30,000.

The return of war to American life allowed Republicans to flex their greatest political asset. When voters were asked which issue mattered most in the election, 26 percent of white women and 23 percent of white men said moral values. But for men, the largest response was the 24 percent who said terrorism, in comparison to 18 percent among women, their second largest response. The only significant gender gap among all the answers was terrorism. The facts entirely countered the analysis following the 2004 election. "Security mom" was another gender gap myth. White women were not consumed with fears of terrorism, at least not to the extent of their concerns about moral values. The lesson of 2004 was said to be a lesson of women. And the story of men was forgotten all over again.

XIX

THE POLITICAL CULTURE OF WHITE MANHOOD
Taxed, Downsized, Emasculated, Dreaming, Believing, and Antagonized

EMASCULATED WHITE MANHOOD

The Incredible Shrinking Man captured the emerging anxieties of some 1950s men. It was the story of a man who becomes smaller, loses his job, his wife, and is unable to keep up with the world. It debuted in theaters the same year that Humphrey Bogart died. Bogart had defined World War II era manhood. Three of his more famous films came out during the war—*The Maltese Falcon, To Have and Have Not,* and *Casablanca.* The American Film Institute's Greatest Male Star of All Time was also one of the most traditionally masculine. In *Casablanca,* Bogart personifies World War II era manhood. He is respected for his simple decisive manner and individual ingenuity, and though he may not be good, once he becomes part of the noble cause, he finds his own noble manhood.

The new man in the 1970s was to be gentler and sensitized. Bogart's characters were to give way to Alan Alda's. But almost immediately as the change was underway, men found themselves wishing they had not signed on. By 1972, an entirely different kind of manhood was now presented in Woody Allen's films. His lead male characters were sensitive, insecure, and indecisive. They felt unable to shape their own lives. In *Play It Again, Sam*, released the year Nixon won reelection, Bogart becomes the alter ego of Allen's character. In order to improve his life, the enfeebled man of the 1970s reaches back for the strength of the idealized man of the 1940s and 1950s.

Social critics were beginning to second-guess the sensitized man by the mid-1980s. An issue of *New Woman* warned: "The Wimp not only eats quiche, he makes it. But you'll have to pay for the ingredients." When the *New York Times Magazine* declared the arrival of "The New Man," one writer compared it to the "new Nixon."[1] Like Nixon, it was only a matter of time until the old man returned.

WHITE MEN CAN'T JUMP

During an ESPN roundtable in June 2005, the last white basketball superstar, Larry Bird, commented that the NBA might benefit from more white stars. "I think it's good for a fan base because as we all know, the majority of the fans are white America," he said on the televised broadcast. "And if you just had a couple of white guys in there, you might get them a little excited." Accusations abounded: Bird the bigot. As columnist Leonard Pitts Jr. pointed out after, "Blacks have become so dominant in the major sports that, according to a 1997 *Sports Illustrated* survey, many white kids have given up competing in the sports. They say they feel intimidated by black players who seem not just faster and stronger, but—key point—'hungrier.'"

The premiere professional sports in the United States are progressively a field of ultra-talented, ultra-elite, and ultra-rich minorities. White men are finding it harder to compete. Steve Nash stands out in part because he is such a clear exception. Consider that four out of five men are white in the United States. In the 2005–2006 NBA season only one out of five players were white men. Blacks make up nearly three-quarters of all players, yet they are only about 15 percent of men in the United States. It was this reality that inspired the film *White Men Can't Jump* (1992), in which the white man, played by Woody Harrelson, perpetually aspires not only to the athletic talent of the black man, Wesley Snipes, but in a more subtle sense, to the calm coolness that Snipes embodies.

While most quarterbacks in the NFL are white—though blacks in this position are increasing—the quarterback is the *only* star position left in which whites dominate. Offensive linemen are the unsung pawns of football. Overall, in the 2005 NFL season, 66 of every 100 men were black and 32 were white (a decrease in white players of 7 percent alone since 1990). In professional baseball, white men's representation falls short of their percent of the population. But they're heavily represented nonetheless, often because baseball is easier to play in rural areas. Six out of ten baseball players are white, three out of ten are Hispanic, and the remaining are black.[2] Yet in the past five years, among the 12 most valuable players in the two divisions of major league baseball, only *one* has been a white male. American white men are all but gone from professional boxing. In golf, the sport of blue-blooded white men, the best player is Tiger Woods, a black man.

The effect is a lessening of white male athletic icons. Auto racing and hockey remain extremely popular across rural and suburban America. They are the last leading sports where white men generally excel. But NASCAR is not a sport of brawn and hockey falls well short of the national stature of basketball, boxing, football, and baseball. White boys and young men may be withdrawing from sports as they find it harder to compete in the premiere athletics. Today, many white boys are forced to look elsewhere for their masculine role models. The soldier becomes one of the last refuges of physical white male stature.

"As a matter of collective ego, the good average white American male had had very little to nourish his morale since the job market had gone bad, nothing, in fact, unless he happened to be a member of the armed forces," Norman Mailer wrote after the onset of the war in Iraq. "For better or worse, the women's movement has had its breakthrough successes and the old, easy white male ego has withered in the glare," Mailer added. "Even the consolation of rooting for his team on TV had been skewed. For many, there was now measurably less reward in watching sports than there used to be, a clear and declarable loss. The great white stars of yesteryear were for the most part gone."[3]

The repercussion may be a withdrawal from athletics. There were signs in 2005 that this was occurring in the marketplace. Based on national tracking of sporting goods sales, the number of American men boxing in the United States fell about one quarter; the decline of those wrestling was more precipitous; football uniform sales did not keep up with population increases beginning in 1987; and shotgun and rifle hunting declined 35 percent between 1987 and 2000.[4] Many white men may seek new expressions of their manhood outside athletics and new masculine role models outside professional sports. The affirmation of traditional masculinity in leadership may become that much more important in presidents, due to its absence in daily life. At the turn of the century it seemed the traditional leading man was fading from film as well.

RECLAIMING WHITE MASCULINITY

Hollywood's young white male stars by 2000 were a more sensitized breed: Leonardo DiCaprio, Joaquin Phoenix, Tobey Maguire, and Jake Gyllenhaal. Termed the "metrosexual," the trend was felt throughout the marketplace. In 1999, men's bath and shower products were a $2 million market. By 2003, it had grown to a $19.3 million market. Over the same period, men's skin care products grew from $3.9 million to $13.8 million.[5] When asked "How important is it to you to be physically attractive?" among whites, fully 78 percent of women say it is "very important" or "somewhat important" and 67 percent of men did also.[6]

As quickly as feminized men sought recognition in adornment, men also sought to regain their manhood. In 1997, *Maxim* magazine came to the United States, with its bikini girl covers, and a "lad fad" of men's magazines followed. On Comedy Central's "The Man Show," Adam Carolla and Jimmy Kimmel featured a beer-guzzling man. The show ended with girls jumping on trampolines. As one person commented, "if you say it's degrading to women you're missing the point." Films released in the same year, such as *Office Space* and *Fight Club*, told the stories of white men awakening themselves from the passive corporate life and combating or challenging that which emasculated them.

The new trend was to be übermasculine. It was an assertion that white men were no longer ashamed to be men, and emulated other earlier movements before them. The 1970s afro had been symbolic of "Black is beautiful." As gay culture had reclaimed the word "queer," white men were reclaiming their manhood.

During the Bush-Kerry race, American men aged 25 to 55 rated society as far more feminine than they rated themselves. Fully 84 percent of men saw themselves as masculine or macho. In comparison, 58 percent of men saw society as feminine while 42 percent saw it as masculine or macho. But in a personal crisis, men still value a quality they view as female: 67 percent said they would turn to a woman.[7]

A decade after *Maxim* hit American newsstands, the revival of traditional masculinity remained a popular motif in advertising. Miller Lite's "Man Laws" featured Burt Reynolds and other famous men sitting around tables discussing pressing issues, like dating a friend's ex and deciding what "man law" dictates is appropriate. *Maxim* began a satirical ad campaign to help men win back their masculinity by creating instructional websites.[8]

Burger King's "Manthem" ad campaign showed a man with a woman seated at a nice restaurant with a petite dish of food. The white man gets up. The girl is confused, as he begins singing, "I am man, hear me roar." He walks out the restaurant's door, adding, "and I'm way too hungry to settle for chick food." His voice lowers as he crosses the street. Suddenly, men of every race and size march in, holding their burgers, singing "yes, I'll admit I've been fed quiche" (aghast, sighs are heard), as one man karate chops a brick, skinny men flex, and they sing, "I will eat this meat!" Fortuitously, cheerleaders appear, as men pull off their own underwear and burn them (a reference to the 1970s feminist movement's burning of bras, to be sure). Then they destroy a minivan, the symbol of modern emasculation. Men hold their burgers high. The voiceover says, "Eat like a man, man."

There was a sad quality within this trend. These men became cartoons of themselves. The classic man has a quiet power and these men were portraying a braggart's masculinity, often pathetically overt. That these were nearly always white men was unmistakable.

DUMB DOWN DADS

Contemporary television shows such as *Married with Children*, *The Simpsons*, and *Everybody Loves Raymond* portray a stupefied, somewhat dysfunctional, and disrespected regular white male. Al Bundy, Homer Simpson, and Raymond Barone are the polar opposites of the glorified father figures of the past. Ward Cleaver, of *Leave It to Beaver*, or Jim Anderson Sr., of *Father Knows Best*, were dignified, wise, and responsible. It is not that those examples were ideal, but today's male characters often represent the opposite extreme. Today, they are little more than incompetent yet lovable fools, contrasting the put together, responsible, modern woman.

In 2002, social psychologist William Pollack asked a focus group of boys ages 7 to 12 to characterize television fathers. Boys said the dads were "funny" and "silly," not nurturing or strong. None of the more recent shows such as *According to Jim*, *Arrested Development*, or *Still Standing* give boys reason to think otherwise.

"Boys will say in a positive way, 'well I like the men because they are funny,'" Pollack says. "But the characters aren't really funny, but kind of ridiculous. And they can't think of too many male characters, other than violent ones, that they can identify with."

It is not that the portrayal of husbands as bumbling is a new phenomenon. *The Flintstones* certainly accomplished that. But when the cartoon strips became real life, in a time when white manhood was portrayed as complicit in every societal ill, the "dumb down dad" sitcom came to reflect a "defrocking" of masculinity. *The Honeymooners*, like *All in the Family*, echoed the negative conception of the working-class white man.

In the 1990s, Robert Bly's writings won a large following, mostly among whites. Father after father, he noticed, were "convinced" they were an "inadequate human being." He observed, "Women have been telling him that for 30 to 40 years. He doesn't know how to talk; he can't express himself; he doesn't know what his feelings are. People hear what they hear. Your father feels that he's okay when he's with a hammer but in every other way he is inadequate." Bly later added, "I would say that the primary experience of the American man now is the experience of being inadequate." At Bly's retreats men played drums, listened to poetry, sat around campfires, went to sweat lodges, and talked. In a PBS special on Bly, when Bill Moyers began asking white men why they attend these retreats, two men answered:

> *Man one:* I feel safer talking with men than I do with women kinda in this vein, that I can tell you what I think about you and if it hurts you somehow that doesn't affect me. But if you are a woman and I told you something that hurt you, somehow I'd be responsible for hurting you. But if you're male, take it.
>
> *Man two:* One of the reasons I came, because there seems to be for years an incredible lack of strong men, clear men, powerful men in this world. And Robert Bly is one of those men of power. And I always grew up believing that nature abhorred a vacuum. And what I see is that we've gotten so close to a complete vacuum of powerful male men in this world, male models of clarity.[9]

Betty Friedan criticized Bly's efforts to toughen feminized males as reactionary. "I'd hoped by now that men were strong enough to accept their vulnerability and to be authentic without aping Neanderthal cavemen," she told one reporter in 1991.[10]

Friedan's criticism betrayed the reason behind Bly's popularity. If these men were reactionary, they were no more reactionary than the women in the movement Friedan had championed decades past. Men sought confidence that manhood was no longer a "liability," as Norman Mailer put it. Bly's movement understood what modern liberalism did not. White men were losing a sense of the masculine role model, as well as of personal manhood. These men were not seeking to find their manhood to control others. They were hoping to find their manhood to have more control over their own lives.

TAXES, RUGGED INDIVIDUALISM, AND THE AMERICAN DREAM

When progressive evangelical preacher Jim Wallis was in Los Angeles on Michael Medved's conservative talk radio show, it turned into a debate over tax policy. After Wallis spoke to the moral obligation for government programs to help the poor, Medved took two calls.

> Quentin in Zimmerman, Minnesota: My big beef with you liberals and Democrats is you like to keep poor people in programs and its' sustainability to keep them poor, like a mother is tied to the baby's umbilical cord. . . . Until that umbilical cord is cut and severed the baby cannot become a child. I don't understand if you really are for the poor why don't you make programs that cease.

> Paul in Amarillo, Texas: Most middle-class Americans, lower-middle class, have worked their butts off to get the little bit that they have and they are sick and tired of people with their hands out. They are sick and tired of the tax money gets taken away from them. Look, most poor people—and this is a fact, ok, this is not me saying it—most poor people are poor by choice. They are poor because they have kids, a lot of them usually, before they are financially able to take care of 'em. And also, they refuse to do what it takes. . . .[11]

The show ends soon after. Medved stands up. He tells Wallis, "It's going to be really tough for people with only a high school diploma to get a job in a postindustrial economy."

Wallis shakes hands with Medved and says goodbye. As we walk out of the studio, Wallis tells me, "The problem with that last caller is that he's blaming from the bottom up. He's looking up and blaming down. I think you should blame up and look down."

White men simply do not blame up. When Americans were asked, "What if the tax was only collected on estates worth more than $1.5 million? Then would you favor or oppose placing this tax on assets when someone dies?" A majority of every class of whites did not favor the tax—69 percent of white men opposed it while 56 percent of white women did as well.

However, slightly over four out of five Americans believe there is "some" tension today between the rich and poor. About four out of ten minorities believe there is "a lot" of class tension while 26 percent of white men and 30 percent of white women feel the same.[12] But moderate class tension, among the vast majority of Americans, does not translate into calls to further tax the well-off. This explains, in part, why conventional economic populism repeatedly fails to win presidencies.

MOBILITY, BIG GOVERNMENT, AND WHITE MALES

Humorist Will Rogers once commented, "You can't lick this prosperity thing. Even the fellow that hasn't got any is all excited over the idea."[13] White men more than any other demographic believe in the "prosperity thing." While white men agree with white women on opportunities in society, they more strongly believe they will be able to succeed in their lifetime.

When asked, "Looking ahead, how likely is it that you will ever be financially wealthy?" and given several options, among whites, fully 51 percent of white men and 36 percent of white women said that they were "somewhat or very likely to become wealthy," 31 percent of men and 37 percent of women said it was "not very likely," while about 16 percent of white men and 24 percent of white women said it was "not at all likely." All tax politics flows from this reality.

When Americans were asked if the "very rich have too much power," 77 percent of white women, 70 percent of white men, and 69 percent of minorities said yes. But white males are not willing to take that power by significantly increasing taxes on rich Americans.

White men, however, are indeed more class conscious than white women. About half of white males believe it is "essential" or "very important" to have a wealthy family to get ahead, while only a third of white women agree. But white women put more emphasis on hard work. Fully 55 percent of women say it is "essential" to success while 47 percent of men say the same. In comparison, 44 percent of white men and 38 percent of white women believe to succeed it is "essential" or "very important" to know the right people.

When whites are asked about their greatest financial concerns, almost half answered either that they don't have enough money, are worried about losing their jobs, or can't afford healthcare. More white women (76 percent) are worried about retirement than are white men (66 percent).[14]

It's difficult to see how Democrats can successfully tout bigger government programs when the summation of these findings is considered. Even during welfare reform in 1996, only about a fifth of whites with less than $30,000 in annual household income, and slightly more women, believed that it "cuts too much."[15]

Republicans compound the issue for Democrats by clouding the effect of tax cuts. During the third debate of the 2004 campaign, Bush said that most of the tax cuts went to low- and middle-income Americans. That was dishonest. A majority went to Americans with incomes in the top 10 percent.[16] For decades, Democrats have seen these inequities as their electoral opening.

"I think the persistent and I think, gross, favoring of extremely rich people in this country is beginning to seep into the consciousness of the people that are not extremely rich," Jimmy Carter tells me from his home in Georgia. "And they are seeing that even at this moment Bush [and his] administration are pushing for tax breaks for the very wealthy while they are cutting veterans benefits and other social issues with which you are familiar." Carter crosses his legs and points his wrinkled hand outward. "At the same time a lot of fiscally conservative people, men and women, see these incredibly great deficits, and I use the word 'incredibly' deliberately—they are hard to believe as a sign of mismanagement or lack of management. And of course, the total subversion of a protectiveness of government services. People see it vividly with what's happening in Iraq and what happened in the Katrina area. . . . I think the misapplication of basic principles in the management of government, including the deficits, and things I need not repeat, are beginning to sink into the country."

But for Carter to be right, government services have to be redefined to focus on need instead of on groups. As long as the white working class, half of the American electorate today, is suspect of government services, they will be suspect of Democrats as well.[17] The problem is fundamentally among white men. Unless white men see government programs that ease their burden, they will stand against all forms of taxation.

Class politics especially fails for Democrats because whites fundamentally do not see class barriers, though they are conscious of divisions. Nine out of ten whites believe it is possible "to start out poor in this country, work hard, and become rich." Four out of ten whites believe they have "already" reached the "American Dream," as they define it (only a quarter of minorities do), while more than a third of whites believe they will "some day."

White men are significantly more optimistic that they will be able to achieve their ambitions. Almost half of white men in the broad middle class, with annual household incomes between $30,000 and $75,000, believe it is "somewhat likely" they will be wealthy some day.[18]

The common belief among liberals is that Republicans win these men by noneconomic means and then make their economic livelihood worse by instituting policies such as Bush's tax cuts. Republicans have offered these men few economic incentives. Demonstrably, GOP tax policy under Bush is bad for the average man. But Democrats have failed to address white men's economic plight and wrongly believe they can rebuff Republican tax policy by placing the rich in adversarial terms. Republicans meet white men's noneconomic desires, while Democrats offer no clear economic cure, and culturally aggravate white males in the process.

The liberal mistake, nonetheless, is presuming that white men will take this insult for the right amount of money in tax policy or safety nets. "How we feel about ourselves, to get up in the morning and be able to sleep at night, counts more than a bunch of numbers that are hard to interpret," William Pollack says. "And I think Americans know they hear the same numbers every four to eight years and nothing much changes for them anyway."

In 2003, Roper pollsters asked the poorest men: "Do you think this tax plan benefits mainly the rich or benefits everyone?" Tellingly, two-thirds believed the plan primarily helped the wealthy but a majority still favored the plan.[19]

The Republicans' lead man on taxes, Grover Norquist, explains that for white men, "You had the same problem in '84 when Democrats were the compassion party. Which is the compassion party? The Democrats. Who you voting for? The Republicans. Why? Because compassion means you may raise my taxes."

"I don't like the nanny state," Republican voter Gaylen Fischer tells me after the midterm elections in 2006, at a diner in Iowa, after I ask why he did not vote Democratic for president, but did locally. He adds, "Most of my friends are self-reliant people," and this, he infers, means they would not favor Democrats.

If part of manhood is the ability to provide, taxes inevitably come to represent a tax on that manhood. When voters were asked in 2004 whether government should do more to solve their problems or less, there was a vast difference between white men and women. For those making under $30,000 a year, 58 percent of white women believed government should do more while only 42 percent of white men believed the same. The middle and upper class polls had almost the same findings.[20] Poor white men agree with rich white men. They see government providing them little assistance while it undermines their well being, so they stand against it.

"That is fascinating," Richard Wirthlin says, after I read him the finding. "It reflects the gender gap, in my view, in ideological terms. The whole issue of governance gets involved in the gender gap. But it also gives an advantage to Republicans running for president for this reason, not that we have to appeal to our own constituencies as openly or as vigorously by declaiming generally, or more specifically that government should do less. But the hook is that the Democrats' constituency—again blue collar, labor, less affluent—those are more likely to be the recipients of government services—will be tethered to an anchor, that will prevent them from rebuffing or inoculating against a Republican who claims— and you've got to be careful about how strongly he claims—but who leans toward government should do less."

White men oppose the taxes that fund big government because, unlike during the New Deal and under the G. I. Bill (when the benefits of big government were theirs too), the 1960s' government programs such as welfare, affirmative action, and Medicaid assist all Americans except, in the great majority of cases, those who are white and male. Social Security was taken for granted by white men as well as most Americans through the dusk of the twentieth century. But for a large majority of those white men not on Social Security or Medicare, there seemed little to gain for losing half their income to taxes.

"Some in the Democratic Party want to go back to the us-against-them seventies populism. And a large part of the *us* would be the working-class white male, but they don't feel part of that *us*," Mark Warner says. "They feel part of the establishment. They view themselves as middle class or will get to middle class in a way and they *don't* believe that the Democrats' social and government-run programs are going to get them there."

THE DOWNSIZED MAN

"Most of the elected Democratic leaders in Ohio were on this platform but I was standing next to John Glenn. John Kerry gave this great talk, about 20,000 to 25,000 people there. Then [Kerry] went down to the field to start shaking hands with a few folks," AFL-CIO's president John Sweeney recalls, resting his arms on the table, scrunched forward, wearing yellow suspender straps and a light blue shirt. Sweeney is bald, with narrow, stern eyebrows. The son of Irish immigrants, he was born during FDR's first term. We sit in the conference room at the union's national headquarters in Washington, the White House directly below, as he recalls a 2004 rally in Akron, Ohio.

"John Glenn and I saw these two young men approaching [Kerry]. They were guys in their late 20s, I would say, who had on Bush T-shirts. And as they got up to Kerry to shake his hand, we saw that Kerry was spending a minute or two more with them than he was with the others that he was greeting. Then we got on the bus to go off to our next stop. I said to Senator Kerry, 'So how was that conversation with those two Bush fans?' He said, 'It was interesting.' In the short time he determined that one was employed and the other was unemployed. One had some form of health insurance but no pension. And the other had no health converge. After their brief stories, he said to them, 'Why are you supporting President Bush?' They said it was about gay marriage; it was about gun control; and it was about the whole abortion question. He said, 'Well what about your jobs, your health care, your retirement security?' They said, 'Those are important but our values are what's driving us.' And I guess," Sweeney adds, "that's the story that we've heard so often."

For decades, it was only unionization that kept some white men Democratic. But the typical white male blue-collar jobs that were unionized are fading. Shortly before I met with Sweeney, Ford Motor Company announced it was cutting its staff by one-third, or 14,000 jobs, and offering buyout packages to all of its 75,000 U.S. factory workers.[21] The fewer industrialized jobs, the fewer male union members. The fewer white men in unions, the fewer white men that are sure Democratic votes. In Iowa, ground zero in presidential politics, only about 10 percent of its workforce was unionized in 2004 compared to about 17 percent in the mid 1980s.[22]

The United States has the lowest level of unionization in 60 years. In the 1950s, 35 percent of the workforce was unionized. During the Bush-Kerry race, according to the Bureau of Labor Statistics, only 12.5 percent of the labor market was unionized. If public sector employees were removed, the percentage fell to 7.9 percent.[23] Making matters worse, in the summer of 2005, the Service Employees International Union (SEIU) and the Teamsters left the AFL-CIO. The splintering among the major American unions has only further diminished Big Labor's ability to counter Big Business. In 1984, for the first time, Democratic candidates earned more contributions from corporations than labor.[24] By 2004, businesses gave $1.5 billion to federal candidates of both parties, while labor gave only $61.6 million.[25] For the blue party, the problem is not merely one of less muscle to organize Democrats, the problem is that there is also less money to pour into the Democratic Party, especially from its one traditional working-class bloc.

The repercussions fall upon the whole of the workforce. At least 46 million Americans are without health insurance (almost 7 million more than in 2000).[26] Defined benefits have also become nearly extinct. In 1980, 28 percent of workers had defined benefit pensions (by 2003, 5 percent), while the median 401K balance for people 55 to 59 was $15,000, not enough to fund a half year, let alone a retirement.[27]

The de-unionization of America correlates both to the loss of defined benefits and the drastically rising wage gap. It is the nature of the wage gap that illustrates why the immense success of a small number of white men is wrongly presumed to reach the majority. In 2004, the real income of the richest 1 percent of Americans surged by almost 12.5 percent, even when excluding capital gains on investments, while the average real income of the bottom 99 percent of Americans rose merely 1.5 percent.[28] In other words, "trickle down" doesn't work.

"The Democratic Party stopped being for unions, stopped being for workers, and those people in the way it had been since the 1930s," says Michael Podhorzer, who helps lead the AFL-CIO's political department. "Rather than putting the emphasis on the fact that the Democrats were now trying to expand what government was doing on behalf of others in America, it was that the Democratic Party was suddenly not coming through for workers, and for unions in particular." He later adds, "As the Democratic Party became less credible to workers, as fewer workers were in unions to mediate all of this, the Republicans discovered and became more and more skilled at exploiting cultural issues."

Unions are attempting to rally unorganized workers, as well as to fight for health care and retirement security, to boost their waning influence. Their efforts to reach beyond the union ranks reflect how anemic they have become. Although union members remain Democratic—65 percent backed Kerry—there are fewer of them. From 1983 to 2003, the number of union members decreased in 36 of the 50 states. Kerry won a majority of whites, men or women, in union households.[29]

The de-unionization of America at the blue-collar level means that the one structural body that kept white men Democrats is dissolving. Sweeney believes that white workingmen can still be reached, if Democrats only recognize that they face economic realities similar to minorities. "Democrats stopped defending the working-class white male's economic interests," he says, adding that "the whole business that Democrats have failed, on message," Sweeney shirks back, waves the idea off like a bug. "They have left the issues that are important to workers!"

The white workingman no longer earns the highest salary of racial groups. Among median weekly earnings of full-time wage and salary workers, Asian men's earnings exceed white men's by about $100 a week. Asian women's earnings also exceed white women's but by a smaller amount.[30] It is as if white America did not have a racist history with Asians (Japanese internment camps in World War II or the terrible Chinese exclusion laws throughout the Old West). Asians are now incorporated in the American dream.

Much of the decline, and stagnation, in white male income began with the recession of the 1970s. By the 1980s, as factories in Pittsburgh and Detroit began downsizing dramatically, it was white men who were hit hardest. They suffered a 53 percent loss of high-paying jobs, while there was a 97 percent increase in low-paid work for white men. "What struck me most," Michael Harrington wrote, "was the psychological impact of the possibility, or reality, of poverty upon them. In a sense it was precisely because they had once been confident members of a white, mainly male, working class that had battled the companies and won, that they were so devastated now. Almost all of them referred to themselves as 'middle class' and it was because of that self-image that they were so demoralized by, say, the fact that they no longer had health insurance (they lost it along with their jobs) and had to worry about medical care for their kids."[31]

Yet liberals paid little attention to white men, as factories closed, as their economic well-being became progressively destabilized, and generations of industrial workers were left to reinvent their livelihood, and therefore, their personal manhood. Democrats' attention was on the emerging movement to lift up women. But white men were facing a lowering concrete ceiling all their own.

"The workingman, he's going bye-bye," Democratic strategist and academic Elaine Kamarck says. "The trend is that they are disappearing. The center of the electorate is a much different electorate. Look whose incomes have lost most in the past 20 years, it's been working-class men, not working-class women. Men are in trouble in this economy and working-class blue-collar men with only high school educations are really in trouble," she continues. "What I say to you is, this is a transitory phenomenon because it is occurring in people who have expectations and see a cultural revolution, mostly a feminist revolution, making them poorer. You know, what Stan Greenberg called Joe-six-pack, they're gone, they're dying," she says, elevating her voice. "They are searching for a reason why they are not rich and in control, why they are making the same amount of money as their wives as opposed to substantially more money. They're looking for reasons. They need something to explain what is going on in their lives. The whole cultural populism thing provides them with a good reason. It's big government. It's these liberals. It's these femi-nazis."

Yet, sons who did not live through the civil rights or feminist movements vote Republican, as their fathers did under Nixon and Reagan, because white male support for the GOP is due far more to worldview than to blowback. Fully 61 percent of white men between the ages of 25 and 29 voted Republican in 2004, and more of that age group supported the GOP in 2000. Whether there is an industrial or information economy, the White Male Gap will continue as long as the political paradigm remains the same. When white men do poorly it does not lead them to Democrats, because dogmatic liberals have for decades pushed Democrats to side against the white workingman. But it is not merely white men who are having problems. Their sons are as well.

LOST BOYS

Boys are over 50 percent more likely than girls to repeat a grade in elementary school, one-third more likely to drop out of high school, and twice as likely to be identified as having a learning disability.[32] Without exception, this boy problem is worse among minorities, though this likely reflects class more than race. As feminists rightly point out, a component of this problem for all boys is the anti-intellectualism within machismo. But it also reflects a system that has focused on girls' educational weaknesses without giving equivalent consideration to boys' weaknesses. There is a striking difference in self-worth and self-expectations between boys and girls.

A 2003 study of schoolchildren found that 76 percent of boys felt their parents put a lot of pressure on them to do well in school, while only 64 percent of girls answered the same. But 90 percent of girls, compared to 85 percent of boys, wanted to go to college, 10 percent more girls said they wanted to go to graduate school (57 to 47), 6 percent more girls said school is a "thing you do to express yourself" (80 to 74), and 79 percent of girls said they received good grades compared to 60 percent of boys.[33] The results are best seen in high school and college as they eventually correlate to job prospects, marriage, happiness, and political persuasion.

Between 1970 and 2001, the number of young women enrolled in colleges went from 42 percent of all college students to 56 percent.[34] Only half of men, compared to six out of ten women, planned to graduate from college. In 1998, there was a 50–50 split of white men and white women in college from the middle class (household incomes of $30,000 to $70,000). By 2005, the proportion of white male college students from the middle class plummeted to 43 percent.[35] Men are less likely to graduate: 57 percent of women graduate college, as do 51 percent of men.[36] In 1948, men were 70 percent of all college students; by 1969 they were 59 percent. By 1979 they were 49 percent. Today, overall, men make up only 42 percent of the nation's two- and four-year college students.[37] Women now earn *more* bachelor's degrees in business than men and fully 100,000 more masters degrees were awarded to women in 2003–2004 than to men (men earned 41 percent of master's degrees that year).[38]

Clearly, this marks a decline in the education of white men since white men are the largest male group in the general population. In 1976, white men were 83 percent of the male college student population. In 2004, they were 68 percent. Among those men earning graduate degrees in the United States, white males have declined from 83 percent in 1976 to 63 percent in 2004.[39] Of all professional degrees—doctors, lawyers, dentists—conferred on males in 1977, 92 percent went to white men; in 1990, the figure was 87 percent. In 2004, 76 percent of professional degrees earned by men went to white men.[40]

More boys drop out of high school than girls.[41] High school boys still score higher than girls on the SATs, primarily due to the math section—the *New York Times* speculated it was "because the timed multiple-choice questions play to boys' strengths and because more middling female students take the test." But in time, the median girls' score will likely exceed that of boys. On the national assessment test, with a more diverse group of students (not merely those planning to attend college), twelfth-grade boys score "slightly better" on the math and science sections while scoring "far worse" than girls on reading and writing. More women graduated from Harvard with honors in the 2006 spring class than did men.[42]

WHITE MEN STRUGGLING

The problems of boys will likely prolong their problems as men. Between 1979 and 2003, women's earnings advanced 12 percent, while men's earnings declined 8 percent for those who did not attend college.[43] Though Democrats once championed the workingman, these men believe the party long ago left them behind.

"It's perceived that we speak for everybody but *them*," Democratic analyst Anna Greenberg puts it. "That we want to give everybody a fair shake but them. And in the meantime, they are getting screwed by the economy."

Joyless work has begun not to pay off for white men. At midcentury, the sacrifice served their family, their country, and their sense of manhood. But as their ability to provide decreases, these white men come to feel downsized in every respect of their life.

In John Updike's first of four Rabbit novels, when Harry leaves his girl, a minister asks why he walked out on her. "She asked me to buy a pack of cigarettes," he replies. When the minister persists, Harry adds that it simply felt too stifling, too mediocre, like a "muddle." "I once did something right," Harry says. "I played first-rate basketball. I really did. And after you're first-rate at something, no matter what, it kind of takes the kick out of being second-rate."[44]

As Norman Mailer tells me, "half of the male working class, particularly those that work with their bodies, could have been athletes, could have been criminals . . . but they decided at a given point in their lives they had a choice to make. Were they going to stick with their own tough gang," he continues, "or were they going to go into the tunnel of 9-to–5 for the rest of their lives and age as they saw the people around them aging—and that produced an unholy wrath in them. The unholy wrath is that 'I'm using up my life.'"

White men not only find it more difficult to make a living today; their sacrifices are disrespected. The grunt is a man to scoff at on television, as the "dumb-down dad," instead of someone to commend. The sacrifice these men make is demeaned. They are often seen as failing to capitalize on "white male privilege." All white men are perceived as starting from second base, instead of home plate. When they strike out, they're failed men. A living is to be made, and they are seen as not man enough for the task.

Today, many single white workingmen are retreating from this pressure. They are not remarrying after divorce and soon become less active civically. By the time men without college educations reach their early 40s, significantly more are unmarried compared to women.[45] Today, unmarried men make up one out of five American citizens. White men are seven out of ten of all unmarried and eight out of ten of all married men. Fewer unmarried men vote than unmarried women, but unmarried women still receive far more attention in registration drives. Unmarried men are 20 percent less likely to own a home than married men and are far less likely to go to church (51 percent of unmarried men never attend compared to 34 percent of unmarried women).[46]

"What happens is these disenfranchised white men may feel fed up with Bush but they don't see anyone on the Democratic or liberal party they'd rather go to," William Pollack says. "You can be up there speaking with your mouth going," Pollack says of a candidate, "but someone is looking at you and fantasizing about whether you really give a damn about who they are!"

"Liberals have to find a way to reach out to these disenfranchised men," Pollack continues. "And simultaneously let them see, these men themselves and the country, that they can also reach out to single mothers who are disenfranchised and that some of that pain is shared. I've actually seen in small townships, in kind of focus groups, where all of a sudden the so-called angry white male will hear from the theoretically radical women's lib single mom. It starts off with hatred and misunderstanding and then they both start talking about how they've been misunderstood and they can't get a job, have a lot of pain, have a lot of struggle, they weren't brought up to be who they turned out to be, they reach out to each other," Pollack says. "Because, as people they realize that they are both stuck in some kind of gender straight jacket that [prevents them from getting] anywhere. Why can't the politicians, particularly the liberal or Democratic politicians, find a way to give both messages? It doesn't have to be either-or."

Meanwhile, national Democrats did not address the effect of industrial outsourcing upon the white male working class. "Some of the first jobs to leave the country were the steel jobs, then the coal jobs," emphasizes John Murtha, who has served in Congress throughout this era. "I think it is about the manufacturing jobs that went away. Those are the kind of jobs men can do. They had to get new jobs that were not as demanding physically, that woman were as good at and could work side by side [with men]."

While seven out of ten Americans are against "outsourcing," they see a wave of it all around them.[47] White men feel it wash over them and pray not to be one more sap pulled under. Harlow Reseburg sees it daily. He's the project coordinator at Milwaukee's only dislocated-worker retraining center, housed in a restored factory beneath an overpass. Reseburg has white hair, long gray sideburns, thick arms, and a belly. His office deals with 1,800 to 2,400 dislocated workers at one time. Milwaukee, like so many cities in America, has graveyards of vacant plants. Reseburg commutes 48 miles daily to work and is a member of three unions, including the steel workers and machinists unions. After jobs are lost, union or not, his office is often the first, if only, network for the newly unemployed.

Dislocated workers are, Reseburg says, "insecure; there is a lot of fear. Press coverage is minimal. Many times when you have a large plant closing, there are suicides. They take the blame on themselves. Corporate America in New York decided to close a plant in Wisconsin," Reseburg tells me in the fall of 2006, in his blue shirt and black suspenders, clasping his POW-MIA coffee cup. He's a Vietnam veteran, as are his two brothers, and behind him are pictures of those brothers, mementos of service, and an American flag. Reseburg sees many white workingmen at their most vulnerable, fresh from being fired, sometimes after a binge at the bar, sometimes years later. It is only then some men reconcile themselves with the reality of being a man, unable to get work, and therefore unable to really be a man.

"Most definitely feel their whole self worth gets threatened," he tells me. "I worked with a human relations person from one of our larger employers and he was unemployed three years before I met him. He [continued to go] to work for 18 months, never told his wife that he lost his job. He spent close to $100,000 that he had in his savings account just to put on the show that he got up every morning and went to work. He went out and looked for work. This was in the mid '90s. He wanted to get the same $140,000 a year that he was making before he became unemployed. His first job that I found him was for $60,000. He lasted six weeks. Then he went to $30,000 and that lasted for six months."

If women had been stuck in a world that relegated femininity to house cleaning and child rearing, men were stuck in a world that relegated masculinity to the ability to provide for that house, for the money to feed the child, for their very happiness. Bill Moyers once recalled, "A male said to me once after years of standing on the platform of a subway, 'I die a little bit down there every day, but I know I am doing so for my family.'"[48]

Eight out of ten white men today believe women have as much responsibility to support the family as men (88 percent of white women agree). Still, in 2001, only 31 percent of married households had a wife as the lead wage earner, while as many men as women get a "real sense of belonging" from time with their family—76 percent of men and 78 percent of women.[49] That many men still have the responsibility of lead wage earner but yearn for more family time presents them with the constant awareness of sacrifice, a sacrifice that was perceived as honorable duty in the 1950s. One 2003 poll found that 65 percent of women are completely satisfied with the flexibility of their hours while 58 percent of men are.[50]

These same men are finding it more difficult to meet their expectations as lead wage earners. Men's earnings in 2005 were lower than their earnings in 1973, when adjusted for inflation.[51] The common workingman, over 25, made $34,532 annually in 1970. By 2003, he made $28,763 (in 2001 dollars).[52] Among those in the working class, and adjusting for inflation, between 1979 and 2003, the wages of men with some college, but no degree, remained stagnant, while women's wages rose by 20 percent.

"I did a focus group of white men who were under 30 for my unmarried project. They would never use the word despair," Anna Greenberg recalls. "But the despair I sensed in that room about what their future was going to look like and the thing they cared about most was a good paying job. And that dominated everything. Everything! They would never articulate it this way, but there is the sense that they are searching for the economic security their fathers had. It affects their ability to think they can get married. Of course, they all hate women. They are a bunch of misogynists," she adds, agitated. "I was just glad that they didn't know a woman was behind the glass. They think we are going to try and spend all their money."

But why wouldn't young men question their capacity to marry without the right job? Why would they not think finances matter to women? The reason is larger than the popular television series *Sex and the City*, in which women who are every bit as professional as Greenberg adore rich, powerful, and handsome male characters.

When men between the ages of 25 and 55 were asked who their role models were, the list betrayed the archetype young men *still* emulate. They were men of money and power. Bill Gates ranked first (28 percent), George W. Bush (22 percent), Derek Jeter (14 percent), Bill Clinton (11 percent), Donald Trump (9 percent), and Sean "P. Diddy" Combs (2 percent).[53]

As Warren Farrell wrote, history books are "500 pages of advertisements for the performer role." He argued that, "Each lesson tells [a man], 'if you perform, you will get love and respect; if you fail, you will be nothing.' To a boy, history is pressure to perform, not relief from pressure. Feminism is relief from the pressure to be confined to only the traditional female role. To a boy, then, history is not the equivalent of women's studies; it is the opposite of women's studies." Farrell continued, "The men who are successful have become the most dependent on success to attract love. When this man loses his success, he often fears he will lose love."[54] And with good reason: Working class men have twice the divorce rate of men with college degrees.[55]

To this day there remains a sense that unemployment falls harder on a man's pride, if only because more of him remains wrapped up in his ability to provide. As writer Jonathan Mahler put it, "women have been hit as hard as men, but white-collar men tend to experience unemployment differently, organizational psychologists say. For most women, survival trumps ego; they simply adapt and find some job. For men, grappling with joblessness inevitably entails surrendering an idea of who they are—or who others thought they were."[56]

STILL ANTAGONIZING THE WHITE MALE

On day two of nominee Samuel A. Alito's 2006 Supreme Court confirmation hearing, a senator directly asked Alito if he was a bigot. Alito baldly answered, "I'm not any kind of bigot." Alito's wife, seated behind him, began to cry and walked out of the proceedings, pushing back tears.

Columnist David Brooks pointed out that if Samuel Alito had been a little older, he probably would have been a Democrat. Alito is an Italian American from Trenton. He was born when Harry Truman was president, at a time when the workingman was a Democrat. During the hearings, Democrats asked about civil rights protections and Republicans asked about rulings that empower law enforcement to fight terrorists. There were Democratic insinuations that Alito was racist (words like "gestapo" were used), and questions were raised about whether he tolerated police brutality. "But those wild accusations don't carry weight any more," Brooks wrote. "Rich liberals have been calling white ethnics bigots for 40 years." Alito took it, answering each question calmly. As hours turned to days, Alito, usually a taciturn man, sat stiffly in his dark suit, pushing up his glasses, unfazed.

"After every defeat, Democrats vow to reconnect with middle-class whites. But if there is one lesson of the Alito hearings, it is that the Democratic Party continues to repel those voters just as vigorously as ever," Brooks wrote. "The big story of American politics, which was underlined by every hour of the Alito hearings, is that sometime between 1932 and 1968, the DNA of the Democratic Party fundamentally changed. In 1932, the Democrats had working-class DNA. Today, the Democrats have different DNA, the DNA of a minority party."[57]

After the 2004 election in which the White Male Gap proved too vast for Democrats to win, the party focused on message and values but ignored the very voters they had lost. By 2006, the Bush administration's mismanaged war in Iraq, as well as GOP scandals, gave Congress to the Democrats. The war will end, and like Iran-Contra, the scandals will fade, just as Ross Perot faded from presidential politics. Yet the same voters, those antagonized white men, will be no nearer to the liberal cause than in 1980. Even when Democrats attempted to reach out to white men it felt like an insult to many.

In 2003, during the Democratic primary race, Howard Dean said, "I still want to be the candidate for guys with Confederate flags in their pickup trucks." Two years later, now president of the Democratic National Congress, Dean derisively referred to Republicans as "a pretty monolithic party. They all behave the same. They all look the same. It's pretty much a white Christian party."[58]

"He wants to appeal to the rednecks driving pickup trucks," Pat Robertson says, chuckling, shaking his head, "and it's just constant insults by the Democratic Party against the American male." In this case, Robertson was right.

In 2007, on the same day that Senator Joseph Biden declared his candidacy for the presidency, he said of his colleague and fellow candidate Senator Barack Obama, "You got the first sort of mainstream African American who is articulate and bright and clean and a nice-looking guy." He immediately apologized for the remarks and their racist implications, but the damage was done.

Not long after, in early February on Fox News Sunday, Juan Williams responded. "I think the difficulty that Biden had is you've got a woman, Hillary Clinton, and a black man, Barack Obama, as the two top leading candidates," Williams said. "I don't think that white males are accustomed to talking about people in a way that's effective without getting into race and gender."[59]

What was a white male viewer supposed to think when a liberal black pundit characterized Biden's comments as indicative of white men's attitudes? The statement that it was solely white males who suffer from the very American problem of seeing the nation through race and gender is not only contradicted by all polling, but is the sort of small slight that irks the white workingman, and reinforces his view that liberals are intolerant of him. One slip-up by a senator and all white men are racist and sexist. It becomes cyclical. Biden's comments elicit similar comments from Williams, while neither man is in any respect racist.

"The liberal Democratic wing," William Pollack says, "didn't take into account the angst that these [white] men felt and to a large extent, they saw them as atavistic, backwater, or a backlash, as being fools—and maybe they were. But that message came across as though they were fools or even worse, as one man felt, and the candidate will remain unmentioned," he says, referring to an interview he did in 2000, "I think that person who represents me [a white man] sees me as a potential perpetrator, child molester, wife beater, and unsupportive person of women's rights."

The antagonism from the left flank took a more offensive form in Michael Moore's 2001 book *Stupid White Men*, which spent 58 weeks on the *New York Times* best-seller list.[60] In it, he listed all the ills of mankind as perpetrated by "always a white guy." His list included the atomic bomb, the black plague, every war America has been in, and then he also mentioned the Holocaust and lethal chemicals. He asked, "Who do you think" decided to "pollute the world" with the internal combustion engine?[61]

That Lise Meitner was instrumental in inventing the bomb as well, that the black plague came from the Middle East, that it was white men who led the war that ended the Holocaust, that it was white men who not only invented lethal chemicals, but also penicillin and the cure for malaria—all that didn't matter to Moore. White men were like the internal combustion engine to him: defined by the worst effects only. Moore is not a radical misfit. He promoted his book on some of network television's leading talk shows. Democrats gave him VIP seating at the 2004 convention. Moore was the personification of the liberal who acted like the white workingman's champion but constantly antagonized him. The one-time champion of the downsized man in Detroit had devolved to the cultural equivalent of the elite he fought. He was the very establishment he believed he stood against. Moore was now Roger.

This antagonism took on a more establishment tone when in 2006, one of the leading liberal minds in politics, Peter Beinart, blamed "NASCAR man"—the liberal euphemism for exurban white men—for the Democrats' decline. That same year, in *The Good Fight*, Beinart made a good argument, challenging dovish liberals to stand strong against national threats. Paradoxically, he was now setting his sights on the very voter who primarily left over the issue. If Democrats were to toughen up, to not be the "nice ass," wrote Beinart, for them to "eradicate" their "self-indulgent niceness," which indeed is a problem, "they must also confront an even bigger scourge," and that was "NASCAR man."

Beinart described him as a man who: "loves guns, pickup trucks, chewing tobacco, and church on Sunday." Imagine if George Will described black men by such stereotypical descriptors. It didn't stop there. Beinart wrote that for Democrats, "NASCAR man" is "the bully everyone wants to appease." It was as if Rush Limbaugh called Gloria Steinem sexist for not being a fan of Limbaugh's rants against "femi-nazis."

Democrats fail, Beinart wrote, because they have to "tailor" their "views to his whims." The argument was that Democrats don't say what they believe on certain liberal issues, like gay marriage, because they fear they'll do worse with "NASCAR man." "Once liberals silence NASCAR man," Beinart wrote, "and all the other blabbermouths who sabotage their efforts at intellectual reconstruction," liberals will find their core set of beliefs.[62]

Americans would then respect liberals, the logic went, for advocating issues they believed in, and the revival would begin. Of course, no one doubted that socialists believed in their own cause. Few doubted that Goldwater, McGovern, or Mondale believed in their causes. They all lost badly. Liberals lack a great idea. But a great idea wins with the people, not in spite of them. Nearly a century after Herbert Croly founded the *New Republic* and helped the progressive era rise by championing the white workingman, among others, a top editor at his magazine was now blaming the white workingman for liberalism's demise. The liberal was blaming the battered. Were conservatives now going to blame black women for the Republicans' loss of Congress in 2006?

That dogmatic liberals then selected the second largest voting bloc, and compared those white men to "blabbermouths," to acting as a "bully," that they often used stereotypical descriptors (such as "chewing tobacco" and church) with an underlying condescension, was not simply antithetical to the liberal credo, it was tactically dumb.

"At least [Republicans] have been telling them that what they are and who they are is legitimate, positive, and good," Pollack says. "Rather than, to pick a comparison, when the Vietnam veterans came back—and it was something I went through in my own life, I wasn't a veteran, I was against the war, I did not go and fight—but here we were spitting on the veterans as though they were the ones who made the war in Vietnam. Now I think men have felt they've been brought up to be a certain way. They've acted that way. And they feel like other men, more liberal men, and women were spitting on them."

These men were no longer "forgotten," as Franklin D. Roosevelt put it. That implies that Democrats accidentally left these men behind. In 1968, liberals began to purposefully disregard white men, and they paid for it. They reaped the whirlwind of their illiberal intolerance in presidential election losses. But then they thought that these losses were simply the byproduct of fighting the good fight. Because, to be sure, the fight for black and female equality was fought and won by Democrats, and it was the greatest of fights. It was true to liberal credo. The true test of that credo was when the "little guy" was no longer

the majority. Democrats were Lincolnesque in their push for black equality especially, but then they made a great mistake.

Liberals blamed all white men for the wrongs of some. It was as if Lincoln
had decided at the conclusion of the Civil War that every former citizen of the
confederacy should be branded with a scarlet letter. But our greatest president
did not do that. His supreme genius was in understanding that only in absolution
could the nation heal and move forward. From Jackson to Franklin D. Roosevelt,
Democrats rose by fighting for the "plain people" and the common man especially. As the American enterprise was extended to all others, Democrats took up
each group's fight one by one. But Democrats did not have to lose those they
first fought for to win all the fights ahead.

Consider the one liberal issue Beinart brought up. The core of the Democratic base, minority women, were the strongest opponents of gay marriage,
not white men. This false generalization was typical of the political left and,
again, is refuted by fact. It is white men today who feel that they are on the receiving end of constant leftist stereotyping. Ironically, because white women
focus more on the nuance of issues and white men focus more upon character,
as exit polling demonstrates, it is white men who most likely would respect a
candidate who disagrees with them on gay marriage, if that disagreement
seemed based in principle.

"Politicians promise the whole world and give you crap," Rodney Mason,
the North Carolina ferry hand, says, "'The Man' nowadays judges people by the
bad and forgets the good." Many working-class white men feel as he did, separate from 'the Man,' in fact, under the Man's metaphorical yoke. They believe
that they are often branded by their failures. The presumption of "while male
privilege" only aggravates their cultural disenfranchisement.

"I feel like [Democrats will] be pretty much one thing and then be something else. Telling people what they want to hear," Mason adds. And this is
where Beinart is correct to emphasize the fact that Democrats need to discover
their core, if not obdurate, beliefs. "I would vote Democratic if I saw a man with
a backbone," Mason continues.

The issues that a party stands upon matter. To simply select leftist causes
without considering the very voters that you have most offended, most abandoned, and most disregarded, is bad democracy and bad politics. The White
Male Gap will only close when Democrats respect the kind of candidates and issues that win these men and a good half of white women as well.

The nomenclature, whether "Joe-six-pack" or "NASCAR Dad" or "Angry White Male," does at least get it right in one respect. There is a common kind of guy in all these men. It is the reason John Travolta can play a working-class Italian kid from New Jersey in *Saturday Night Fever* and later a working-class "good old boy" from Texas in *Urban Cowboy*.

When Stan Greenberg was in Macomb County, talking with blue-collar whites who left the Democratic Party to vote for Reagan, what he found were voters who "wondered why they weren't the central drama of the Democratic Party. They should be honored, not shunned," he wrote of their common belief. Those working-class whites saw Democrats who were, "even contemptuous of their values, their fears, and their simple suburban ways."[63]

"I think there are a number of left liberal candidates who know that these working white men, these angry white men, really have had a tough time of it and are very confused and want to reach out to them," Harvard's William Pollack says. "But they are afraid that reaching out will be seen as too politically conservative. They won't get their liberal base, and they will have no base."

Most Democrats no longer overtly antagonize white men. The vilifying of them has lessoned since the 1970s, '80s, and '90s. But white men watch with the third eye. They notice what is not said but implied. They see the liberal presumption that they are backward, slow, intolerant. They see the overt efforts to reach every group but white men. They notice that Democrats still see color over economic plight. They see a progressive urban media immediately assume that wealthy white boys at Duke did rape a poor black girl (reporters say "alleged" but convey likely guilt). They hear that leading white male radio commentator, Don Imus, make a cruel quip about a team of black female college basketball players, calling them "nappy-headed hoes." They see the media deem it unforgivable and believe it is only unforgivable because a white male said it. They notice the very same critics of Imus hardly denounce the media's assumption that the Duke students were rapists, even after all charges are dropped the same week Imus is fired. White men see two kinds of ugly stereotyping receiving two different reactions in the liberal mainstream. They watch Barack Obama and Hillary Clinton denounce Imus, but read that both Democratic candidates raised millions from the music community that popularizes the very language Imus spoke. They see Bill Clinton advocate a centrist Democratic Party but immediately push divisive liberal social issues, like his removal of a ban on abortion counseling in federally funded health care clinics on the first day of his presidency. They see an intelligent liberal argue for a stronger Democratic Party on national security but then blame white men, who left over the issue, for the downfall of the party. They see John Kerry vote against authorizing the first Gulf War in 1991 but support the second, and then turn away from that support, and they wonder: What does he stand for? What do Democrats stand for? Does God and country mean to Democrats what it does to *us?* Then they see many liberals treat their faith, their Americanism, as juvenile or merely rhetoric. Men died for that faith. Children went without fathers for that faith. Each step on the American flag was a step on that sacrifice. They see Al Gore talk about the "people versus the powerful" but believe, after three decades of living through dogmatic liberalism, that Gore doesn't really mean *them* in the "people." They watch Hillary Clinton vow to run a presidential campaign of "listening," but question whether, unlike leading Democrats before her, she'll listen to them as well. Ralph Waldo Emerson once said, "What you do speaks so loud that I cannot hear what you say." It's the actions that white men await.

RECONCILIATION
White Men and Democrats,
Toward 2008 and 2012

Jim Webb lifted the framed black and white image of his father and pointed to the lean figure in uniform. He spoke about his dad flying cargo planes during the Berlin airlift, and how for three years as a small boy he used to take the photo to bed with him, every night, while his father was deployed overseas. The camera zoomed in, as the newly elected Virginia senator spoke of how he was "proud to follow in his [father's] footsteps." He sat stiffly, in a dark blazer and red tie. Webb's voice tightened. He became austere, his eyes narrowing, as he spoke of his service as a Marine in Vietnam, his brother's military service, as well as his son's, who currently was a Marine in Iraq. Webb said that his family served like others because "we love our country" and "we trusted the judgment of our national leaders," but that "they *owed* us sound judgment." And as this man who admires Andrew Jackson spoke of President Bush taking the nation to war "recklessly," listing "disregarded warnings," Webb embodied all that Democrats were and could be again.[1]

Perhaps that was why he was chosen to give the Democratic response to President Bush's 2007 State of the Union address. It was not Webb's stance against the war that was of a different mold. It was who he was, a military man from a military family. He was not reflexively antiwar or referencing world opinion to justify his cause. In his view, Iraq was ruining the nation from within. Bush had dishonored his country, Webb implied, and aggressively patriotic in his tone and in the squint of his eye, he seemed sincere.

Webb's honor was beyond repute and therefore, like Pennsylvania Representative John Murtha before him, the confrontational words were upheld by the grit of the man. Only weeks before the address, there was an offhand confrontation between Webb and Bush in the East Wing of the White House.

"How's your boy?" Bush asked.

"I'd like to get them out of Iraq, Mr. President," Webb responded.

"That's not what I asked you," Bush said. "How's your boy?"

"That's between me and my boy, Mr. President," Webb replied, as the men parted ways.[2]

Webb embodied the strong masculinity missing from what Kevin Phillips termed the "feminine party" after Johnson took manhood down with the Vietnam War. Webb spoke in straight choppy sentences and seemed to have too much starch in his collar. But it was his plain speech and earned manhood that was of the vital Democratic old school. In his recent book, *Born Fighting: How the Scots-Irish Shaped America*, Webb wrote:

> From the perspective of the activist Left, [rednecks] are the greatest obstacles to what might be called the collectivist taming of America, symbolized by the edicts of political correctness. And for the last fifty years the Left has been doing everything in its power to sue them, legislate against their interests, mock them in the media, isolate them as idiosyncratic, and publicly humiliate their traditions in order to make them, at best, irrelevant to America's future growth.[3]

Webb's response to the president was defined by his determination to restore the honor to those white men who were "born fighting." As he spoke to the nation, Webb never mentioned that he had been Ronald Reagan's secretary of the Navy. He only recalled his small days, when he was a grunt, a Marine, because he was also a novelist, and novelists are, at their core, students of character. Webb understood the symbolism of the dutiful common man. It represented what white men sought most in the modern day: honor and strength of character. When the reverence for grit seemed to become purely Republican, so did the common man. Webb was a Reagan Democrat who dropped the prefix. He was the sort of leader, Democrats hoped, white men would follow back to the party that they, or their fathers, once called their own.

Presidents transform parties. The contenders represent the possibility of that change. Yet with the 2008 election underway Democrats are not standing behind nominees capable of leading their party's revival. In substance, the leading candidates are significantly closer to the Democrats who led the party since 1972 than to those of the days of JFK or FDR. Their gender and color may be different. But their platforms and perspectives are not.

That did not mean Democrats would lose in 2008. "George Bush is handing us our Hoover moment. But we'll only build a lasting majority if we put in place and carry out an agenda that works," DLC president Bruce Reeds says. Indeed, every historical indicator, from the quagmire in Iraq to a remarkably unpopular two-term president, meant Democrats should have a "big year" in 2008, as DLC founder Al From puts it, sitting beside Reed over eggs and roasted tomatoes with reporters in the summer of 2007. "We'd have to work really really hard to screw that up." But if modern Democrats have proven capable of one action, it's screwing up.

"If you see blue sky, go for it," John F. Kennedy once said. Democrats found blue sky in 2006 with the election of many Democrats of the old school, like Webb. Twelve years earlier, when Republicans won back Congress in 1994, the national nature of the contest emulated the presidential vote exactly, leading 63 percent of white male voters to back Republicans in House contests. In 2006, the next fully national midterm election, only 53 percent of white male voters supported House Republican candidates. This does not mean 2008 will emulate 2006. There were two lessons of the midterms. Candidates like Virginia Senator Jim Webb and Montana Senator Jon Tester possessed the right stuff; and of equivalent consequence, Democrats did not win voters' allegiance.

Shortly after the election of 2004, approximately 45 percent of white male voters said they were Republicans. By January 2007, only about 32 percent of white men still considered themselves Republicans. Over the same period, white women's affiliation with the Republican Party dropped from 41 percent to 29 percent. Yet Democrats made no significant gains with white men, and only increased 4 percent with women in party affiliation. Nearly all those who left the Republican Party became Independents.[4]

Presidential elections are not only a contest in character, but also a contest between two characters. Unless Democrats understand what white men believe on issues of war and safety, their skepticism of government programs, and their visceral feelings of patriotism, grit, and reverence for honor, the political left will continue to be barred from permanent majority status.

"It will be a long time before it will be mathematically possible to be the majority party without being competitive for the white vote," Bruce Reed says, later adding, "Democrats are reluctant to do what it takes to win back the white male vote, unnecessarily so in most cases."

If Vietnam ruined the Democratic Party, the war in Iraq offers it the opportunity for redemption. National security is the ideal issue for dispelling the poor perception of liberalism because the issue highlights three negative conceptions of the political left: that they are weak, that they lack grit, and that they are apologists for national interests, often caricatured as the "blame America first" party, as Jeane Kirkpatrick branded the "San Francisco Democrats" in 1984.

But it will take more than rhetoric. Historically, Americans largely trust soldiers to make peace. If Adlai Stevenson had said "I will go to Korea," voters would have thought little of it. Tough talk was not going to replace the ability to envision the outcome. Voters want to believe that the contender has fought a hard fight. This is the dramatic advantage of Rudy Giuliani, due to September 11. It was the advantage of Eisenhower in 1952 and even Nixon in 1968. Certainly, it was the advantage that President Bush enjoyed in 2004 as well.

Americanism is fundamentally a belief in individualism, capitalism, strength, and a better future, and white men are the truest believers. Their faith in the country cannot be overstated. Yet, with the 2008 primary race well under way, Democrats are attempting to bandage their greatest weakness rather than heal it. To date, they have not provided a leading candidate to refute the perception that theirs is the "feminine party." The lesson of 1972 and 2004 was that a decorated veteran was not enough to win. Yet Kerry's and McGovern's failures did not mean that candidates like Jackson and Eisenhower and Kennedy were not winning electoral archetypes. There is a misunderstanding on the political left that the public discontent over the war in Iraq is going to sway the pendulum of public opinion toward dovish Democrats. It might elect a Democrat for a term—but it won't enlist new Democrats. Among several mistakes of the Kerry campaign was that it argued diplomacy foremost, therefore substantiating the perception of the Democratic Party as a party of Neville Chamberlains. The conception may neither be fair nor true, but it's prevalent.

As the 2008 primary race heated up, a consensus began forming that the "daddy party" was too much of a man, and now the "mommy party" would clean up the mess. But that is the stuff of sitcoms, not wartime. The irony of the 2008 election is that Democrats have candidates who can win, but the party remains stuck in its passions rather than its pragmatism. Bill Clinton once quoted a friend of his: "In every presidential election, Democrats want to fall in love; Republicans just fall in line."[5] On this matter, Democrats are compelled by the lessons of history to find their inner Republican.

"A rational man acting in the real world may be defined as one who decides where he will strike a balance between what he desires and what can be done," columnist Walter Lippmann once wrote.[6] The realism that had allowed Democrats to win back Congress in 2006 was fading by the month in 2007. There was no issue like national security to provide the opportunity to close the White Male Gap—it was defense issues that had widened it above all else. And it will not be closed without the party's antiwar base offering concessions.

Domestically, a candidacy based on the fight to economically uplift the working- and middle-class cannot lead a campaign, as has been demonstrated by the historical failures of economic populism. But such populism can be joined with a platform based on national security. When Webb spoke to the nation during the response to the State of the Union address, he pointed out that it now takes the average worker more than a year to earn what his boss makes in one day. If a candidate like Webb ties this economic cause with the American cause, as John F. Kennedy accomplished in linking civil rights to the cold war defense of freedom, the potential remains for a winning Democratic "meat and potatoes" agenda.

H. W. Brands observed that trust in the federal government has always been easiest to win in wartime. "No one does defense like the feds," he quipped. As Peter Beinart ably advocates, liberalism is neither the isolationism of traditional conservatism nor the international hawkish activism of neoconservatives. He pointed out that "if conservatives worry that Americans do not see their own virtue, liberals worry that Americans see only their virtue."[7] And if Americans, especially white men, must choose, most will lean toward the candidate that seems to value the best actions rather than the worst mistakes. Nearly six decades after Arthur Schlesinger Jr. challenged the emerging "doughface progressive," more than three decades after the doughface won the Democratic Party with McGovern, it is time that the antiwar left flank realized they are not *the* Democratic Party but only a constituency of it.

Liberalism's rebirth begins not by becoming hawks. A Wilson, Roosevelt, or Kennedy liberal does not favor war as the means to diplomatic ends. But liberals are compelled to resurrect the principle that to speak softly, you need the big stick. Negotiations to avert war without the threat of force are merely empty rhetoric. The left wing is compelled to consider that there is cause for war, that some causes are worth defending, and that the American nation has defended many worthy causes. To recognize this larger historical truth amid a terrible war that is dominating present debate would be truly brave. Yet if the debate over war is limited to Bush's war, if it is stuck in deceptions leading up to war or discussed in partisan tones, it will only push white men further to the right. If war can win honor and if the act of a "just war" is the defense of that which is worth honoring, then a bad war can be challenged as constituting a dishonoring of the nation and of those who died in its service. This is one of the tragedies of Iraq. Another sad outcome of the war is that the failed use of force in Iraq has actually emboldened America's enemies like Iran and Al Qaeda. America's bluff appears to have been called.

"The Democratic Party can coalesce a grand coalition again, as it did under Franklin Roosevelt," Democratic strategist Tad Devine believes. "The way we get [white men] back is we have to convince them that these guys that they have put in power are ruining their country and ruining their lives. That's how we get them back. We don't get them back with a positive message. We convince them that the Republicans are ruining the country, doing it by war in Iraq, doing it by deficits that go on the heads of their children. And these guys, they're responsible, most of them work. They're out there, trying to make ends meet and when you convince them that the government that they've elected is at odds with everything that is part of their lives, they will reject the government." But he adds, "We got to convince people that we'll do a good job protecting the country. I think that has to be a fundamental value."

There will be issues other than Iraq in 2008 and 2012 that will dominate American national security. The resurgence of the Taliban in Afghanistan and the revival of Al Qaeda undermines the Republican narrative on national security. Then there is Iran. If one accepts the supposition that there are some hostile governments that the United States cannot allow to go nuclear, then it seems Iran is a case in point. The Democratic Party can argue for a stronger *and* smarter stance on Iran, but it also must demonstrate it concretely. Democrats should, as they have advocated, push for an Apollo-like national security plan on oil that would decrease our dependence on the volatile Middle East. The program should fund alternative fuel research, dramatically increase mileage standards through legislation, offer large tax breaks for purchasing hybrid or fuel-efficient cars, and possibly include a carbon tax, all with the intent of weaning the United States off of the Organization of Petroleum Exporting Countries (OPEC). Such energy policies with benchmarks would do more to strengthen U.S. security than possibly any other issue—rallying white men along with others to a cause that favors Democrats. Republicans would be forced to oppose it, due both to their ties to the oil and gas industries and to their allegiance to fiscal conservative fundamentalists, who are absolutist about the free market. There are other issues—from the worsening Palestinian-Israeli conflict, to North Korea, which exploded a nuclear device on George W. Bush's watch—that weaken Republican dominance in the defense debate.

"The challenge for the Democrats, though, is to point out the problems with Bush and Republicans but not spend the whole time being the party of anger," former Virginia Governor Mark Warner says. "And not allow yourself to default into, I do think there is a blame-America-first crowd. Don't totally spend all your time attacking Bush, or God knows, attacking country. But say where are you going to go from here."

And then there is China. There is room for a candidate to call for a declaration to defend Pax Americana against the emerging concern of Pax China. For all the criticism of the United States, it stands not only for capitalism, but has also defended liberty more than any nation before it. Whereas China, most visibly in Darfur, uses the bottom line to define its ends and means in world affairs. Liberals need to recognize this truth. Democrats need to discover what future they are running against as well as fighting to realize.

Above all other security issues, the poor state of the armed forces themselves requires addressing. "Rebuilding the military will be a big issue for Democrats in the next election," DNC president Bruce Reed says. "Everything Dick Cheney said in 2000 about the military being hollowed out was a crock then, but is true now that the military is stretched thin, the reserves and the national guard have been overtaxed, and the Rumsfeld strategy of defense transformation has been a fiasco," Reed adds. "If Democrats are smart they will make a case that they are the ones who will offer a bigger, stronger armed forces."

White men were the sole voting bloc appearing to stick with the president during the war in Iraq in 2007, not because they liked the war, nor because they thought the war was going well, but because *the nation was at war*. They followed the war closely in the news and though they may not have been optimistic, they saw the world as they had learned on the playground—retreat may embolden the adversary. They believed that the best defense is a good offense. Their support for the armed forces was tied up in their patriotism. But even their support, polling demonstrated, was waning by the month.

"Reagan may have secured the presidency in 1980 when in the debate he turned to Carter and said, 'Are you better off today than you were four years ago?' The country said, 'stagflation, Iranian hostage crisis, no of course not,'" George Will says. "And the question is whether in 2008 the Democratic candidate will be able to turn to the country and use the Republican Party's issue against it—'Are you safer today then you were four years ago?' And the country says, good heavens no."

But George Will knows that it depends on who is asking the question. Yet, the opportunity exists for Kennedy's "missile gap" to be converted to a Republican "security gap." It takes only one candidate, with a strong vice president at his or her side, to redefine forty years of national security politics.

George W. Bush's presidency, likely not to be redeemed by history, has given Democrats openings well beyond national security. The criticism of President Bush's addition of trillions to the national debt has led Democrats to reclaim the issue of fiscal responsibility. The question is, as with defense, can they do so credibly? The proof will be in the platform and the politician.

While sincerity must underpin any stance, Democrats, like Republicans, are best served by championing issues that directly refute the negative stereotypes of their party. Every Democratic candidate has to contend with the presumption that he or she is soft on defense and crime, advocates higher taxes, ignores the middle class, and cares more for civil liberties than for combating terrorists. Democrats are compelled to undercut these perceptions, and to do so successfully the party must induce its liberal base to compromise. Social conservatives have been the largest galvanizing electoral force for Republicans over a quarter century, but they have not won their central issue, the abolition of abortion—or at least the overruling of the *Roe v. Wade* decision. Liberals are compelled by realism to follow the religious right's lead. The religious right's pragmatism has won the judges it desires to the Supreme Court. Conversely, by putting cause before coalition, dogmatic liberals bear responsibility for conservative jurists and their rulings.

As the Pew Research Center found in its surveys, not only do liberals hold a dimmer view of Democrats compared to the Republican base's opinion of the GOP, but the liberals are also less likely to put coalition before cause because of their skepticism of hierarchy, which makes compromise more difficult.

There is a tax agenda awaiting Democrats that could also help dismiss negative stereotypes. By 2010, the alternative minimum tax will affect more than four-fifths of Americans with incomes between $100,000 and $500,000 annually, yet it will affect only about a third of taxpayers with incomes exceeding $1 million.[8] Among voters in the 2004 election, as many as 22 percent of white men and 18 percent of white women were vulnerable to this tax, and it requires attention. But the focus, firstly, should be on the middle and working classes. One option is an elimination of the taxes on the working class, those making less than $50,000 in household income, which would include 39 percent of men and 43 percent of women among the white voters in 2004. Alternatively, as Rahm Emanuel and Bruce Reed suggest, there should be a maximum 10 percent flat tax for all Americans making under $100,000 in household income.[9] Such a tax break would alleviate the tax burden of eight out of ten white voters, and an even higher percent of minorities.[10]

Due to the decline in defined benefits, former Clinton-era national economic advisor Gene Sperling believes that Democrats should push for a "Universal 401(K)." Sperling emphasizes that Democrats need to advocate empowerment fiscal policies over safety nets.

Issues of modern medical care are gradually undermining the middle and working classes. One quarter of white men lean strongly Republican but occupy the center of the electorate. Those very same men favor government guaranteed health insurance for all Americans, but it is a slim majority. Universal health insurance remains a hard sell to white men, who have only known a lifetime of big government's failure to reach them. Redefining this view of big government will not occur through rhetoric but through a Democratic presidency that succeeds in redefining the party as Clinton intended. Though health insurance has not proven a rallying cry for Americans in the past, it is an indispensable second-tier component of the Democratic platform.

There is an economic platform to be argued without the "us against *them*" class language, which will fail on impact. The ultrarich cannot be treated in antagonistic tones. Americans are aspirational about their politics—they vote on the next election not the last—and they are aspirationial about their chances in life—white men most of all. Yet the income statistics are startling: While most white men's wages remained stagnant and much of America struggles to get by, the richest 1 percent went from holding 8 percent of the nation's total income in 1980 to fully 16 percent in 2004.[11] The answer is a platform of tax breaks for everyone *except* the ultrarich. What follows thereafter can be decided in the White House. The loss to the treasury can be corrected by putting an end to corporate welfare, among a myriad of options. Such fiscal policies, combined with tax credits for education and retraining, would gradually reshape the sense of the Democrats' priorities.

On the other fronts, Democrats, already strong on environmental issues, should advocate for further protection of wildlife grounds for hunting and fishing. To dispel the conception that Democrats give little credence to cultural issues—seen most vividly in the mockery of Dan Quayle's advocacy of traditional marriage—the liberal party should put forward a platform to protect children from "cultural pollution," while remaining true to their emphasis on civil liberties. Internet, cable, and cell phones have revolutionized the basics of parenting. In 1950s America, when inside the home, a parent could maintain a good amount of control over the degree to which the outside world affected their children. Today, the startling availability of online pornography, hate speech, and weapons websites leaves parents feeling powerless. The party that comes up with reasonable strategies to empower parents to have more control over their children's media and devices will be rewarded at the polls. This policy would necessitate challenging the civil liberty absolutists on the left wing. But it is those challenges that earn the respect of the far larger non-ideological portion of voters.

Possibly no step would do more symbolically to heal wounds with white men than a Democratic declaration that race- and gender-based affirmative action has run its course. The policy would put to rest among white men the persistent question: Why should middle-class black men or rich white women be given preference over poor white men? A new affirmative action focused solely on economic need would continue to disproportionately assist minorities and would also reach those poor white men who have come to believe government can and will do little for them. Should Democrats reform affirmative action, they would begin to change many of those men's minds.

A cross-racial movement will only begin when policies no longer focus on difference, but emphasize instead a common struggle. Ending race-based affirmative action, combating stagnant wages, explicitly including the white workingman in the rhetoric of *us* (because they have been implicitly excluded in the past) will go a long way toward convincing white men that Democrats really are the people's party. After four decades of electoral decline, the political paradigm could be upended.

Yet, for many, the effort to win back some white men feels antithetical to liberalism itself. Although Democrats have never won a sustainable majority without white men, this fact causes remarkably little concern among many liberals. That too must change for real change to be realized.

"It's always harder for a party to get as excited about cutting its losses as it is running up wins," Bruce Reed says. "And what Clinton understood, and other Democrats have had more trouble understanding, it's just as important to shore up your weaknesses—in many ways it's more important to shore up your weaknesses—than it is to remind people of your strengths."

Modern liberalism is compelled to realize that it is not the purpose of democracy to make some people feel better about being different. Quarrels over Christmas decorations only pit leftists against the mainstream, and liberalism never fails to lose that bout. The radical in one party is always a handmaiden to the opposition. When one federal court ruled that "under God" should be taken out of the Pledge of Allegiance, the mainstream suddenly felt that the courts really were going too far. Liberalism must reconcile itself to the fact that beginning in the late 1960s the bulk of Americans, white men primarily, came to believe in the tyranny of the minority. In democracies, the "fact of pluralism" also means tolerating the majority.

Yet, policies do not make presidencies. Republicans begin every contest for the presidency arguing from a platform based on the "four F's": faith, family, force, and freedom. Democrats need not challenge any of these principles but could reclaim them as their own—family and force especially. It's the broad unifying themes that win elections.

With Americans working far harder today than they once did, there is a personal void unfilled by the routine. The typical two-parent family works 12 weeks more per year than in 1969.[12] That leaves working men and women with an emptiness, filled best by faith and cause, and beliefs often rooted in God and country.

What Roosevelt, Nixon, and Reagan fundamentally did was honor the regular American family and offer honor to the workingman. Democrats are compelled to advocate authentic, thematic statements of cause to defend and uphold the quiet duty and strength of regular working men and women.

"Campaigns are written and won not on the basis of past performance but on the kind of vision a candidate or campaign takes and how congruent that vision is with the public," Richard Wirthlin says. "And second, how achievable the implementation of that vision comes across."

The plan for action will only be trusted if the character of the candidate defines the person as worthy of trust. Disparagements of character, for this reason, are the most urgent fight for the left. Democratic campaigns from, Dukakis to Kerry, were fatally wounded by misconceptions and reticence. "The Greeks say *Pathima Mathima*, you learn from your experiences," Mike Dukakis tells me. Americans like fighters and Dukakis, above all, regrets that he did not fight back. Kerry expresses the same regrets. White men respect the fight in the man. Half of white men may live in the suburbs but many are purchasing pickup trucks and rate John Wayne among the greatest actors. The western man did not vanish with the frontier. The Democrats' best branch of peace to white men is to back candidates who personify the frontier mythology as intrepid repositories of grit and honor.

"I think that 2008 could be a threshold election in the same frame that 1980 was," Warner says. "Maybe not necessarily the working class white male, but the chamber of commerce, or the main street, white male Republican, small business owner, medium level corporate guy. I think there is almost an unprecedented opportunity for Democrats to win them," he adds. "Because undermining the Republicans at this point—let me take Iraq off the table—I think that chamber of commerce crowd is scared about America's diminished stature in the world."

Politics await a Democrat who can stand up to the left flank and therefore appear larger than liberalism. But it equally awaits a candidate who can revive a proudly American liberalism. The answer is in history. Woodrow Wilson, Franklin Delano Roosevelt, and John F. Kennedy were not perfect, but their pragmatism offered Democrats their only winning direction. The classically liberal appeal will only occur, though, with a candidate who is unapologetically American and affirms the struggle for all.

American poet Maya Angelou once wrote, "I've learned that people will forget what you said, people will forget what you did, but people will never forget how you made them feel."[13] Even if white men do not recall the details of what transpired over the last four decades, they recall the way liberalism made them feel. They were branded with the sins of the nation's forefathers. Yet today, once and for all, white men must be allowed to move on. To be sure, white men must acknowledge and learn about America's bad past along with its good. But they must no longer be blamed for other white men's sins. Each impolitic, even hurtful, statement by a white man cannot be held to a higher set of standards and criticism than all others. If Lincoln could welcome the South back into the Union, liberalism can welcome back white male America. To some, this may seem like sentimental nonsense. It's not. For some forty years, phrases like "the Man," "male chauvinist pig," "white male privilege," "dead white males," "angry white male," and the actions behind them have led to an entire vocabulary of blaming white men for the nation's worst ills. White men heard every word, kept it to themselves, and turned away from the political party they once built.

"Liberals have to say you are not the enemy," psychologist William Pollack believes. "What you were brought up on wasn't wrong, although things are changing. There are some inherent values that are good. Let's talk about those that are good. I mean, heroism, caring for others, classical male values."

It is striking that the White Male Gap remains the Achilles' heel of Democrats. Three times Democrats have tried to salvage their party. There was the formation of Americans for Democratic Action by FDR Democrats in 1947. After the drubbing of George McGovern in 1972, the Coalition for a Democratic Majority was formed. At the height of the Reagan era in 1984 came the dawn of the Democratic Leadership Council. One group faded and another rose. None has succeeded in reforming the party base.

"It's really hard for a party to recognize what both parties have to recognize, which is that they are not going to win unless they show the electorate that they are better than the electorate thinks they are," Bruce Reed says. "Remember, George Bush's campaign in 2000 was about how he was better, that he wasn't a Gingrich conservative, that he was in fact, a compassionate one."

To Republican strategist Frank Luntz, the Democrats' pragmatic attempts to reorient their party failed because they "saw this as an issue of ideology and I'm going to say that it's an issue of authenticity." Issues matter, but the substance of the character beneath matters more.

Simply put, however, Is the liberal reformation possible? Liberals account for half of all Democrats. The Democratic Party revival will only succeed if the liberal base supports the effort to reach beyond it. The leadership supported the war in Afghanistan while the base stood against it. In too many similar instances, the left wing of the Democratic Party has chosen the "lost cause" over the larger cause. The true test will come when a candidate in the image of John F. Kennedy runs for the Democratic nomination. Political coalitions compel compromise, and Democrats cannot succeed if liberals put every battle before the war. Until that changes, nothing will change for the political left. To rebuild itself, the Democratic Party *must* find its convictions and vision. It must champion candidates who have a compelling vision and authentic convictions. But first, it must understand on whose behalf they stand.

In the decades between John F. Kennedy and John F. Kerry, workingmen were not conned into voting Republican. Liberalism did *not* decline for lack of assertiveness. There was little that was timid about George McGovern or Walter Mondale. The Democratic revival cannot occur without reaching out to those they lost. But white men will only respect the outreach when they believe the reasons they left the party are respected. Until that day, American conservatives will continue to win the majority of workingmen.

At the close of the 2004 Democratic Convention in Boston, conservative commentator Sean Hannity was walking alone out of the Fleet Center. It was dusk. Two janitors were changing bags in the garbage cans that lined the fluorescent lit hallway. During the Republican convention Hannity was a star. "We love you Sean!" screamed one GOP delegate. But in Boston, among Democrats,

Hannity kept to himself as he left for the night, his bag slung over his shoulder. The middle-aged janitors saw Hannity leaving. One man pointed to the other, excitedly—"Is that Hannity?" The two white men stopped working and approached him. They shook his hand, patted him on the back, and expressed what an honor it was for them to meet him, as if he was the heroic quarterback of their boyhood and part of their lives was tied up in him. Hannity smiled, chatted, and after a couple of minutes went on his way. The two janitors returned to work. And as the leading Democratic politicians passed by, all they had to do was stop, look back, and notice that the Democratic Party's future was behind them, in two ordinary men working late into the night.

APPENDIX OF STUDIES

The White Male Gap study (W. M. G. study) used four main types of data sources:

1. The ANES data set. The American National Election Studies (www.electionstudies.org).
    The 1948–2004 ANES CUMULATIVE DATA FILE [data set]. Stanford University and the University of Michigan [producers and distributors], 2005.
2. CBS, NBC, ABC, NY Times, & LA Times (LAT) exit polls
3. The PEW Research Center for the People & the Press (http://people-press.org/)
4. Gallup Polls (http://www.galluppoll.com/)

In the section that follows are sample sizes for most of the data sets used in this book. The sample sizes for the ANES data that we used are:

	1948	1952	1956	1960	1964	1968	1972	1976	1980	1984	1988	1992	1996	2000	2004
Count	662	1899	1762	1181	1571	1557	2705	2248	1614	2257	2040	2485	1714	1807	1212

The sample sizes for the exit polls used by ABC are:

   1980 National Election Day Exit Poll; ABC NEWS; Sample Size = 9,742
   1984 National Election Day Exit Poll; ABC NEWS; Sample Size = 20,637
   1988 National Election Day Exit Poll; ABC NEWS; Sample Size (National) = 95,167
   (Only 22,785 were available for the national election analysis.)

The sample sizes for the exit polls used by CBS are:

   1972 National Election Day Survey; CBS NEWS; Sample size = 17,595
   1976 National Election Day Survey; CBS NEWS; Sample size = 15,300
   1980 National Election Exit Poll; CBS NEWS & NY TIMES; Sample size = 15,201

1984 National Election Exit Poll; CBS NEWS & NY TIMES; Sample size = 9,175
1988 National Election Exit Poll; CBS NEWS & NY TIMES; Sample size = 11,645

The sample sizes for the exit polls used by NBC are:

1984 National Election Day Exit Poll; NBC NEWS; Sample Size = 11,671
1988 National Election Day NBC NEWS/Wall St Journal Poll; Sample Size = 11,703

The sample sizes for recent exit polls are given below:

1992 National Election Day Exit Poll, Voter Research and Surveys; Sample Size = 15,482
1996 Voter News Service; Sample Size = 16,637
2000 National Election Pool; Sample Size = 13,259
2004 National Election Pool; Sample Size = 13,718
[There was more than one data set in 2004.]

The sample size for a few of the Pew data sets is now given:

Jul 2003 Values Update Survey #23054; Sample Size = 9822.
Dec 2004 Political Typology Survey #24086; Sample Size = 2000
Jul 2005 Religion And Public Life Survey #25052; Sample Size = 2000

The sample size for some Gallup polls are given below:

Gallup Poll # 1948–0432: Taft-Hartley Act/Russia/Senate Pensions/Marshall Plan/Politics; Sample Size = 3,027
Gallup Poll # 1952–0508: Presidential Election/Eisenhower; Sample Size = 3,003
American Institute of Public Opinion; Survey number: AIPO 637 Gallup Poll; 1960 Sample Size = 2,988
Gallup Poll # 1968–0770: Presidential Election/Political Party; Sample Size = 1,605

Where survey weights were provided in the data sets, they were used in the analysis. In some of the surveys in which no weights were provided, the following approach was used: For three possible Presidential vote outcomes (*Democratic*, *Republican* or *third party*), voters were assigned one of three possible weights, depending on their vote. The weights were chosen so that the computed vote outcomes from the sample matched the actual outcomes.

Given below is a list of surveys where weights were computed in this manner:

Gallup Poll # 1948–0432: Taft-Hartley
Gallup Poll # 1952–0508: Presidential Election/Eisenhower
Gallup Poll; October 18–23, 1960; Survey Number: Aipo 637
NYTimes Poll # 2005–03a: Taxes/Getting Ahead In Life/Social Class

In the case of the University of Michigan American National Election Studies the weighting variable was used but was multiplied by a constant depending on the vote to create a new weight, so that the sample total vote would match the actual total vote as closely as possible. This is similar to the procedure used by Ruy A. Teixeira and Joel Rogers. *America's Forgotten Majority: Why the White Working Class Still Matters* (New York: Basic Books, 2000), 188.

In this book whites are often compared with non-whites. American Jews are almost all Caucasian. However, because the voting pattern of American Jews is far more similar to that of minorities than other whites, they were included with minorities rather than whites in all the comparisons, unless otherwise noted. White generally means Gentile (non-Jew) or Christian of European descent. To include Jews among whites in this study would have skewed the objective, which was to empirically understand the white men who left Democrats. Most Jews have been loyal Democrats, both men and women, since Franklin Delano Roosevelt. Like minorities, they also live in heavily populated urban areas, unlike most whites.

Hispanics, many of whom are white, are also considered non-white in this book.

Importantly, when Hispanics and Jews were moved from the white group to the non-white group in the media exit polling of presidential elections from 1972 to 2004, it causes only an approximate 2 percent change in the percent of whites who voted Democratic.

Most of the percentages were computed using SPSS CROSSTABS. When using weighting, that procedure computes percentages by first rounding the numerators and denominators to integers before dividing. This causes a small rounding error, which is generally much less than the random sampling error.

Computer data analysis and statistical analysis was performed by Robert M. Kuhn, PhD. Methodology of study, data interpretation, and analysis of findings was by David Paul Kuhn and Robert M. Kuhn.

ACKNOWLEDGMENTS

I owe my father the greatest debt of gratitude. His statistical research was an indispensable component of this book. I will always be thankful for his months of work, as well as his devotion. I am also particularly grateful to Celinda Lake. Her general assistance at the outset of this study will not be forgotten. I am thankful for her belief in the value of this research, her selfless generosity, and her expert advice.

I am grateful to both Michael Chiaverina for opening my world to journalism in high school and Catherine Small, who sadly died far too young in 2007. Ms. Small introduced me to Henry David Thoreau, Herman Melville, Langston Hughes, and a world of words as a teenager. Her appreciation of Americana and inspirational emphasis on being a "literate American" remains the foundation of my writing. I owe a debt of gratitude to several of my college professors: David Hansen for teaching me about serendipity; Gerald Conner for teaching me to listen; John Ullman for demonstrating that I need not limit myself; and to Brett Greider for all those hours discussing philosophy and religion when I served as his teaching assistant. I am also grateful to my first editor, Chris Carr, who took a chance on a freshman and supported my early journalism.

Professionally, I have had many mentors. I am grateful to Carole Buia, Elaine Rivera, Tammy Drummond, and Ed Barnes for taking a young intern at *Time* under their wing, as well as Stephen Koepp for his continued direction. I am especially grateful to Jacob Margolies for his editorial guidance over the years. He has been my most constant intellectual sparring partner and a good friend. I owe a great debt of gratitude to Dan Collins and Mary Murphy for hiring me at CBS News. It was that opportunity which made this book possible. I am also extremely grateful to Dotty Lynch, Kathy Sciere, and Allen Alter for their editorial direction and personal support. I also wish to thank Joel Roberts, a sharp and incisive editor, and Dick Meyer for emphasizing succinct copy and, more so, his guidance over the years.

Many people assisted me throughout the book. I am grateful to Riva Froymovich for gathering journal articles as well as assisting me with transcribing a half dozen interviews, and to Adam Graham-Silverman for assisting with some last minute reporting. I am particularly grateful to Lee Bob Black, Amy Merrick, Barry Granoff, and my mother, Evelyn Kuhn, for reading part or all of the manuscript and offering the advice that readers give best. I also wish to thank my friends Dave and Jessica Mancini, who took me into their home in Iowa to escape Manhattan for my first few weeks of writing. I am grateful to Brian Vrabel (for his levity), Sara Bergreen (for her resolute and stirring spirit), and Megan Petrus (for challenging me with candor). I owe a special thank you to Emily Gould who assisted me in closing out this book. She truly was an edifice of moral support.

I owe my editor, Jake Klisivitch, a particular debt of gratitude for his patience throughout the process and his editorial direction. I would also like to thank Joanna Mericle and Alan Bradshaw for their assistance in moving this book to press. And lastly, never least, is my literary agent. It is customary to thank agents but Joy Tutela is all a writer could hope. She has been my constant advocate, offering encouragement when it was most needed and crucial editorial guidance along the way. I will forever be grateful for her belief in me.

NOTES

Note: All interviews by author between 1 August 2005 and 30 September 2006. "W. M. G." is the White Male Gap study—see Appendix for further details.

INTRODUCTION

1. Frank Trippett, "Up and Away in a Down Year," *Time*, 5 January 1981.
2. Michael Barone, "He Stands in History," *U.S. News and World Report*, 21 June 2004.
3. W.M.G. study of CBS News Exit Polling.
4. W.M.G. study of data compiled by the University of Michigan American National Election Studies.
5. U.S. Census Bureau State Rankings, Personal Income per Capita in Constant (2000) Dollars, 2004; and author's study of a 2004 National Election Pool exit poll.
6. W. M. G. study of a 2004 National Election Pool exit poll.
7. Author's longitudinal study of media exit polling. See Appendix.
8. Alan Brinkley, "The Road Ahead," *The American Prospect*, December 2004.
9. Emily Kaiser and Howard Goller, "Don't Meddle with CEO Pay, Economist Says," Reuters. Also, Institute for Policy Studies and United for a Fair Economy, 7 Feb. 2006–7 February 2007.
10. H. W. Brands, *The Strange Death of American Liberalism* (Pennsylvania: Keystone, 2003), 175.
11. W.M.G. study of 2004 National Election Pool exit polling.
12. W.M.G. study of results from University of Michigan American National Election Study.
13. U.S. Census Count 2005, Non-Hispanic white males.
14. W.M.G. study of 2004 National Election Pool exit polling and general election vote. More than 122.2 million Americans voted in the general election. According to the W.M.G. study of media exit polling, roughly 35.2 percent, or a little over 43 million, are estimated to be white males as defined in the study. A 5 percent improvement would yield 5 percent of this quantity, which is slightly over 2.15 million; this rounds to 2.2 million. The estimated percent of minority males is 11.2 percent, which is less than one third of the number of white males.
15. Bill Peterson, "Women Shifting Sharply Away from Reagan, Republican Party," *The Washington Post*, 29 March 1982.
16. Walter Shapiro, "What Do Women Want?" *Newsweek*, 19 September 1983.

17. Richard S. Dunham, "Can the GOP bridge the gender gap?" *Business Week*, 19 December 1994.
18. Warre Farrell, *The Myth of Male Power* (New York: Berkley, 1993), 208.
19. Michael Harrington, "The Invisible Poor: White Males," *Washington Post*, 15 February 1987.
20. Betty Friedan, *The Feminine Mystique* (New York: W. W. Norton, 1963), 18.
21. Donna Britt, "Listening To Voices Of Anger," *The Washington Post*, 10 November 1992.
22. David Gates, "White Male Paranoia," *Newsweek*, 29 March 1993.
23. David Brooks, "Report From Philly: Why the GOP is Playing Nice," *Newsweek*, 3 August 2000.
24. Susan Faludi, *Stiffed: The Betrayal of the American Man* (New York: HarperCollins, 1999), 7–13.
25. Ruy A. Teixeira and Joel Rogers, *America's Forgotten Majority: Why the White Working Class Still Matters* (New York: Basic Books, 2000), 31–33.
26. In 2003, roughly 39 percent of both white male and female 2004 voters made between $50,000 and $99,999 in household income. Even among those white voters who are single, the difference in this middle-income bracket is small. The household income bracket of $100,000 to $199,999 included 18 percent of white male voters and 14 percent of white female voters (for singles, it was 9 percent of white males and 6 percent of white females).
27. W.M.G. study done on National Election Pool media exit polling, 2000 and 2004.
28. For these reasons, the author mined the trove of exit polls, University of Michigan, Pew, and Gallup data, and often excluded Jews among whites, as with Hispanics.
29. Yankelovich Monitor Inc., private study, 2003.
30. W.M.G. study of Pew Research Center for the People & the Poor survey, "2004 Political Landscape," 5 November 2003.
31. W.M.G. study on Pew Research Center for the People & the Poor survey, "Beyond Red vs. Blue," 10 May 2005.
32. Karen M. Kaufmann and John R. Petrocik, "The Changing Politics of American Men: Understanding the Sources of the Gender Gap," *American Journal of Political Science*, Vol. 43, No. 3 (July 1999): 864–887.
33. Stanley B. Greenberg and Anna Greenberg, "Memo to Friends of Democracy Corps on Winning Back Men," 24 July 2000.
34. W. M. G. study of 2000 National Education Pool media exit polling.
35. W.M.G. study of 2004 National Education Pool media exit polling.
36. W.M.G. study of Pew Research Center for the People & the Press, "Beyond Red vs. Blue"; "The 2005 Political Typology," 10 May 2005.
37. Pew Forum on Religion & Public Life, "Pragmatic Americans Liberal and Conservative on Social Issues," 3 August 2006.
38. Thomas Frank, *What's The Matter With Kansas? How Conservatives Won The Heart Of America* (New York: Henry Holt, 2004), 245.
39. Henry Steele Commager, *The American Mind* (New Haven: Yale University Press, 1959), 342.
40. Ibid., 51.
41. Ellen Goodman, "It's About Gender, Not Race," *Boston Globe*, 9 November 2003.
42. Michael Kazin, *The Populist Persuasion: An American History* (New York: HarperCollins, 1998), 246.

43. Albert R. Hunt, "Democrats See Victory in U.S. House Races, Senate Within Reach," *Bloomberg*, 28 August 2006.

44. Colleen J. Shogan, "The Contemporary Presidency: The Sixth Year Curse," *Presidential Studies Quarterly* 13, Vol. 36 No. 1, 89.

45. W.M.G. study of state-by-state 2000 National Education Pool media exit polling, compared with CNN 2006 Election exit polling. Whites includes Jews in the 2000 to 2006 comparisons.

46. Jeffrey H. Birnbaum and Chris Cillizza, "'Mortgage Moms' May Star in Midterm Vote," *Washington Post*, 5 September 2006.

CHAPTER I

1. Michael S. Kimmel, *Manhood in America: A Cultural History* (New York: The Free Press, 1996), 225.

2. Richard M. Nixon, "Checkers" campaign speech, available at http://www.americanrhetoric.com/speeches/richardnixoncheckers.html

3. Geoffrey Nunberg, *Talking Right* (Mass.: Perseus Books Group), 45–46.

4. Michael Kazin, *The Populist Persuasion: An American History* (New York: Harper-Collins, 1995), 186.

5. John Micklethwait and Adrian Wooldridge, *The Right Nation* (New York: Penguin, 2004), 50–51.

6. William F. Buckley Jr., "Publisher's Statement," *National Review*, 29 June 2004.

7. Richard Hofstadter, *Anti-Intellectualism in American Life* (Toronto: Knopf, 1963), 3–4.

8. Colleen J. Shogan, "Anti-Intellectualism in the Plebiscitary Presidency: A Conservative Populism?" Paper, annual meeting of American Political Science Association, Philadelphia, 27 August 2003.

9. Paul F. Boller Jr. *Presidential Campaigns* (New York: Oxford, 2004), 283–287.

10. K. A. Cuordileone, "Politics in an Age of Anxiety," *Journal of American History*, September 2000: 515–545.

11. Bruce Curtis, "The Wimp Factor," *American Heritage Magazine*, Vol. 40, No. 7 (November 1989).

12. Chrystia Freeland, "Dumb America?" *Financial Times*, 15 July 2006.

13. Shogan. "Anti-Intellectualism in the Plebiscitary Presidency."

14. Theodore Roosevelt, "The College Graduate and Public Life," *The Atlantic* (August 1894).

15. Curtis, "The Wimp Factor."

16. Henry Steele Commager, *The American Mind* (New Haven: Yale University Press, 1959), 9–10.

17. *Manhattan*. Directed by Woody Allen. 1979. United Artists.

18. Jimmy Carter TV Ad, 1976 Democratic Presidential Campaign Committee, Jimmy Carter Presidential Library.

19. Richard Wolffe, "Bush Regains Mastery of the Linguistic Lapse," *Financial Times*, (21 October 2000).

20. "Piling on Mr. Bush," *Economist*, 23 September 2000.

21. George W. Bush, Yale Commencement Address, delivered 21 May 2001. Available at http://www.yale.edu/lt/archives/v8n1/v8n1georgewbush.htm

22. Author's study of 2004 National Election Pool exit poll.

23. Peter Beinart, "A Fighting Faith," *New Republic*, 2 December 2004.

24. Arthur M. Schlesinger Jr., *The Vital Center: The Politics of Freedom* (New Jersey: Transaction Publishers, 1997), 40–41.

CHAPTER II

1. Bill D. Moyers, "What a Real President Was Like," *The Washington Post*, 13 November 1988.
2. Susan Faludi, *Stiffed: The Betrayal of the American Man* (New York: HarperCollins, 1999), 150.
3. Michael Kazin, *The Populist Persuasion: An American History* (New York: Harper-Collins, 1998), 229–237.
4. Stan Greenberg, *Middle Class Dreams* (New York: Times Books, 1995), 106 and http://www.pbs.org/wgbh/amex/wallace/index.html
5. Earl Black and Merle Black, *The Vital South: How Presidents are Elected* (Cambridge, Massachusetts: Harvard University Press, 1992), 107–108.
6. Tom Reiss, "The First Conservative; How Peter Viereck Inspired—and Lost—a Movement," *New Yorker*, October 2005. Quote from *Saturday Evening Post* cited in John Micklethwait and Adrian Wooldridge, *The Right Nation* (New York: Penguin, 2004), 256.
7. W.M.G. study of 1964 data compiled by the University of Michigan American National Election Studies.
8. Alan J. Lichtman, *Great Presidents Lecture Series*, Teaching Company, American University.
9. Paul, F. Boller, Jr., *Presidential Campaigns* (New York: Oxford, 2004), 163–166.
10. Henry Steele Commager, *The American Mind* (New Haven: Yale University Press, 1959), 51.
11. Ibid.
12. Doris Kearns Goodwin, *Lyndon Johnson and the American Dream* (New York: St. Martin's Press, 1991), 219.
13. Lichtman, *Great Presidents Lecture Series*.
14. Cornel West, *Democracy Matters* (New York: Penguin Press, 2004), 33–34.
15. U.S. Census Bureau, available at http://www.census.gov/hhes/poverty/histpov/hstpov2.html
16. Department of Health and Human Services; Administration for Children, Youth and Families, "Biennial Report to Congress; The Status of Children in Head Start" (Head Start Bureau, 2003), 16.
17. H. W. Brands, *The Strange Death of American Liberalism* (New Haven: Yale University Press, 2003), 18.
18. Sean J. Savage, *JFK, LBJ, and the Democratic Party* (New York: SUNY Press, 2004), 139.
19. Lichtman, *Great Presidents Lecture Series*.
20. Richard M. Scammon and Ben J. Wattenberg, *The Real Majority: The Classic Examination of the American Electorate* (New York: Coward-McCann,1992), 50; and Jeffrey Kahn. Reagan quotation from University of California Berkeley News Center report on Reagan's death, 8 June 2004.
21. Michael Lind, *Next American Nation: The New Nationalism and the Fourth American Revolution* (New York: Free Press 1996), 111.
22. U.S. Department of Justice; Office of Justice Programs; Bureau of Justice Statistics Online Database. Sources: FBI, Uniform Crime Reports as prepared by the National Archive of Criminal Justice Data, 4 March 2007. (Murder rate includes "non-negligent manslaughter.")
23. Gary Gerstle, *American Crucible: Race and Nation in the Twentieth Century* (Princeton, New Jersey: Princeton University Press, 2001), 353.

24. John Updike, *The Rabbit Novels, Volume One, Book Two* (New York: Random House Publishing Group, 2003), 204.
25. Lois Palken Rudnick, Judith E. Smith, and Rachel Rubin, *Identities, An Introductory Textbook* (Massachusetts: Blackwell Publishing, 2005), 141.
26. Michael Shafer, *The Legacy: The Vietnam War in the American Imagination* (Massachusetts: Beacon Press, 1992), 69.
27. Richard L. Strout, "Cronkite Steps Down," *Christian Science Monitor,* 5 March 1981.
28. Theodore Harold White, *America in Search of Itself: The Making of the President, 1956–1980* (New York: Warner Books 1986), 114.
29. Ibid., 111.
30. "Rampage & Restraint," *Time,* 19 April 1968; Faludi, *Stiffed,* 110.
31. Ralph Waldo Emerson, "American Civilization." *Atlantic Monthly,* April 1862.
32. PBS, *American Experience: The Kennedys.* Executive producer Elizabeth Deane.
33. Robert Mason, *Richard Nixon and the Quest for a New Majority* (University of North Carolina Press, 2004), 27.
34. PBS, *American Experience: The Kennedys.*
35. "Do the Polls Help Democracy?" *Time,* 31 May 1968.
36. Norman Mailer, *The Time of Our Time* (New York: Random House, 1999), 1045.
37. Arthur Jr. Schlesinger, *Robert Kennedy and His Times, Volume II* (New York: Houghton Mifflin Company, 1978), 920–921.
38. Ibid., 836.
39. Mailer, *The Time of Our Time,* 642.
40. W.M.G. study of 1968 University of Michigan American National Election Studies survey.
41. Richard M. Nixon, Acceptance Speech for the Republican Nomination, 8 August, 1968. Available at http://www.pbs.org/wgbh/amex/presidents/37_nixon/psources/ps_accept68.html
42. Scammon and Wattenberg, *The Real Majority,* 164.
43. Mailer, *The Time of Our Time,* 681–689.
44. Boller, *Presidential Campaigns,* 322–323
45. Mailer, *The Time of Our Time,* 693.
46. Scammon and Wattenberg, *The Real Majority,* 164.
47. "The Fear Campaign," *Time,* 4 October 1968.
48. Scammon and Wattenberg, *The Real Majority,* 167–168.
49. Thomas B. Edsall, "Karl Rove's Juggernaut," *New Republic,* 25 September 2006.
50. Scammon and Wattenberg, *The Real Majority,* 62.
51. Ibid., 161–162.
52. Ibid., 62 and 57–58, respectively.
53. Teddy White, *The Making of the President* (New York: Athenaeum Publishers, 1961), 332.
54. "Nixon's the One," *Time,* 18 Oct. 1968.
55. Boller, *Presidential Campaigns,* 323.
56. David Halberstam, *The Best and the Brightest* (New York: Random House, 2001), 531.
57. Boller, *Presidential Campaigns,* 325.
58. Scammon and Wattenberg, *The Real Majority,* 183.
59. Greenberg, *Middle Class Dreams,* 114.

60. Kevin Phillips, *The Emerging Republican Majority* (New York: Arlington House, 1969), 91.
61. W.M.G. study of 1968 University of Michigan American National Election Studies survey ("middle class" means middle third income bracket). The Michigan study only gave the third party vote, but not the Wallace vote in 1968. The Wallace estimate is based on the multiplication of third party voters from the Michigan study and the percentage of third party voters from the vote count itself.
62. E. Black and Merle Black, *The Vital South*, 169.

CHAPTER III

1. Author's longitudinal study on media exit polling.
2. Andrew Hacker, "What's the Matter With Democrats?" *New York Times*, 1 October 2006.
3. Matt Labash, "Hunting Bubba," *The Weekly Standard*, 20 June 2005.
4. Author's study on Pew survey 2004 Political Landscape, 5 November 2003.
5. U.S. Census Bureau, State Rankings, Poverty of People, By region, Table 9, Historical and Kaiser Family Foundation on uninsured.
6. Unionization data comes from the U.S. Department of Labor Union Members Summary, 20 January 2006; gun ownership statistics from W.M.G. study of 2000 and 2004 exit polling; church attendance statistic from the Pew Forum on Religion & Public Life, "A Faith-Based Partisan Divide, 2006," p. 10; Individualism statement and satisfaction statistics from Colleen J. Shogan, "Anti-Intellectualism in the Plebiscitary Presidency: A Conservative Populism?" Paper, annual meeting of the American Political Science Association, Philadelphia, 27 August 2003; Military comment from Alan Brinkley, *American Prospect*, December 2004. On megachurches, Brad Wilcox, *Soft Patriarchs, New Men: How Christianity Shapes Fathers and Husbands* (Chicago: University Of Chicago Press 2004), 65; the statistics on social conservatives in the South is from The Pew Research Center for the People & the Press, "Beyond Red vs. Blue," 2005 Political Typology; 10 May 2005.
7. Kevin Phillips, *The Emerging Republican Majority* (New York: Arlington House, 1969), 212.
8. W.M.G. study of 1952–1968 data compiled by the University of Michigan American National Election Studies.
9. Malcolm Ritter, "If You Must Insult Someone, Pick a Northerner," *Los Angeles Times*, 15 September 1996.
10. Ibid.
11. Paul F. Boller Jr., *Presidential Campaigns* (New York: Oxford, 2004), 225–26.
12. Associated Press, "2 Strategists Had 100 White House Meetings," *New York Times*, 21 September 2006.
13. Daniel Casse, "A Party of One: Clinton and the Democrats," *Commentary Magazine*, July 1996.
14. Author's study of 1968 data compiled by the University of Michigan American National Election Studies.
15. Richard M. Scammon and Ben J. Wattenberg, *The Real Majority: The Classic Examination of the American Electorate* (New York: Coward-McCann,1992), 63.
16. Ibid., 226–227.

CHAPTER IV

1. Lois Palken Rudnick, Judith E. Smith, and Rachel Rubin, *Identities, An Introductory Textbook* (Massachusetts: Blackwell Publishing, 2005), 139–40.
2. Richard M. Scammon and Ben J. Wattenberg, *The Real Majority: The Classic Examination of the American Electorate* (New York: Coward-McCann, 1992), 223–24.
3. Jerry Lembcke, *The Spitting Image: Myth, Memory, and the Legacy of Vietnam* (New York: New York University Press, 2000), 50.
4. Pete Hamill, "The Revolt of the White Lower Middle Class," *New York*, 14 April 1969, 24–29.
5. Nixon Presidential Materials, National Archives in College Park, Md. (Staff; White House special files; Staff member and office files; President's office files; president's handwriting), May 1969.
6. Jerome M. Rosow, Assistant Secretary of Labor, "The Problem of the Blue-Collar Worker," 16 April 1970. National Archives in College Park, Md. Nixon Presidential Materials Staff.
7. Homer Bigart, "War Foes Here Attacked by Construction Workers," *New York Times*, 9 May 1970.
8. Michael Kazin, *The Populist Persuasion: An American History* (New York: HarperCollins, 1998), 249
9. Ibid., 250–53.
10. Daniel J. Balz and Ronald Brownstein, *Storming the Gates: Protest Politics and the Republican Revival* (New York: Little Brown, 1996), 64.
11. "Man and Woman of the Year: The Middle Americans," *Time*, 5 January 1970.
12. Kevin P. Phillips, *Boiling Point: Democrats, Republicans, and the Decline of Middle-Class Prosperity* (New York: HarperCollins, 1994), 67.
13. "Remembering Agnew," *MacNeil/Lehrer News Hour*, PBS, 18 September 1996.
14. Lance Morrow, "Family Values," 31 August 1992.
15. Richard Nixon, "Annual Message to the Congress on the State of the Union," 22 January 1971, available at http://www.presidency.ucsb.edu/ws/index.php?pid=3110.
16. Balz and Brownstein, *Storming the Gates*, 64.

CHAPTER V

1. Robert Mason, *Richard Nixon and the Quest for a New Majority* (Chapel Hill: The University of North Carolina Press, 2003), 172.
2. "Campaign Teardrops," *Time*, 13 March 1972.
3. Wallace won Florida with 42 percent of the vote, Tennessee with 68 percent, North Carolina with 50 percent, as well as in Michigan with 51 percent and Maryland with 39 percent, demonstrating his wide appeal. "Wallace for President," available at http://www.pbs.org/wgbh/amex/wallace/maps/map_1972.html#topofmap.
4. "Introducing . . . the McGovern Machine," *Time*, 24 July 1972.
5. Richard M. Scammon and Ben J. Wattenberg, *The Real Majority: The Classic Examination of the American Electorate* (New York: Coward-McCann,1992), 74
6. Eileen Shields-West, *The World Almanac of Presidential Campaigns* (Strongsville, Ohio: World Almanac Education, 1992), 218.
7. Democratic Party Platform of 1972, available at http://www.presidency.ucsb.edu/showplatforms.php?platindex=D1972

8. Matthew D. Lassiter, *The Silent Majority: Suburban Politics in the Sunbelt South* (Princeton: Princeton University Press, 2005), 311.

9. Shields-West, *The World Almanac of Presidential Campaigns*, 219.

10. W.M.G. study of CBS News Exit Polling, 1972.

11. Ibid.

12. Ibid.

13. H. W. Brands, *The Strange Death of American Liberalism* (New Haven: Yale University Press, 2003).

14. John Micklethwait and Adrian Wooldridge, *The Right Nation* (New York: Penguin Group, 2005), 68.

15. Ibid., 70.

16. Peter Beinart, *The Good Fight* (New York: HarperCollins, 2006), 55–56.

17. Michael Kazin, *The Populist Persuasion: An American History* (New York: HarperCollins, 1995), 246.

18. Paul F. Boller Jr., *Presidential Campaigns* (New York: Oxford, 2004), 342.

19. David Shribman, "Senator Henry M. Jackson is Dead at 71," *New York Times*, 2 September 1983.

20. Robert M. Hardaway, *America Goes to School: Law, Reform, and Crisis in Public Education* (Connecticut: Praeger Press, 1995), 124.

21. Beinart, *The Good Fight*, 57.

22. Carter improved a striking 23 percent on Hubert Humphrey's white male support (rising from 35 to 58 percent) within the lower third of earners, and 17 percent among middle income white men (rising from 33 to 50). W.M.G. study of data compiled by the University of Michigan American National Election Studies.

23. With white men, Carter improved 20 percent in the South compared to 10 percent in the non-South between 1968 and 1976. This difference in improvement from the South and non-South appears to have come from 1968 Wallace voters who switched to Carter (there were significantly more Wallace voters in the South). W.M.G. study of data compiled by the University of Michigan American National Election Studies.

24. W.M.G. study of CBS News exit polling, 1976 and subsequent exit polling.

25. Ibid.

CHAPTER VI

1. Louis Menard, *American Studies* (New York: Farrar, Straus and Giroux, 2003), 150.

2. Howell Raines, "Reagan Jokes Stir Aides' Concern," *New York Times*, 2 March 1982.

3. Donald Regan, *For the Record* (New York: Harcourt, 1988), 246–248.

4. Isaiah Berlin, *The Hedgehog and the Fox: An Essay on Tolstoy's View of History* (New York: Simon and Schuster 1966). This hedgehog and fox analogy to Reagan was made first by Allen Lichtman of American University in Washington, D.C.

5. Stanley B. Greenberg and Anna Greenberg, memo re: Winning Back Men, 24 July 2000, Friends of Democracy Corps.

6. Edmund Morris, *The Rise of Theodore Roosevelt* (New York: McCann & Geoghegan Inc, 1979), 60.

7. J. A. Mangan and James Walvin, *Manliness and Morality: Middle Class Masculinity in Britain and America* (New York: St. Martin's Press, 1987), 24.

8. K. A. Cuordileone, "Politics in an Age of Anxiety," *Journal of American History* 87, September 2000: 515–545.

9. Susan Faludi, *Stiffed: The Betrayal of the American Man* (New York: HarperCollins, 1999), 20.

10. Theodore White, *The Making of the President* (New York: Athenaeum Publishers, 1961), 377.

11. Michael Kazin, *The Populist Persuasion: An American History* (New York: Harper-Collins, 1995),170.

12. Cuordileone, "Politics in an Age of Anxiety."

13. Faludi, *Stiffed*, 25.

14. Alan J. Lichtman, *Great Presidents Lecture Series;* Teaching Company; American University.

15. David Halberstam, *The Best and the Brightest* (New York: Modern Library, 2001), 533.

16. Michael S. Kimmel, *Manhood in America: A Cultural History* (Oxford: Oxford University Press, 1996), 269.

17. Ibid., 271.

18. Halberstam, *The Best and the Brightest*, 531–532.

19. Ibid.

20. Bruce Mazlish, *In Search of Nixon* (New York, Basic Books, 1972), 116.

21. Garry Wills, "Nixon Was an Equal-Opportunity Hater," *Albany (NY) Times Union*, 15 November 1999.

22. Arlie Hochschild, "NASCAR Dads Fuel Strategies for Bush in '04," *Los Angeles Times*, 5 October 2003.

23. Joe McGinniss, *The Selling Of the President 1968* (New York: Penguin Group, 1969), 64.

24. John Micklethwait and Adrian Wooldridge, *The Right Nation* (New York: Penguin Group, 2005), 230.

25. Kenji Yoshino, "The Pressure to Cover," *New York Times Magazine*, 15 January 2006.

26. Michael Duffy and Karen Tumulty, "Gore's Secret Guru," *Time*, 8 November 1999.

27. Jay Root and Ron Hutcheson, "President Bush entertains Russian President Vladimir Putin at his ranch near Crawford," *Fort Worth Star-Telegram*, 15 November 2001.

28. Dana Milbank, "Another Ol' Hickory in the White House?" *Washington Post*, 17 September 2002.

29. Ibid.

30. Nikki Finke, "Who is America's Favorite Movie Star?" available at http://www.deadlinehollywooddaily.com/whos-americas-favorite-movie-star.

CHAPTER VII

1. ABC News Transcripts, 23 September 1980.

2. David Paul Kuhn, "The Gospel According to Jim Wallis," *Washington Post Magazine*, 26 November 2006.

3. Peter Beinart, *The Good Fight* (New York: HarperCollins, 2006), 59.

4. Tom Reiss, "The First Conservative," *The New Yorker* (24 October 2005).

5. Arthur Schlesinger Jr., " Forgetting Reinhold Niebuhr," *New York Times*, 18 September 2005.

6. Author's study of The Pew Research Center for the People & the Press, "Beyond Red vs. Blue," *2005 Political Typology*, 10 May 2005.
7. John Halpin and Ruy Teixeira, "The Politics of Definition, Part IV," *American Prospect Online*, 27 April 2006, available at http://www.prospect.org/web/page.ww?section=root&name=ViewWeb&articleId=11455, accessed 1 March 2007.
8. Theodore Harold White, *America in Search of Itself: The Making of the President, 1956–1980* (New York: Warner Books 1986), 119.
9. Edwin Warner, "New Resolve by the New Right," *Time*, 8 December 1980.
10. W.M.G. study on 2004 media exit polling.
11. Ibid.
12. William James, *The Varieties of Religious Experience: A Study in Human Nature* (New York: Penguin American Library 1982), 84.
13. John Micklethwait and Adrian Wooldridge, *The Right Nation* (New York: Penguin, 2004), 12.
14. White, *America in Search of Itself*, 16.
15. Romesh Ratnesar, "Bedeviling an Empire," *Time*, 8 March 1983, available at http://www.time.com/time/80days/830308.html.
16. Walter Isaacson, "Reagan for the Defense; Monday," *Time*, 4 April 1983.
17. "The Jesus Factor," *Frontline*, PBS, available at http://www.pbs.org/wgbh/pages/frontline/shows/jesus/, accessed 1 March 2007.
18. W.M.G study; Pew, 2004 Typology.
19. 2004 media exit polling, as analyzed by Pew's John C. Green, by request of author.
20. Cathy Young, "Venus at the Ballot Box: Women and Social, Economic, and Foreign Policy," *Reason* 32, 1 February 2001, 17.
21. Curtis Hutson, *Mothers* (Tennessee: Sword of the Lord Publishers, 2000), 144.
22. Michael Kazin, *The Populist Persuasion: An American History* (New York: HarperCollins, 1995), 171.
23. J. A. Mangan and James Walvin, *Manliness and Morality: Middle Class Masculinity in Britain and America* (New York: St. Martin's Press, 1987), 81.
24. *The Colbert Report*, first broadcast 8 May 2006 by Comedy Central. Ben Karlin, executive producer.
25. "The State of Man," *GQ*, 17 November 2004.
26. Brad Wilcox, *Soft Patriarchs, New Men: How Christianity Shapes Fathers and Husbands* (Chicago: University of Chicago 2004), 58.
27. James Risen, "Christian Men hold Huge Rally on D.C. Mall," *Los Angeles Times*, 5 October 1997, and Ann Scales, " Men fill D.C. Mall in Huge Gathering," *Boston Globe*, 5 October 1997.
28. Ron Stodghill II, "God of our Fathers," *Time*, 6 October 1997.
29. Wilcox, *Soft Patriarchs, New Men*, 58.
30. Southern Baptist Convention, "The Baptist Faith and Message," available at http://www.sbc.net/bfm/default.asp.
31. Don Browning, "Good Christian Men: How Faith Shapes Fathers," *The Christian Century*, 11 January 2005.
32. U.S. Census Bureau, Historical Poverty Table, Table 19, Percent of Persons in Poverty, by State: 2003, 2004, 2005.
33. Paul Krugman, "True Blue Americans," *New York Times*, 7 May 2002.
34. Micklethwait and Wooldridge, *The Right Nation*, 411.

35. Edwin McDowell, "Books are Proliferating on the Care of Children," *New York Times*, 29 August 1984.

36. Robert Reich, *Reason: Why Liberals Will Win the Battle for America* (New York: Vintage 2005), 27.

37. "Parents and Experts Split on Spanking," *New York Times*, 19 June 1985.

38. W.M.G. study of Pew survey, "Religion on Public Life," 2004 Political Landscape, 5 November 2003.

39. Samuel P. Huntington, *Who are We? The Challenges to America's Identity* (New York: Simon & Schuster, 2005), 352.

40. Micklethwait and Wooldridge, *The Right Nation*, 12.

41. W.M.G. study on Pew survey, "Religion on Public Life," 5 July 2005.

42. "Pursuing Happiness," *The Economist*, 1 July 2006.

43. Robert B. Reich. "Keeping the Faith," *American Prospect* (6 December 2004).

44. W.M.G. Pew 2005 August.

CHAPTER VIII

1. Reagan for President Campaign Plan 1980.

2. W.M.G. study of data compiled by the University of Michigan American National Election Studies for 1960 and 1980.

3. Lee Walczak, "Reagan's Push for Worker Support," *Business Week*, 13 October 1980.

4. Bruce Curtis, "The Wimp Factor," *American Heritage Magazine*, Vol. 40, No.7, November 1989.

5. Carter-Reagan Presidential Debate, 28 October 1980.

6. W.M.G. study of 1980 ABC News exit polling.

7. W.M.G. study of 1980 CBS News exit polling. Reagan improved about 7 percent with liberal, moderate, and conservative white men compared to 1976. In total, conservative white men favored Reagan by about 60 percentage points, and moderate white men favored Reagan by about 20 percentage points. Together, about 85 percent of white male voters in 1980 were now moderate or conservative. His loss of liberal white men only amounted to 15 percent of the electorate. Among women, Carter did worse with white women among moderates and liberals than he had four years earlier. Carter won roughly 60 percent of liberal white women in 1980. But liberals were less than half the number of moderates within the white female electorate. Moderate white women favored Reagan by at least 10 percentage points, while conservative white women favored Reagan by about 50 percentage points. Together, moderates and conservatives equaled about eight out of ten white female voters. In the ensuing years, as the media discussed Reagan's problem with women, it was only liberal white and minority women whom Republicans continued to lose.

8. W.M.G. study of 1980 CBS News exit polling.

9. Among whites, both men and women gave highest priority to balancing the federal budget. White men gave second highest priority to inflation and the economy while white women gave second priority to jobs and unemployment. Those who voted primarily on the issue of Iran actually supported Carter, but only 15 percent of white women and 12 percent of white men did.

10. Equally notable, 57 percent of Democratic white men agreed while only 38 percent of Democratic white women did. The gap was about half that among Republican white men and women, though more men still favored a more forceful

stance. Seven out of ten white voters, male or female, who said they believed the United States should take a more forceful stance, supported Reagan. The results suggest, however tenuously, that among whites, Reagan's perception as a "strong leader" was favored by men over women, and this comported with the stronger national security stance white men favored. The suggestion was that as Republicans championed the traditional man, it won male voters, while not turning off large portions of the female vote. At least half of female voters in this feminist age seemingly preferred the traditional man.

CHAPTER IX

1. Michael S. Kimmel, *Manhood in America: A Cultural History* (Oxford: Oxford University Press, 1996), 263.
2. Kate Millett, *Sexual Politics* (New York: Simon and Schuster, 1969), 319.
3. Daniel Yankelovich, *New Rules* (Washington: Random House, 1981), 101.
4. Norman Mailer, *The Time of Our Time* (New York: Modern Library, 1999), 207.
5. Millett, *Sexual Politics*, 244.
6. "Ready for a Woman President?" CBS News, 5 February 2006, available at http://www.cbsnews.com/stories/2006/02/03/opinion/polls/main1281319.shtml.
7. Millett, *Sexual Politics*, 330.
8. Henry Allen, "The Real 1980s: How Life Went On," *Washington Post*, 14 November 1989.
9. Millett, *Sexual Politics*, 43–46.

CHAPTER X

1. Fred Siegel, "The Statist Temptation," *National Review*,14 August 2000.
2. *The Federalist Papers*, number 51, available at http://www.foundingfathers.info/federalistpapers, accessed 1 March 2007.
3. Russell Kirk, *The Conservative Mind: From Burke to Eliot* (Washington: Regnery Publishing, 2001), 42.
4. Ralph Waldo Emerson, "American Civilization," *Atlantic Monthly*, April 1862.
5. Kirk, *The Conservative Mind*, 219.
6. Henry Steele Commager, *The American Mind* (New Haven: Yale University Press, 1959), 9–10.
7. W.M.G. study of Pew Research Center for the People & the Press, survey, "Beyond Red vs. Blue," 10 May 2005.
8. Samuel P. Huntington, *Who Are We: The Challenges to America's National Identity* (New York: Simon and Schuster, 2004), 274–75.
9. Ronald Reagan, Inaugural Address, 20 January 1981.
10. Geraldine Ferraro, "1984 Vice Presidential Acceptance Address," available at www.americanrhetoric.com.
11. Ronald B. Rapoport, Walter J. Stone, and Alan I. Abramowitz, "Sex and the Caucus Participant: The Gender Gap and Presidential Nominations," *American Journal of Political Science*, 34, August 1990, 3, 725–740.
12. David Hoffman, "Reagan, Invoking History, Urges Democrats To Abandon Party," *Washington Post*, 20 September 1984.
13. Reagan won about seven out of ten white men without a college education; he won about half of all others without a college education. Seven out of ten married white

men voted for Reagan, while 65 percent of married white women supported him. Reagan won about three out of four southern white men. Reagan did so well with white women, again because of the southern female vote. Reagan won 55 percent of the white female vote in the East while winning 70 percent in the South. Reagan won all three household income brackets of whites. Also, by about a 10 percent gap, white men cared more about a strong "U.S. defense" and white women cared more about "arms control or threat of war." W.M.G. study on 1984 CBS media exit polling.

14. Stan Greenberg, *Middle Class Dreams* (New York: Times Books, 1995), 46.
15. Bruce Curtis, "The Wimp Factor," *American Heritage Magazine* 40 (November 1989): 7.
16. Kate Zernike, "Kerry's Lesson: Lambeau Rhymes With Rambo," *New York Times*, 19 September 2004.
17. W.M.G. study of Pew survey, "2004 Political Landscape," 5 November 2003.
18. Karlyn H. Bowman, "The Gender Gap, Real or Hype?" 1 January 2002 and "Ex Femina; Gender Gap Calculus," 21 September 2000, both available at www.IWF.org.
19. Louann Brizendine, "The Female Brain—Excerpted First Chapter," *New York Times*, 10 September 2006.
20. Caitlin Flanagan, "We're Here, We're Square, Get Used to It," *Time*, 30 April 2006.
21. Nancy Gibbs, "The War Against Feminism," *Time*, 9 March 1992.
22. Charlotte Allen, "The return of the happy housewife," *Los Angeles Times*, 5 March 2006.

CHAPTER XI

1. ABC *20/20*, "State of the Nation; A Country Divided," *ABC News Transcripts*, 30 June 2006.
2. W.M.G. study of longitudinal CBS exit polls—by region.
3. *The Colbert Report*, first broadcast on January 9, 2006 by Comedy Central. Ben Karlin, executive producer.
4. John B. Judis and Ruy Teixeira, *The Emerging Democratic Majority* (New York: Simon & Schuster, 2004), 147.
5. Ronald Brownstein, "GOP Plants Flag on New Voting Frontier," *Los Angeles Times*, 22 November 2004.
6. David Paul Kuhn, "The Year In Politics," CBSNews.com, 23 December 2004, available at http://www.cbsnews.com/stories/2004/12/20/politics/main662099.shtml.
7. Mark Gersh, "Micro-Politics," *DLC | Blueprint Magazine*, 15 March 2005.
8. Author's study of 2004 media exit poll.
9. W.M.G. longitudinal study of media exit polling.
10. Val E. Limburg, "The Fairness Doctrine," Museum of Broadcast Communications, available at http://www.museum.tv/archives/etv/F/htmlF/fairnessdoct/fairnessdoct.htm.
11. David Paul Kuhn, "Senator Franken?" *Salon.com*, 28 April 2005.
12. W.M.G. study on Pew survey, 2004 Political Landscape, 5 November 2003.

13. David Cole, "My First (and Last) Time with Bill O'Reilly," *Nation Magazine*, 13 July 2004 available at http://www.thenation.com/doc/20040719/coleweb, accessed 1 March 2007.

14. Paul Krugman, "Reign of Error," *New York Times*, 28 July 2006.

15. ABC *20/20*, "State Of The Nation; A Country Divided," *ABC News Transcripts*, 30 June 2006.

16. "Belief that Iraq Had Weapons of Mass Destruction Has Increased Substantially," Harris Poll #57, 21 July 2006.

17. The Pew Internet & American Life Project; Online News; March 2006.

18. W.M.G. study of The Pew Research Center for the People & the Press, "Beyond Red vs. Blue," The 2005 Political Typology, 10 May 2005.

19. The Pew Internet & American Life Project, "The State of Blogging," January 2005. The percent of white female and male bloggers is from a Pew survey in January 2006. Whites includes Jews and 2006 blog readership and writing given directly from Pew.

20. Mark Halperin and John F. Harris, "Clinton Politics vs. Bush Politics Book Excerpt," *DLC | Blueprint Magazine*, 4 January 2007.

CHAPTER XII

1. Associated Press, "'Mr. Gorbachev, Open This Gate, Tear Down This Wall'; President's Challenge in Berlin Talk," *Los Angeles Times*, 12 June 1987; Gerald M. Boyd, "Excerpts From Reagan's Talk At The Berlin Wall And Raze Berlin Wall," *New York Times*, 13 June 1987, available at http://ronaldreagan.hagbergmedia.com/video_and_audio/ and http://www.britannica.com/presidents/art–13685.

2. Joe McGinniss, *The Selling Of the President* (New York: Penguin Group, 1969), 26.

3. John Balzar, "Reagan Legacy," *Los Angeles Times*, 7 June 2004.

4. Shankar Vedantam, "Hidden Biases," *Washington Post*, 30 January 2006.

5. John F. Kennedy, *Profiles in Courage* (New York: Harper and Row, 1963), 207.

6. Arthur Schlesinger, Jr. *Robert Kennedy and His Times, Volume II* (New York: Houghton Mifflin Company, 1978), 848.

7. Joe Klein, *Politics Lost: How American Democracy Was Trivialized By People Who Think You're Stupid* (New York: Doubleday, 2006), 79 and 145.

8. George Breitman, *Malcolm X Speaks; Selected Speeches and Statements* (New York: Grove Press, 1990), 20.

9. Clarence Page, "2008 'Head Game' Starts Now," *Chicago Tribune*, 16 October 2006.

10. Aristotle, *Rhetoric*, trans. W. Rhys Roberts, book I, 3–7 and 17, available at http://www.public.iastate.edu/~honeyl/Rhetoric/index.html

11. Ibid., book II, chapter 21.

12. Ron Fournier and Trevor Tompson, "Poll: Character Trumps Policy for Voter," *Associated Press*, 11 March 2007.

13. W.M.G. on 2000 and 2004 exit polls.

14. W.M.G. study of 1980 CBS News/*New York Times* exit polling.

15. CBS, *60 Minutes*, 14 January 2007.

16. *The American President*, first broadcast on 9 April 2000 by PBS. Philip B. Kunhardt, producer.

17. NBC News Transcripts, *The Today Show*, 25 January 2006.

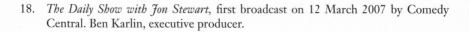

18. *The Daily Show with Jon Stewart*, first broadcast on 12 March 2007 by Comedy Central. Ben Karlin, executive producer.

CHAPTER XIII

1. Susan Faludi, *Stiffed: The Betrayal of the American Man* (New York: HarperCollins, 1999), 316.
2. "Bush Depicts Dukakis as Out of Sync With Partner," *Washington Post*, 23 July 1988.
3. David Hoffman, "Bush Seeks To Sew Up Flag Vote," *Washington Post*, 21 September 1988, and *Associated Press*, 20 September 1988.
4. Bernard Weinraub, "Loaded for Bear And Then Some," *New York Times*, 14 September 1988.
5. George W. Bush campaign speech, Waukesha, Wisconson, 14 July 1004.
6. Ibid.
7. Russell Kirk, *The Conservative Mind: From Burke to Eliot* (Washington: Regnery Publishing, 2001), 223.
8. Author's study of Pew Research Center for the People & the Press, "Beyond Red vs. Blue," 2005 Political Typology, 10 May 2005.
9. Ibid. Fourteen percent of white men and 13 percent of white women are "upbeats," the first centrist group. They believe government "does a better job than people think" (68 percent compared to 45 percent nationally), that elected officials care about them, believe "most corporations make a fair profits (64 percent to 32 percent nationally), and three out of four are strongly optimistic about the nation's ability to solve its problems, believe immigrants strengthen the nation, and that corporations make reasonable profits. They also favor preemptive military action against threats. While 56 percent identify as Independent, 39 percent Republican, and 5 percent Democratic, about three out of four lean Republican and supported Bush 63 percent to 14 percent for Kerry.

   "Disaffecteds" include 11 percent of white male voters and 9 percent of white female voters. Seven out of ten have no college degree, which explains why eight out of ten believe "immigrants today are a burden on our country because they take our jobs, housing and government." Even more believe most elected officials don't care about what they think, while half believe hard work does not guarantee success, compared to a quarter of Americans who agree. Despite the financial strain, they only moderately support welfare for the poor, likely because fully seven out of ten believe government is "always wasteful and inefficient." Only 2 percent are Democratic, while 30 percent are Republican, and 68 percent are Independent. Bush won 42 percent of their vote while Kerry won 21 percent. The traditional Democratic coalition, under FDR and JFK, would no doubt have reversed these numbers.
10. Tim Grieve, "Hollywood Searches for a Democratic Star," *Salon.com*, 2 December 2003.
11. Matt Bai, "Beverly Hills Coup," *New York Times*, 13 November 2005.
12. Dwight R. Worley, "Senator Hillary Clinton Blasts Bush Assassination Film," *The Journal News*, 16 September 2006.
13. Maureen Dowd, "Bush, Sensing Landslide, Ridicules Rival," *New York Times*, November 1988.

14. Michael Barone, "The New Politics of Cultural Values," *The Public Perspective*, May 1990 / June 1990.
15. Cathleen Decker, "Politics 88," *Los Angeles Times*, June 23, 1988.
16. "George Bush and Willie Horton," *New York Times*, November 4, 1988.
17. W.M.G. study of 1988 CBS News/*New York Times* exit polling.
18. Ibid.

CHAPTER XIV

1. W.M.G. study of 1992 VNS exit polling.
2. The 1988 and 1984 Perot voter responses are informed estimations, taking into consideration that voters demonstrated an apparent bias to overestimate their Republican support in past contests.
3. Consider Reagan in 1980. While a third party candidate earned 8 percent of the vote, Reagan showed improvements with key portions of the electorate when compared with the 1976 election. He improved among moderate white males while holding the same level of support with moderate white women. He made gains in both the Democratic unions and the Jewish vote. Even among black voters, he improved by about 5 percent. But his gains were largely among whites. In the South, he improved by 13 percentage points among white men and by 7 percent among white women, in comparison to Ford.

    Furthermore, in 1968, the last election with a major third-party candidate, Democrats saw their middle-class white male support drop in half compared to 1964 and still fall 13 points compared to 1956, their previous low. This was the beginning of the White Male Gap, when white men began deserting Democrats at significantly higher levels than they deserted Republicans. It was a time of antiwar protests, rising crime, the counterculture, when white men began to feel especially estranged from liberalism. By 1992, when Clinton won the presidency, he showed no significant improvement with any income bracket of white men or women. For his part, Bush showed drastic declines among whites, from 20 to 25 percent across middle-class and poor white male income brackets and 10 to 20 percent among the same groups of women.

    In 1968, it was Nixon who made inroads among whites and this gave experts reason to assess that Wallace's vote would have split 70 to 30 in Nixon's favor. There were no inroads to be found with Clinton's numbers and hence, however you cut the vote, Bush suffered nearly all the losses. Clinton in 1992 looked like Dukakis in 1988.
4. E. J. Dionne Jr., "After 12 Years of Conservatism, a New Era Emerges," *Washington Post*, 4 November 1992.

CHAPTER XV

1. Steven Stark, "Gap Politics," *The Atlantic Monthly*, July 1996.
2. Warren Farrell, *The Myth of Male Power* (New York: Berkley, 1993), 172, 190, 191, 208, 187, 390–398.
3. Susan P. Dalessandro, Lisa A. Stilwell, and Lynda M. Reese, "Law School Admission Council Research Report Series; LSAT Performance with Regional, Gender, and Racial/Ethnic Breakdowns: 1997–1998 Through 2003–2004 Testing Years," 13, 17, 26.

4. Althea K. Nagai, Research Fellow, Center for Equal Opportunity, "Racial and Ethnic Admission Preferences at the University of Michigan Law School," 21.

5. W.M.G. study on *New York Times* Poll # 2005–03A: Taxes/Getting Ahead in Life/Social Class; *New York Times* Survey Organization.

6. Daniel J. Balz and Ronald Brownstein, *Storming the Gates: Protest Politics and the Republican Revival* (New York: Little Brown & Co., 1996), 122.

7. Richard Morin and Barbara Vobejda, "'94 May Be the Year of the Man: GOP Is Powered By Male Support," *Washington Post*, 10 November 1994.

8. Rick Lyman, "Ann Richards, Plain-Spoken Texas Governor Who Aided Minorities, Dies at 73," *New York Times*, 14 September 2006.

9. William A. Degregorio, *The Complete Book of U.S. Presidents* (New Jersey: Barricade Books, 2005), 762.

10. Facts on File World News Digest, "Republicans Win Control of U.S. House and Senate; Dominate Congress for First Time in 40 Years," 10 November 1994.

11. "Who Voted, State-by-State Breakdown," *The Hotline*, 11 November 1994.

12. Alan I. Abramowitz, "Issue Evolution Reconsidered: Racial Attitudes and Partisanship in the U.S. Electorate," *American Journal of Political Science*, February 1994.

13. Ruy A. Teixeira and Joel Rogers, *America's Forgotten Majority: Why the White Working Class Still Matters* (New York: Basic Books, 2000), 85.

14. David Gates, "White Male Paranoia," *Newsweek*, 9 March 1993.

15. Tatsha Robertson and Sarah Schweitzer, "Howard B. Dean," *Boston Globe*, 21 September 2003.

16. Michael Zwieg, *The Working Class Majority: America's Best Kept Secret* (Cornell: ILR Press, 2000), 64–65.

17. "A Doubtful Bet on Living Standards," *Baltimore Sun*, 23 December 1994.

18. Jeff Madrick, "The Way to a Fair Deal," *New York Review of Books*, Volume 53, Number 1, 12 January 2006.

19. Zwieg, *The Working Class Majority*, 53–54.

20. Gates, "White Male Paranoia."

21. Arthur M. Schlesinger, *The Disuniting of America* (New York: Norton, 1992), 4.

22. Ibid., 122.

23. National Center on Educational Statistics, Table 249, Bachelor's degrees conferred by degree-granting institutions, by discipline division: Selected years, 1970–71 through 2003–04.

CHAPTER XVI

1. Edwin Chen, "Dole to Quit Senate to Devote Time to Presidential Race," *Los Angeles Times*, 16 May 1996.

2. Edwin Chen and Maria L. LaGanga, "Clinton Taxes Victimize Families, Dole Charges," *New York Times*, 3 October 1996.

3. W.M.G. Longitudinal media exit polling. Among white men who had voted for Perot in 1992, 36 percent stayed with Perot, 17 percent shifted their support to Clinton and 45 percent to Dole. For white women who voted for Perot in 1992, 28 percent stayed, 26 percent shifted to Clinton and 45 percent to Dole. By 2000, among white men who said they voted for Perot in 1996, 22 percent voted for Gore and 70 percent voted for Bush, while among white women 29 percent voted for Gore and 61 percent voted for Bush.

4. W.M.G. study of 1996 media exit polling.

5. Charles Peters, "The Rich and the Rest," *New York Times*, 6 November 2005.
6. CNN, President Bill Clinton address, 17 August 1998.
7. T. S. Eliot, *The Hollow Men* (Golden, Colorado: Fulcrum Press, 2000).
8. David Remnick, "The Wanderer," *The New Yorker,* September 2006.

CHAPTER XVII

1. Sean Wilentz, *The Rise of American Democracy* (New York: Norton, 2005), 487–488.
2. Eileen Shields-West, *The World Almanac of Presidential Campaigns* (Strongsville, Ohio: World Almanac Education 1992), 62.
3. William A. Degregorio, *The Complete Book of U.S. Presidents* (Fort Lee, NJ: Barricade Books, 2005), 144–145.
4. Michelle Mittelstadt, "Republicans pounce on Gore's claim that he created the Internet," *Associated Press*, 12 March 1999.
5. W.M.G. study of longitudinal media exit polling.
6. Ibid.
7. A fifth of white women called themselves liberals, half said they were moderate, and 28 percent were conservative. Among white men, at the turn of the century, only 15 percent said they were liberals, half said they were moderate, and 36 percent said they were conservative.
8. Bush narrowly won white women earning between $30,000 and $50,000 and won white women with a household income between $50,000 and $75,000 by a margin of 12 percent (still short of the 28 percent win of white men among this same group). Among affluent white women with household incomes of $75,000 to $100,000, Democrats actually won these women by a margin of 3 percent, while losing these same white men by a margin of 31 percent. For those making over $100,000, Republicans won white men by 33 percent and white women by 8 percent. For the poorest whites, those making less than $30,000 in household income, Republicans won these men and lost women by nearly the same margin. White males supported the GOP by 13 percent among those under $15,000, but white females in that income bracket backed Gore by roughly the same margin. Republicans won by a 21 percent margin among those white men between $15,000 and $30,000, but Democrats won these same white women. Poor white women likely leaned Democratic for financial reasons and social safety nets. Poor white men likely leaned Republican for cultural reasons, far more over grit, security, guns, and some over social conservative values, but above all, it was an issue of masculinity. But what was interesting, was that for values reasons, white women leaned Democratic in the second largest income bracket.
9. W.M.G. 1992 media exit polling. Among white men, Democrats lost union members by 5 percent compared to non-union members by 35 percent. Among white women, Democrats won union members by 15 percent (slightly less than, but about quarter of the white female electorate), and lost non-union members by 8 percent
10. Readership and income statistic from *Field & Stream* demographic records.
11. Richard Goldstein, "Butching up for Victory," *Nation*, 26 January 2004.
12. W.M.G. study of 2000 and 2004 exit polling.
13. For whites making under $30,000 annually, 62 percent of men opposed gun control and 68 percent of women supported it. Wealthier white men were less opposed, but their opposition never fell below about 55 percent, and wealthier white women were more supportive, as high as three out of four among those with

household incomes over $75,000. Education level followed the same pattern. Among white men who opposed further control, 77 out of every 100 supported Republicans, while among those white women who supported further gun control, 57 percent supported Democrats.

14. Mary Leonard-Ramshaw, "The Primary Source," *Boston Globe*, 18 January 2004.
15. Kathleen Kenna, "Money Talks," *Toronto Star*, 5 November 2000.
16. David M. Halbfinger, "Shotgun in Hand, Kerry Defines His Gun-Control Stance," *New York Times*, 1 November 2003.
17. Judy Wilgoren, "Kerry on Hunting Photo-Op to Help Image," *New York Times*, 22 October 2004.
18. W.M.G. study on Pew Research Center survey, "2004 Political Landscape," 5 November 2003.

CHAPTER XVIII

1. *The American President*, first broadcast on 9 April 2000 by PBS. Philip B. Kunhardt, producer.
2. CQ Staff Directories, CQ Electronic Library, CQ Congress Collection, available at http://library.cqpress.com/, accessed November 5, 2006.
3. Barbara Ehrenreich, "The Warrior Culture," *Time*, 15 October 1990.
4. Steven J. Nider, "The Military Challenge." *DLC | Blueprint Magazine*, 12 July 2001.
5. Study of Pentagon data on cross-racial/gender death count for Global War on Terrorism, 20 January 2007.
6. United States Government Accountability Office Report to Congressional Requesters, "Military Personnel Reporting Additional Service Member Demographics Could Enhance Congressional Oversight," September 2005.
7. W.M.G. study of Pew News Interest Index, January 2007.
8. Ibid.
9. W.M.G. study of Pew polling from July 2003, December 2005, and January 2007.
10. W.M.G. study of Pew survey 2004 Political Landscape; 5 November 2003.
11. W.M.G. study of Pew News Interest Index, February 2006.
12. Clyde Wilcox, Lara Hewitt, Dee Allsop, "The Gender Gap in Attitudes Toward the Gulf War: A Cross-National Perspective," *Journal of Peace Research*, Vol. 33, No. 1, February 1996, 67–82.
13. CNN 2006 Election Exit Polling. Whites includes Jews.
14. W.M.G. study of The Pew Research Center for the People & the Press, "Beyond Red vs. Blue," 2005 Political Typology; 10 May 2005.
15. W.M.G. study of Pew survey "Beyond Red vs. Blue."
16. Ehrenreich, "The Warrior Culture."
17. Matt Bai, "Beverly Hills Coup?" *New York Times*, 13 November 2005.
18. John Micklethwait and Adrian Wooldridge, *The Right Nation* (New York: Penguin, 2004), 410.
19. CBS News/*New York Times* Poll, October 1–3, 2004.
20. David Paul Kuhn, "The Year In Politics," 23 December 2004, available at http://www.cbsnews.com/stories/2004/12/20/politics/main662099.shtml, accessed 1 March 2004.
21. Kate Zernike, "Kerry's Lesson: Lambeau Rhymes with Rambo," *New York Times*, 19 September 2004.
22. W.M.G. longitudinal study of media exit polling.

23. After the 2004 election, of those polled, only one out of four white men were now Democrats, while a third of white women were. About half of white men were Republican, compared to 43 percent of white women. Among whites, 16 percent of men considered themselves liberals, compared to 21 percent of women, while 44 percent of men were moderates (46 percent for women), and 40 percent of men were conservative, compared to a third of women.

24. As was the case in other modern presidential contests, more minority women voted Democratic than men. Fully 76 percent of minority women and 71 percent of minority men supported Kerry. But overall, Bush had still done better with minorities in 2004 than in 2000.

25. Kerry split white women in the West. He won white women by 2 percent in the East. He lost white women in the Midwest by 8 percent. But he won *only* 31 percent of white women in the South. Bush won fully 69 percent. Since 1988, southern white women were far more Republican than their sisters in other regions.

CHAPTER XIX

1. Curt Suplee, "Dawn of the Wimp You Asked for It," *Washington Post*, 10 September 1984.

2. Institute for Diversity and Ethics in Sport at the University of Central Florida, 2005.

3. Norman Mailer, "The White Man Unburdened," *New York Review of Books*, 17 July 2003.

4. Simon Kuper, "American Masculinity Takes a Prolonged Time-Out," *Financial Times*, 29 January 2005.

5. Jim Rendon, "A Man's World Is at the Spa or Salon," *New York Times*, 28 March 2004.

6. W.M.G study of *New York Times* Poll # 2005–03A, "Taxes/Getting Ahead in Life/Social Class," Survey Organization: *New York Times*.

7. *"The State of Man," GQ*, 17 November 2004.

8. Sam McManis, "Manly Men," *Miami Herald*, 24 June 2006.

9. Robert Bly with Bill Moyers, "A Gathering of Men," PBS.

10. Paul Zakrzewski, "Daddy, What Did You Do in the Men's Movement?" *The Boston Globe*, 19 June 2005.

11. *Michael Medved Show*, February 6, 2006.

12. W.M.G study on *New York Times* Poll # 2005–03A: Taxes/Getting Ahead in Life/Social Class, Survey Organization: *New York Times*.

13. Eileen Shields-West, *The World Almanac of Presidential Campaigns* (Strongsville, Ohio: World Almanac Education, 1992), 166.

14. W.M.G. study of *New York Times* Poll # 2005–03A: Taxes/Getting Ahead in Life/Social Class, Survey Organization: *New York Times*.

15. W.M.G. study of 1996 exit polling.

16. David Cay Johnston, "Richest Are Leaving Even the Rich Far Behind," *New York Times*, 5 June 2005.

17. John Halpin and Ruy Teixeira, "The Politics of Definition," *American Prospect Online*, 20 April 2006, available at http://www.prospect.org/web/page.ww?section=root&name=ViewWeb&articleId=11455, accessed 1 March 2007.

18. W.M.G study of *New York Times* Poll # 2005–03A: Taxes/Getting Ahead in Life/Social Class; Survey Organization: *New York Times*.

19. Arlie Hochschild, "NASCAR Dads Fuel Strategies for Bush in '04," *Los Angeles Times*, 5 October 2003.

20. W.M.G. study of 2004 exit polling.
21. Reuters, "Ford to cut $5 bln in Costs, Third of Salaried Staff," 15 September 2006.
22. Thomas Beaumont, "Campaign Organization Must Improve, Labor Says," *Des Moines Register,* 8 June 2006.
23. Robyn E. Blumner, "Democrats Should Look for the Union Label," *St. Petersburg Times,* 6 February 2005.
24. Michael Lind, *Next American Nation: The New Nationalism and the Fourth American Revolution* (New York: Free Press 1996), 187.
25. David R. Francis, "Big labor's split matters—even to nonunion America," *Christian Science Monitor,* 1 August 2005.
26. Economic Policy Institute.
27. Rahm Emanuel and Bruce Reed, *The Plan: Big Ideas for America* (New York: PublicAffairs, 2006), 88–89.
28. Paul Krugman, "Left Behind Economics," *New York Times,* 14 July 2006.
29. Blumner, "Democrats Should Look for the Union Label." White males includes Jews.
30. U.S. Department of Labor, Table 2, Median weekly earnings of full-time wage and salary workers by union affiliation and selected characteristics, 20 January 2006.
31. Michael Harrington, "The Invisible Poor: White Males," *Washington Post,* 15 February 1987.
32. Richard Whitmire, "Boy Trouble," *The New Republic,* 23 January 2006.
33. Yankelovich Monitor Inc., 2003.
34. "Gender Differences in Participation and Completion of Undergraduate Education and How They Have Changed Over Time," National Center for Education Statistics.
35. Richard Whitmire, "Boy Trouble," *New Republic,* 23 January 2006.
36. Chronicle of Higher Education Almanac of Higher Education 2006.
37. National Center for Education, Statistics, available at http://nces.ed.gov/programs/digest/d05/tables/dt05_169.asp.
38. National Center for Educational, Statistics, Table 252. Bachelor's, master's, and doctoral degrees conferred by degree-granting institutions, by sex of student and field of study: 2003–04.
39. National Center for Educational Statistics; Table 205. Total fall enrollment in degree-granting institutions, by race/ethnicity, sex, attendance status, and level of student: Selected years, 1976 through 2004.
40. National Center for Educational Statistics; Table 270. First-professional degrees conferred by degree-granting institutions, by racial/ethnic group and sex of student: Selected years, 1976–77 through 2003–04.
41. National Center for Educational Statistics, Table 105. Percentage of high school dropouts (status dropouts) among persons 16 to 24 years old, by sex and race/ethnicity: 1960 through 2004.
42. Tamar Lewin, "The New Gender Divide; At Colleges, Women Are Leaving Men in the Dust," *New York Times,* 9 July 2006.
43. Eduardo Porter and Michelle O'Donnell, "Facing Middle Age With No Degree, and No Wife," *New York Times,* 6 August 2006.
44. John Updike, *The Rabbit Novels, Volume One, Book One* (New York: Random House Publishing Group, 2003), 204, 213–92.
45. Porter and O'Donnell, "Facing Middle Age With No Degree, and No Wife."

46. Women's Voices, Women's Vote, "The State of Unmarried America: A Demographic, Lifestyle, and Attitudinal Overview of America's Emerging Majority," February 2006.

47. Pew 2005, "Beyond Red vs. Blue, Republicans Divided About Role of Government—Democrats by Social and Personal Values."

48. Warren Farrell, *The Myth of Male Power* (New York: Berkley, 1993), 197.

49. Yankelovich Monitor Inc., 2003.

50. AEI Public Opinion Study the State of the American Worker 2005: Attitudes About Work, Chores, and Leisure in America (Updated 30 August 2005).

51. U.S. Census Bureau, Income, Poverty, and Health Insurance Coverage in the United States, 2005; 38.

52. U.S. Census Bureau, Table P–16. Educational Attainment—People 25 Years Old and Over by Median Income and Sex: 1991 to 2003.

53. GQ Poll, The State of Man, 17 November 2004.

54. Farrell, *The Myth of Male Power,* 172–173.

55. Porter and O'Donnell, "Facing Middle Age With No Degree, and No Wife."

56. Jonathan Mahler, "Commute to Nowhere," *New York Times*, 13 April 2003.

57. David Brooks, "Losing the Alitos," *New York Times*, 12 January 2006.

58. Carla Marinucci, "Dean calls GOP 'a white Christian party'," *San Francisco Chronicle*, 7 June 2005.

59. *Fox News Sunday* Roundtable, 4 February 2007.

60. Judy Bachrach, "Moore's War," *Vanity Fair*, March 2005.

61. Michael Moore, *Stupid White Men . . . And Other Sorry Excuses for the State of the Nation* (New York: Regan Books, 2004), 58–59.

62. Peter Beinart, "Nice Ass," *New Republic*, 22 May 2006.

63. Stan Greenberg, *Middle Class Dreams* (New York: Times Books, 1995), 34.

CHAPTER XX

1. Democratic Response to the State of the Union Address, CNN, 24 January 2007.

2. Michael D. Shear, "In Following His Own Script, Webb May Test Senate's Limits," *Washington Post*, 29 November 2006.

3. James Webb, *Born Fighting: How the Scots-Irish Shaped America* (New York: Broadway, 2004), 295.

4. W.M.G. study of Pew polling November 2004 and January 2007

5. CNN transcript, *Late Edition with Wolf Blitzer,* 14 September 2003.

6. Walter Lippmann, *The Public Philosophy* (London: Little, Brown & Company, 1956), 40.

7. Peter Beinart, *The Good Fight* (New York: HarperCollins, 2006), 190.

8. David Cay Johnston, "Richest Are Leaving Even the Rich Far Behind," *New York Times*, 5 June 2005.

9. Rahm Emanuel and Bruce Reed, *The Plan: Big Ideas for America* (New York: PublicAffairs 2006), 145.

10. W.M.G. study on 2004 election exit polling.

11. "Inequality in America," *Economist*, 17 June 2006.

12. Peter Beinart, "The Rehabilitation of the Cold-War Liberal," *New York Times Magazine*, 30 April 2006.

13. Elizabeth H. Dole, *Hearts Touched With Fire: My 500 Most Inspirational Quotations* (New York: Carroll & Graf Publishers, 2004), 92.

INDEX